BOYS WILL BE BOYS

SPRING-HEELED JACK,
THE TERROR OF LONDON.

"SIR ROLAND," SAID SPRING-HEELED JACK, "THIS IS A MERRY NIGHT FOR US TO MEET"

E. S. TURNER

BOYS WILL

the story of Sweeney Todd, Deadwood Dick,

BE BOYS

Sexton Blake, Billy Bunter, Dick Barton, et. al.

WITH AN INTRODUCTION BY CAPT. C. B. FRY

London
MICHAEL JOSEPH

First published by
MICHAEL JOSEPH LTD
26 Bloomsbury Street,
London, W.C.1
1948

SECOND IMPRESSION NOVEMBER 1948
THIRD IMPRESSION NOVEMBER 1948
FOURTH IMPRESSION NOVEMBER 1948

*Set and printed in Great Britain by Unwin Brothers Ltd. at the
Gresham Press, Woking, in Fournier type, eleven point, leaded,
on paper made by John Dickinson and bound by James Burn.*

CONTENTS

AUTHOR'S NOTE

IN THIS BOOK I have used the terms 'blood' and 'penny dreadful' as far as possible to refer only to the Victorian penny publications which first inspired—I will not say deserved—these descriptions. Even down to the present day the terms have been freely used by parents and teachers to describe almost anything, however innocuous, that a boy reads for his own recreation. Boys themselves even took a certain delight in calling their magazines 'bloods,' rather in the spirit which prompted soldiers of World War One to call themselves the 'old contemptibles.' However, as far as this book is concerned, 'bloods' and 'penny dreadfuls' died out with the nineteenth century.

I am indebted, for permission to reprint extracts and illustrations, to the Directors of the Amalgamated Press, to Messrs. D. C. Thomson and Co., to the editors of *The Tatler* and *Horizon*, and to Mr. George Orwell. Many of the stories from which I quote are out of copyright. In other instances it would be a daunting task to trace who (if anyone) holds the copyright; if I have unknowingly transgressed, I ask indulgence. I am grateful also to Mr. Neil Tuson of the B.B.C. for valuable assistance in preparing the chapter on Dick Barton.

Finally, I would like to express my thanks to Mr. Philip Youngman Carter who, at the right moment, stimulated my ripening interest in these neglected by-ways of literature; with the result that I decided there and then to write this book.

INTRODUCTION

by

CAPTAIN C. B. FRY

> O monstrous! but one half-pennyworth of
> bread to this intolerable deal of sack!
>
> —KING HENRY IV

THAT IS WHAT Shakespeare wrote, and he might have written it about the 'Blood' and 'The Penny Dreadful.'

On the other hand, he might have used this literature as he used North's translation of *Plutarch's Lives*. He might have made immortal plays out of some of them.

Why not? Ben Jonson, almost literally and word for word, transmuted the stiff and angular love letters of philosopher Philostratus (written in Greek prose to some Alexandrine lady) into *Drink to me only with thine eyes*, one of the loveliest lyrics in our language.

An important point. For it proves the accepted notion that the content of a literary product may be excellent while the manner of its communication is atrocious. And, of course, though neither Will nor Ben affords us an example of it, the process may travel vice-versa.

Here may I interpolate that I know well enough I was not invited to write these comments because of my status as a literary critic (though I wager I could move timber with most of the bretheren) but because I have for forty years been responsible for the training of youth. Youth desirous of a successful career in the sea-services, consequently in all likelihood blessed with adven-turous spirit, and con-comitantly and *a fortiori* addicted to vicarious excitement in print.

We will come to that; but first of all let us consult some authorities.

What did Dr. Samuel Johnson say? I guess you do not know he delivered the following pronunciamento, quite suddenly in the middle of quite alien topics; and the words from Boswell are as follows:—

After this tempest had subsided, I recollect the following particulars of his conversation. 'I am always' he said 'for getting a boy forward in his learning; for that is a sure good.

'I would let him at first read any English book which happens to engage his attention, because you have done a great deal when you have brought him to have entertainment from a book.

'He'll get better books afterwards.'

First round then goes to 'Blood and Thunder.'

But there is corroboration quite up-to-date. For you must know that in response to an urgent request made in the spring of 1946 the Ministry of Education (since my Sea-training Establishment N.T.S. *Mercury* is registered by the Ministry as a Secondary School and is in receipt of the princely grant of £200 a year towards a total cost of nearly £16,000) kindly carried out in October 1947 a Full Inspection ; very kindly and sympathetically. And the six H.M.I.s who came were able men, masters of their job. So I earnestly consulted the English expert on how on earth to teach the modern illiterate product of Council and other Schools some modicum of competence in expressing itself in its mother tongue, so after cross-questioning me about the facilities afforded to our youths in 'free reading,' he strongly advised me to let them read anything they would, Bloods, Thrillers and all. In fact in his own well-chosen words he repeated the burden of Dr. Johnson's fiat. So on very strong authority the second round goes to 'Blood and Thunder'—and I use the names respectfully.

Now I must tell you that in my ship we inherited from the Founder a solemn ban upon 'Bloods and Penny Dreadfuls.' We faithfully adhered to our Founder's practice because he was not only a good man but exceptionally successful in promoting youth towards success in after-life both with the Royal Navy and with the Merchant Service. He was, in fact, one sort of genius.

Consequently, Bloods and Dreadfuls were banned; and as in my ship people do what they are told, this type of literature was for some years scarcely visible. Then thrillers grew to be plentiful and these were not banned. But I confess this was quite blind. For all we knew the booklets were wholesome, if exciting, stories. We had no evidence against them. None whatever.

It happens that never in my life have I properly read a Blood or a Dreadful. At my Public School, Repton, during my six years there I never even saw one. Nobody, even Lord Kindersley, who was my football fag, ever possessed one. There was too much else to do. And the public schoolboy is nothing if not critical.

At Charterhouse where I was a Classical master for two years, I never saw or heard of any such publications.

So I cannot claim to be an experienced judge of the matter. But I, as well as Dr. Johnson, have a reasoned opinion based on purely theoretical grounds, not indeed against solid 'Blood' and tangible 'Dreadful' but against a modern fungus growth of another kind. And hereupon I beg to be allowed a digression.

What I think is this. Silly cinema, cretinous croon-words have a deleterious effect. The cinema of the baser sort and the moronic verbosity of the crooner, are ten times worse than any Blood could be.

The evil they do is this. They have a wide influence by fixing in the mind of youth crude and inappropriate attitudes, i.e. artificial tendencies to respond to situations. As a modern philosopher, Professor Ivan Richards, has said, 'Even the decision as to what constitutes a pretty girl or a handsome young man, an affair apparently natural and personal enough, is largely determined by magazine covers and movie stars.'

I am told that the technique of kissing has changed quite a lot since Hollywood sent us all to school again.

Now it is certain that the result of these artificial low-grade fixations is deplorable. General taste is vitiated. Youth and maiden are induced to substitute the world of Cinema and Crooner for the real world. They become functionally unable to face things as they are. They simply project their stock attitudes, fictions absorbed from these primitive and under-bred sources, into the world of everyday life. They live cinema; they feel croon-song. They dream their workaday life. Don't talk to me about Bloods!

I admit that never in all my forty years' experience can I recall one single instance in which any youth in my ship went astray by imitating in action anything from any Blood, Dreadful or Thriller. That is not the catch at all, if any catch there be.

The catch is how they express themselves when they write and how they look at life and the living thereof. And I am sorry to say I cannot absolve the gallant composers of our literature of all tendency to extravagance.

I doubt if Dr. Johnson ever in his life had charge of ten youths at a time, or even one. Still less of about two hundred. So though no doubt he thought himself into a profoundly settled opinion about 'let 'em read anything,' he never saw the results of such libertarian self-education.

The eminent H.M.I., whose verdict is recorded above, was, I am quite sure, concerned entirely with the writing and speaking of English. He knew the difficulty presented by the modern youthful mind, empty of all sustenance from reading. He was not thinking of the moral disposition induced, he was thinking only of the mental furniture obtainable by reading. No reading, no furniture.

What surprises me is that nobody now reads Fenimore Cooper, Marryat and Henty. Not to mention Sir Walter Scott—whom, by the way, I heard in a broadcast by Mr. John Brophy summarized as an 'overrated writer.' Ye gods . . . and little fishes!

It may be that youth does not genuinely read the Blood, the Dreadful and the lesser Thriller—youth may run its eye across page after page and pick up by eye what is happening. That may be the charm; one exciting event after another. Just like Dick Barton, visible instead of audible. But the atmosphere is pervasive; the theme-song adhesive; the total effect pardonably doubtful in the eyes of the trainer of youth.

Come to think of it, however, whether we regard the Horrific Thriller, the Adventurous Shocker or the Mock Heroic Boy, there is the difficulty that *Ivanhoe*, *Treasure Island* or *The Tower of London* could by rapid compression be turned into Bloods. How are we to draw a line determining where the legitimate ends and the illegitimate begins? Then, how place Rudyard Kipling's *Stalky?*

There is, indeed, one sort of boy-read story of which I can never approve. It is the fantastic sort of school-story in which small boys are portrayed as for ever successful in making fools of school-masters, who are already congenital morons.

This sort of fantasy is objectionable in the same sense as it is objectionable to guy Clergymen or even Policemen on the stage— and over the radio. B.B.C. beware!

Any influence on the young encouraging them against authority is nowadays highly undesirable. Indiscipline, irreverence and disrespect are rife enough without further encouragement. There are quite enough children who boss their parents and waste the time of magistrates.

Still one may pause and wonder whether these curious books and booklets matter so much after all. It may be, not.

Let us consider one's own case. Wilfred Walter, the Shake-spearian actor, took me once to the Elephant and Castle Theatre to see *Maria Martin, or The Murder in the Red Barn*. It was melodrama, tragic and extreme; truly tragic by intention. But I found it excruciatingly funny. I have never been so amused by any presentation of comedy.

Again what could be more effectively inducive of melancholy than many a musical comedy? *No, No, Nanette* is calculated to make one sadder and sadder act by act and scene by scene.

Is it then certain that the sort of book and story we are considering really deceives their youthful reader?

The skilful author of the present treatise has not examined that aspect of his theme. I am inclined to allow that maybe we credit our youthful 'addicts' of Blood and Dreadful with less insight and intelligence than they actually possess. Is it possible they read tongue in cheek?

Anyway, the whole subject is as tangled as some of the plots of Shocker and Thriller. A dozen Brains Trusts would produce many shades of divergent opinion and of contrary valuation. The Distinguished Anonymous Psychologist would, I guess, produce some longish technical terms on the subject—these in the nature of what we called at Oxford Question-begging Appellatives.

There remains that to the majority of its readers this present very interesting book will be a book of many revelations.

My summary is 'Who'd have believed it?'

Who would have believed that English literature contained so many hidden treasures?

Who would have believed that so many fortunes were founded on the discovery of so many Treasure Islands?

Meanwhile what about Edgar Allen Poe and *The Mystery of the Rue Morgue*?

How many of you have read it?

*   *   *

P.S.—I shall probably seize and devour the next 'Blood' I see stuffed into a crack in the deck to keep the wind away or the rats out.

C. B. FRY

IN THIS BOOK the reader is invited to take a backward plunge into the new mythology—the mythology of Sexton Blake and Deadwood Dick, of Jack Sheppard, Jack Harkaway and Billy Bunter; of all the idols of boyhood from Charley Wag down to Dick Barton.

It should not be necessary to do as Alfred Harmsworth did in 1894 when he launched *Union Jack*, and assure the reader: YOU NEED NOT BE ASHAMED TO BE SEEN READING THIS BOOK!

Of the adult population of these islands, it is doubtful whether half of one per cent could truthfully claim that they had never dipped in their youth into what undiscriminating parents called 'bloods.' The writer's hope is that many will welcome the opportunity to look back, if not sentimentally, then critically or even shudderingly, at the he-men, the ape-men and the bird-men whose adventures they followed under cover of Hall and Knight's Algebra or in the precarious privacy of bed.

It was a pity that this type of reading had to be associated with a feeling of guilt (though it may well be that this went to heighten the reader's appreciation). Probably there is no product of the human brain which has been the object of such remorseless and misconceived abuse as the boy's thriller. On no theme have magistrates, clergymen and schoolmasters talked more prejudice to the reported inch.

As long ago as 1901 Mr. G. K. Chesterton in *The Defendant*
brought down a withering fire on the critics who were branding
'penny dreadfuls' as criminal and degraded in outlook. He had
grown impatient with the thesis that a boy who could not read
stole an apple because he liked the taste of apple, but that a boy
who could read stole an apple because his mind was aflame with
a story about Dick Turpin. No less muddle-minded, he pointed
out, were the critics who charged the authors of 'penny dreadfuls'
with romanticizing outlaws, and yet praised the works of Scott,
Stevenson and even Wordsworth who had done the same thing
in the name of literature. Any reader who wished to revel in
corruption, Chesterton pointed out, could do so by buying a full-
length novel by a fashionable author. Such literature could not
be bought at one penny, for if it were published at that price the
police would seize it.

Critics had also urged, said Chesterton, that boys' thrillers
ought to be suppressed because they were 'ignorant in a literary
sense,' which was like complaining that a novel was ignorant in
the chemical sense, or in the economic sense. He said:

The simple need for some kind of ideal world in which fictitious
persons play an unhampered part is infinitely deeper and older than the
rules of good art, and much more important.

The Times has been sensibly tolerant on the theme of boys'
fiction. In 1918 the *Literary Supplement* deplored the parental
policy of foisting on schoolboys 'pietistic powder concealed in
jam':

Boys of school age have not yet arrived at writing books for themselves; but at least as the instinct of self-protection asserts itself they can
kick; and the kick is the unconscious healthy protest of youth that its
mind shall not be pauperized by well-meaning seniors.

The same leading article was critical of four boys' writers
hitherto regarded as unimpeachable: W. H. G. Kingston, for 'the
curse of condescension' which sometimes afflicted him; R. M.
Ballantyne, who 'sank to insufferable goody-goody'; Fenimore
Cooper, whose *The Last of the Mohicans* only just passed muster
because realistic-minded schoolboys knew him to be the author also

of the notorious *The Pilot*, which was a regular prize at dames'
schools; and Captain Marryat—'To palm *Masterman Ready* upon
a child and to hold *Peter Simple* up your sleeve was no better
than a trick.' *The Times Literary Supplement* had a weak corner
for 'penny dreadfuls.' There was a leader in 1941 regretting that
the famous collection of the late Mr. Barry Ono—which that
hospitable collector was so proud to display to his friends—was
henceforth to be hidden away in the caverns of the British Museum.

In recent times Mr. George Orwell has seen fit to lay waste
the field of boys' thrillers on the ground that they are 'sodden
in the worst political illusions of 1910.' At first thought, he admits,
the idea of a left-wing boys' paper makes one slightly sick; no
normal boy would look at it. Then he remembers that in Spain
of pre-Franco days there were some successful examples of adventure fiction with a leftist slant.[1] Even if this cannot be done here,
he says, there is no reason why every boys' paper should be guilty
of snobbishness and gutter patriotism. (For Mr. Orwell's blast and
Mr. Charles Hamilton's counter-blast, see Chapter XIII.)

It may be that as the reader scans the ensuing chapters he will
begin guiltily to try to assess how much of his present-day outlook
was conditioned by the peculiar codes of the bravos of his boyhood, or to what extent his class prejudices were sharpened by
the tales of one school or another, or whether he voted Conservative
because he was pretty sure that was how Sexton Blake voted in
'The Great Election Mystery.' If this kind of self-examination
distresses him, he should lay the blame on Mr. Orwell, who brought
the question up.

This book, it must be emphasized, is purely a refresher course.
It has no other object than to transport the sentimental reader
back to that agreeable period when steam men puffed across the
prairie trampling Indians underfoot; when the elect of Britain's
boarding schools set off every other week by balloon or submarine
to discover a lost city or a vanishing island; when almost every
Northcliffe boys' paper carried a serial describing the invasion of

---

[1] It may discourage Mr. Orwell to know that a Victorian 'penny dreadful' with
the promising title of *Socialist Girl* is dismissed by Montague Summers in *A Gothic
Bibliography* as 'pseudo-pornography.'

Britain by Germans, French or Russians; when wellnigh every tramp, ice-cream vendor, organ grinder or muffin man turned out to be Sexton Blake; and when every self-respecting football team had its mysterious masked centre-forward.

The writer, researching through back numbers, found that memories were powerfully evoked by the advertisements alone: the coveted Daisy air rifle; the monster watch—'yours for sixpence, chain free'; the singing scarf pins, shocking coils, multiplying billiard balls, solaphones, plurascopes, chella-phones, tubogliders, stink bombs and pocket picture palaces of a pre-atomic generation. (What manufacturer would to-day think it worth while to cut up surplus cinema film into individual frames for displaying in a monocular contraption to be held up to the light?)

But it may be remembered that not all the advertisements were aimed at the adolescent. Stop blushing—yes. Watch yourself grow—yes. Learn ventriloquism—yes. Join our Christmas Chocolate Club—yes. But who was the advertiser getting at when he promised 'Red noses completely cured,' when he urged 'Banish hair poverty,' or undertook to cure the smoking habit in three days? Alongside an appeal for recruits to the Armed Forces would appear the exhortation: 'Write to the Editor of *Answers* if you are not getting your right pension.' It would seem that the readers covered all the ages of man from childhood to second childhood, from pimples to rheumatism. And somewhere in this span—it is not certain where—were the readers who were expected to apply for the secret of making their hair curl ('Mine curled at once,' writes Major).

It may be that some readers will look through these pages in vain for some mention of their favourite character. The writer can only plead the vastness of the field. Take detectives alone. Then take only those detectives who, like Sherlock Holmes, had one-syllable surnames and two-syllable Christian names (with the accent on the first syllable): Sexton Blake, Nelson Lee, Falcon Swift, Ferrers Locke, Dixon Hawke, Martin Track and a dozen others. It is impossible to give a chapter on each. The best plan seemed to be to concentrate on Blake, the doyen of them all, and to lump the others together. This is perhaps a bit hard on Nelson

Lee, whose peculiar fate it was to become a detective-schoolmaster, and on Nick Carter, who was sufficient of an individualist to have a one-syllable first name and a two-syllable surname, but no other course was easily feasible. Regretfully but firmly one had to omit the *Jester's* tireless Hawkshaw, who saved so many buxom somnambulists from ghastly deaths.

The *Jester* and the other 'comics' have been touched on only very lightly. They are nevertheless a rewarding study and it will be no surprise if some day a sociologist turns in a tome on Weary Willie and Tired Tim.

It would have been easy to fill this volume with an account of Victorian 'penny dreadfuls' alone. The temptation has been resisted, partly because the number of readers who can remember following the adventures of Spring-Heeled Jack and Jack Sheppard must by now be limited. But it is important, as well as oddly fascinating, to examine the kind of literature from which the later boys' thrillers sprang. Whatever its faults, the 'penny dreadful' was a work of vivid imagination, as Wells and Barrie have seen fit to testify. And if the shockers of those days seem altogether gorier, it must be remembered that our grandfathers were that much nearer to an age of crude violence and crude superstition, of dwarfs and mis-shapen things, of legalized atrocity. The gibbet was abolished only in 1834. In 1839 the following sentence was passed by one of Her Majesty's judges on three convicted Chartists:

'That each of you, John Frost, Zephaniah Williams and William Jones, be taken hence to the place from whence you came, and be there taken on a hurdle to the place of execution, and that each of you be then hung by the neck until you be dead, and that afterwards the head of each of you shall be severed from his body, and the body of each, divided into four quarters, to be disposed of as Her Majesty shall think fit; and may the Lord have mercy upon your souls.'

The sentence was not carried out, and the young Queen was spared the problem of deciding what to do with twelve bleeding portions of three of her dissident subjects. But much later than this special trains were put on by the railways in order that all those interested should be able to witness a public execution.

It would have been easy, too, to have written more about the

Boy's Own Paper, *Chums* and *The Captain*, which were the kind of journals that parents wanted their sons to read. Many lads, however, preferred to put off perusal of these until they had acquired (at half price) from the boy next door all the journals they knew their parents did not want them to read.

It may surprise the ordinary reader to know that there is to-day an international trade in 'bloods,' from *Varney the Vampire* to the last *Nick Carter*, and that this trade is fostered by a variety of amateur magazines. Of these the *Collector's Miscellany*, published from Saltburn-on-the-Sea, is a good example, containing as it does sentimentally reminiscent articles about the boys' fiction of yore and all kinds of data of interest to collectors. One researcher described in its pages how he spent many months during the early part of the late war in examining the school stories of the *Magnet* and the *Gem*, and determining which were written by Charles Hamilton and which were not; a feat of literary research which may yet receive wider recognition. New discoveries about the origins of Sweeney Todd and Sexton Blake are eagerly passed on from reader to reader. Long-concealed identities hidden behind pen names are triumphantly revealed. Occasionally there is a quiz containing questions like: 'What was the title of the first school story in the *Boys' Realm* and who wrote it?' and 'Name the Eskimo who was a prominent character in several *Boys' Friend* serials.'

Britain has no monopoly of these specialist publications. In Fisherville, Massachusetts is published *Reckless Ralph's Dime Novel Round-Up*, which contains advertisements offering the *Champion* and *Nelson Lee Library*, in addition to such native wares as *Bowery Boy* and *White Slavery Up-to-Date*. From Manitoba in 1947 came a handsome offer to post *The Story Paper Collector* free to anyone in the sterling area until the sending of funds became easier.

Independent of these publications, there are groups who meet to discuss the journals of their boyhood, and pen acquaintances who correspond with each other exchanging newly discovered lore. Some of them bring a keen business sense to the collecting of old 'bloods'; in the past there have even been accusations of sharp practice in this innocent-seeming hobby, certain dealers allegedly

introducing into their lists fictitious titles of 'penny dreadfuls' as
a come-on device. Every year, unhappily, the existing stocks are
depleted, thanks to the activities of spring-cleaning wives or
impatient executors.

Some day perhaps there will be a book about boys' thrillers
from the inside. It will be highly informative and disillusioning.
It will contain the real reason why such-and-such a magazine
was killed, why such-and-such a character was slain in his apparent
prime. It will describe the editorial conferences at which story
policy was decided, at which old taboos were discarded or new
ones introduced; at which the circulation staff made their periodic
demand that a popular character should be made to undergo
adventures in Birmingham, Liverpool, Glasgow or Leeds; at which
the decision was made to put someone on to dusting off old plots
and giving them a new lease of life; and at which everyone, from
general manager to office boy, was invited to suggest ways of
injecting adrenalin into a flagging serial. They were shrewd men
who ran the fiction factories both north and south of the Tweed.
They did not make many mistakes, and when they did they passed
them off as triumphs. Was there ever a boys' paper which was
discontinued on the ground that it lacked support? Two weeks
before a journal was due to be pole-axed would come the warning
'Watch for a Sensational Surprise!' In the last issue would appear
a dozen warnings—'Don't ask for So-and-So next week, ask for
Such-and-Such!' The reason given was always that So-and-So
had proved so popular that it had been decided to extend it and
include in it a variety of features never before assembled in any
magazine. In the thrill of this news nobody bothered to ask why
the title was being changed. Perhaps it is too much to hope for a
behind-the-scenes book. There are too many tricks of the trade
which it would be impolitic to give away.

Many boys' thrillers died in the fatal early summer of 1940 and
may never be revived. But some of the hardier weeklies—notably
the *Sexton Blake Library*—kept going. The extent of the slaughter
is to be deplored, for never were lusty home-made products more
necessary to offset the encroachment of 'Yank magazines' and the
feebler imitations put out by traditionless firms in this country.

It is true that the best of the American thrillers are very good indeed. Luckily we do not often encounter the worst of them. Anyone with a morbid desire to see how far the detective story or the 'western' can be debased should turn to the writings of that fearless explorer of the literary bad lands, Mr. S. J. Perelman. In his book *Crazy like a Fox*, Mr. Perelman exercises a sophisticated wit at the expense of an American detective magazine which he describes as 'the sauciest blend of libido and murder this side of Gilles de Rais.' Given only the paper our own publishers could entrench themselves firmly against any threat from the peddlers of spice-and-thunder—even if (*pace* Mr. Orwell) it did mean steeping another generation in the worst political illusions of 1910.

Meanwhile (*pace* Shakespeare) *Summon up the blood!*

CHAPTER I

GOTHIC HANGOVER

CHARLES ADDAMS, the macabre-minded artist of *The New Yorker*, has a sketch of a sinister-looking building which bears a notice: 'Beware of the Thing.' That notice is a fair expression of the Gothic mood in which the boys' 'blood' was born, more than a hundred years ago.

Popular fiction of the early nineteenth century was steeped in darkness and diablerie: spectres gliding in a green phosphorescence, hags picking over the bones of charnel houses, deathsheads in closets, heirs to great estates chained in dungeons, forests stuffed with robbers and werewolves, graves creaking open in the moonlight to let the vampires out—these were the stock-in-trade of the Gothic, and bogus Gothic, novelist. The vogue for these romantic horrors had been set by Horace Walpole (*The Castle of Otranto*), Ann Radcliffe (*The Mysteries of Udolpho*) and Matthew Gregory Lewis (*The Monk*); and there were plenty of pens ready to imitate, translate, paraphrase or purloin for the benefit of the literate fringe of the working classes. In rising spate, and at ever cheaper cost, came romances set in clammy castles in the German forests or in convents ruled by degenerate nuns who wielded the knout upon their novices. The atmosphere of all of them was oppressive. Neither indoors nor outdoors was there a stirring of fresh air. In the turrets of castles censers smoked before unholy altars; no one opened a window, unless to jump from it. Out of doors the air was foul with the reek of gibbets.

There was one basic plot running through the Gothic thrillers. Indeed it grew to be the basic plot of the nineteenth century. It was that of the young and rightful heir deprived of his birthright by evil-scheming relatives or guardians. So that the reader might be sure that he was receiving the familiar prescription, the plot was frequently outlined at length in the sub-title of the story. For example:

Lovel Castle, or the Rightful Heir Restored, a Gothic Tale; Narrating how a Young Man, the supposed son of a Peasant, by a Train of Unparalleled Circumstances, not only discovers who were his Real Parents, but that they came to Untimely Deaths; with his Adventures in the Haunted Apartment, Discovery of the Fatal Closet, and Appearance of the Ghost of his murdered Father; relating also how the Murderer was brought to Justice, with his Confession and the restoration to the Injured Orphan of his title and estates.

This plot was gratefully taken up in the 'thirties and 'forties by the popular low-priced magazines which began to compete for the pence of the masses, and by the publishers of penny parts—to be known all too soon as 'penny dreadfuls'—which for the next half-century were to provide sorely needed escapism in humble homes.

The first 'penny dreadfuls' were not aimed at the juvenile market, but the scalp-tingling subject-matter readily seduced the young from their lukewarm loyalty to *Robinson Crusoe* and *Quentin Durward*. Edward Lloyd (founder of *Lloyd's Newspaper*), who put out a wide range of penny-a-week Gothic shockers during the 'forties, was not sufficiently hypocritical to pretend that he was publishing for adults only. It has been put on record by Thomas Frost (*Forty Years' Recollections*, 1860) that Lloyd, if in doubt whether a manuscript held the elements of popular appeal, would deliberately 'try it out on the office boy.' The procedure was explained to Frost, who was hoping to sell a story for publication in penny parts, by Lloyd's manager—'a stout gentleman of sleek costume and urbane manners':

'Our publications circulate among a class so different in education and social position from the readers of three-volume novels that we sometimes distrust our own judgment and place the manuscript in the hands of an illiterate person—a servant, or machine boy, for instance. If they pronounce favourably upon it, we think it will do.'

Lloyd surrounded himself by a small group of writers of demoniac imagination, prodigious output and an engaging lack of scruple. Outstanding among them was Thomas Peckett Prest, supposedly a relative of a Dean of Durham, who for all his industry —and notoriety—rates no mention in the reference books of to-day. His chief claims to notice are that he was the creator of Sweeney Todd, a legend destined to span the generations (see next chapter); and that he was almost certainly the head of the group who, at Lloyd's behest, plagiarized the works of Dickens as fast as they came out. The law of the day offered friendly shelter to literary pirates, and Lloyd was able to make the nucleus of his fortune by putting out the *Penny Pickwick, Oliver Twiss, Nickelas Nicklebery, Martin Guzzlewit* and others as thinly disguised. Enthusiasm for Dickens was so great and uncritical that it readily embraced all his imitators. 'Bos' was the pseudonym under which Prest and his associates laboured. According to Montague Summers, the original idea had been to ascribe the piracies to 'Boaz,' but this name was ruled out on the peculiar ground that it was more dangerously close to Dickens's 'Boz' than was 'Bos'; and also on the ground that it was too Biblical.[1]

Before he took on the mantle of 'Bos' Prest had edited *The Calendar of Horrors* (which included a story called *Geralda the Demon Nun*). He continued to write many tales in the same vein for Lloyd. The grand catalogue of his works contains such inviting titles as *The Maniac Father, or The Victims of Seduction,* and *Vice and Its Victims, or Phoebe the Peasant's Daughter*.

A characteristic of Prest and all Lloyd's writers was that they could turn their pen to any kind of fiction. Most of their stories were published anonymously and in consequence it is almost impossible to distinguish one man's work from that of another; bibliographies are sadly contradictory. Between them these writers who constituted the Salisbury Square School piled up a library of

---

[1] Dickens fulminated in vain, not only against Lloyd but against dramatists like Stirling and Moncrieff who produced complete stage versions of his novels before he himself was in sight of the last chapter. His threat to hang his imitators 'on gibbets so lofty and enduring that their remains shall be a monument to our just vengeance to all succeeding ages' was greeted with derision. He took some of the pirates to court, but, in his own words, 'I was treated as if I were the robber instead of the robbed.'

Gothic delights which included *The Black Monk, or The Secret
of the Grey Turret; Almira's Curse, or The Black Tower of Brans-
dorf; The Ranger of the Tomb, or The Gypsy's Prophesy;* and *The
Castle Fiend.* But Lloyd's most ghoulish and goriest publication
was probably *Varney the Vampire* (which preceded Bram Stoker's
Dracula by nearly half a century). The British Museum attributes
this work to the astonishing James Malcolm Rymer, who was
reputed to keep as many as ten serials running at the same time.

Varney the Vampire had as its alternative title *The Feast of
Blood,* which was if anything an understatement; the story was an
unmitigated shocker. The opening illustration showed a buck-
toothed horror sinking its jaws deep in the throat of a fair young
woman lying prostrate over her bed; in the background was a
portrait of a saturnine cavalier who surveyed the scene with relish.
Here is an excerpt from the first chapter:

The figure turns half round, and the light falls upon its face. It is
perfectly white—perfectly bloodless. The eyes look like polished tin;
the lips are drawn back, and the principal feature next to those dreadful
eyes is the teeth—projecting like those of some wild animal, hideously,
glaringly white and fang-like. It approaches the bed with a strange
gliding movement. It clashes together its long nails that literally appear
to hang from the finger ends. No sound comes from its lips. . . .

The storm has ceased—all is still. The winds are hushed; the church
clock proclaims the hour of one; a hissing sound comes from the throat
of the hideous being and he raises his long gaunt arms—the lips move.
He advances. The girl places one small foot from the bed on the floor.
She is unconsciously dragging the clothing with her. The door of the
room is in that direction—can she reach it?

With a sudden rush that could not be foreseen—with a strange howling
cry that was enough to awaken terror in every breast, the figure seized
the long tresses of her hair and twining them round his bony hands he
held her to the bed. Then she screamed—Heaven granted her then the
power to scream. Shriek followed shriek in rapid succession. The bed
clothes fell in a heap by the side of the bed—she was dragged by her
long silken hair completely on to it again. Her beautiful rounded limbs
quivered with the agony of her soul. The glassy horrible eyes of the figure
ran over the angelic form with a hideous satisfaction—horrible profana-
tion. He drags her head to the bed's edge. He forces it back by the long
hair still entwined in his grasp. With a plunge he seizes her neck in his
fang-like teeth—a gush of blood and a hideous sucking noise follows.
The girl has swooned and the vampire is at his hideous repast!

The incomparable Mr. Rymer kept this tale going for 220 chapters. He gloated on the lustrous eyes and rosy cheeks of the happy, well-fed vampire; on the shot vampire reviving in the first rays of moonlight; on the impaling of suspected corpses of young women with a wooden stake (an illustration shows a spectator with a fine sense of fitness raising his hat during this proceeding); on a covey of vampires dragging a new corpse into the moonlight and inciting it to deeds of mischief; and on a couple of gibbering resurrectionists fleeing from an opening casket in the vaults of a church. At length came the written confession of Sir Francis Varney, that unhappy miscreant perpetually deprived of what the author called 'the downy freshness of Heaven's bounty.' In other words, although he had died several times Sir Francis could not lie down. His second 'death' was suffered at the hands of Charles the Second and Rochester, who wanted no surviving witnesses to one of their whoring expeditions in Pimlico. Finally there was a postscript recording the visit to Naples of an ugly, wealthy Englishman, who asked for a guide to Vesuvius. Briefing this guide amid the poisonous odours of the volcano, the stranger said:

'You will say that you accompanied Varney the Vampire to the crater of Mount Vesuvius, and that, tired and disgusted with a life of horror, he flung himself in to prevent the possibility of a reanimation of his remains.'

Before the guide could utter anything but a shriek Varney took one tremendous leap and disappeared into the burning mouth of the mountain.

The only light relief in these 828 closely printed pages was that provided by fire, shipwreck, cliff falls, collapse of great buildings and fantastic thunderstorms. But from the length of the story it is obvious that it had an insatiable following. Nor do the critics appear to have been hostile. At the end of a preface to the reprinted work in 1847 Rymer said: 'To the whole of the Metropolitan Press for their laudatory notices the author is peculiarly obliged.'

Sometimes Rymer wrote under the name of Errym. He is credited with being the author of *Ada, the Betrayed, or the Murder at the Old Smithy*. Some of his works defy classification; for instance, *The Unspeakable, or The Life and Adventures of a Stammerer*.

Edward Lloyd also published a number of domestic romances with titles like *Fatherless Fanny, or The Mysterious Orphan*, and *Alice Horne, or the Revenge of the Blighted One*, full of go-and-never-darken-this-door-again and dead-dead-and-never-called-me mother. Prest and Rymer turned these out with accomplished ease.

Nor did Lloyd overlook the historical romance. Here, however, he had the field by no means to himself. Pierce Egan, for instance, rarely lacked a publisher for his ponderous and bloodthirsty romances. Historians accuse him of a contempt for fact and a predilection for scenes of cruelty and slaughter, but acquit him of any 'immoral or irreligious' tendencies. The editor of the *London Journal* sought to dispense with Egan's gory romances in 1859 and began printing Sir Walter Scott, but had to recall Egan hurriedly; not the first or the last time that Scott was soundly defeated in the lists of popular fiction.

Egan's style was floridly prolix. His characters would stand and apostrophize each other in melodramatic metaphor for columns on end. Here is an extract from *Quintin Matsys, the Blacksmith of Antwerp*, which introduced a band of German vigilantes known as the *fehm-gerichte:*

'To Satan with thee! thou croaking frog—thou blot on our 'scutcheon —thou canker in our flower—thou worm upon a green leaf. I hate to look on thee, thou ugly weed in our garden! Thou ever comest as a blight. I know whenever I see thy sneaking, paleface visage that I must pray the devil for help, for there is some cursed disaster sure to follow thy appearance. Out of my sight, thou venom-jawed reptile, or I may forget thou'rt my brother and strangle thee.

'Degenerate descendant of a family that had no stain upon its character until thou hast placed it there; unworthy follower of an art itself so elevated that its votaries should be the soul of honour! Base, unmanly, evil-minded knave! who hast crawled into the bosom of my peaceful home to void that poison on all within thy influence, quit my sight and never let my eyes suffer the disgrace of gazing on one so false and vicious!'

In spasmodic demand from the 'forties onward was the sea story—usually a tale of buccaneers or smugglers. There was precious little ozone or salt spray in the earlier stories, however. One of Lloyd's titles was *The Death Ship, or The Pirate's Bride and the Maniac of the Deep*. The seas were cluttered with spectral barks and gallows ships (with men hanging from every available spar from the yardarms to the flying jib boom). When the hero, cheated of his inheritance, eventually put to sea there were hags in the hold and hunchbacks in the rigging. The pirate chief would prove to be a buck negro, glittering with jewels as big as pigeons' eggs, who would dine in his saloon with half a dozen skeletons, all that remained of the masters and midshipmen of His Majesty's sloops sent to take him. Setting up skeletons for the captain's table was only one of a score of gruesome tasks for the ship's surgeon under the Skull and Crossbones; he had to be an anatomist of no mean attainments.

The writers of these tormented sea stories made no strong claims to nautical knowledge. They were happiest when they could bring the hero ashore to a sorceress's cabin where snakes curled above altars laden with skulls and the word 'Death' was embroidered menacingly on the altar drop. The pirates' cavern was another favourite haunt. Here, surrounded by the loot of the seven seas, the robbers would stage spectacular carousals. Tired of swilling rare wines down their gullets, they would crave something more exciting:

'Fill up your glass,' cries the Captain, '*and this time we will drink it in flames!*'
All the lights are extinguished, splinters of wood are kindled, and the flaming goblets set fire to and quaffed by the whole band at a single gulp.

That there were certain dangers in this sort of practice is seen by an extract from the innocently titled story *The Darling of Our Crew* which appeared under the imprint of Edwin Brett in 1880 (even at that date it was still hag-ridden):

She (Mother Shebear) made her way to a keg which stood before the fire.
From this she took a pint of raw brandy and put it over the fire, until it seemed on the point of exploding, and a blue lambent flame floated on the top.
Chuckling fiendishly as she regarded this, she blew out the flame and drank half of it at a draught.
Now madness glared in her eyes unmistakably.
She drank off the remainder of the fearful potion and danced.

Her face assumed a frightful colour.

She stretched forth her long talons, yelling in the fierce grip of delirium tremens, as she advanced to where Jack was, to fling him into the flames, shrieking—

'Now, boy, you shall be my victim. Ha! Ha! Ha!'

Hitherto he had stood horrified and fascinated.

But the instinct of self-preservation was strong within him.

He stepped back and drew his pistol to fire.

But there was no necessity for him to use his pistols.

A sight which no pen can adequately describe greeted him.

The hag paused in her rush and pressed her hand over her breast.

Then the fearful sounds she was uttering came forth no more.

Their place was taken by a bluish lambent flame that came forth from her mouth and curled in fearful fantastic wreaths about her face.

The boy covered his face with his hands.

He could gaze no more.

The sight was too awful.

Moments passed.

Centuries they seemed to him.

Again he ventured to look up.

She was still standing there but another change had come over her.

Now the features that had likened her to humanity had disappeared.

She was an incandescent mass of matter like a statue, burning and glowing like the centre of a fire.

He sprang forward.

There was some water in a bucket.

He seized it and poured it over what had once been a woman.

The water turned at once to steam and flew off.

But it had no perceptible effect in quenching the burning mass.

Again and again he tried.

The result was the same.

Water had no power to put out the burning mass!

He sat down in sheer despair.

The fearful effluvia cast off by the burning body made him ill.

And so he sat there sick with horror and watched the mass turn from red to dull blue and finally go out altogether.

Most of the writers of 'penny dreadfuls' went in for romance unadulterated; others had axes to grind. The redoubtable G. W. M. Reynolds, Chartist sympathizer and founder of *Reynolds Weekly Newspaper* (1850), used every opportunity to play up the violent contrast between Wealth and Poverty. His marathon work, *The Mysteries of London*, inspired by Eugene Sue's *The Mysteries of*

Paris, ran for the best part of a decade, though after the first two volumes other pens took over. It professed to be an exposure of voluntary vice in high places and involuntary vice in low places, of the system in which 'the daughter of a peer is nursed in enjoyments and passes through an uninterrupted avenue of felicity from the cradle to the tomb; while the daughter of poverty opens her eyes at her birth upon destitution in all its most appalling shapes and at length sells her virtue for a loaf of bread.'

Reynolds left little to his readers' imagination. His slums were incestuous, pox-ridden hells in which pigs ate the bodies of newly-dead babes and hardened undertakers' men fainted at the sights which met their eyes. Hump-backed dwarfs, harridans and grave-robbers groped past against a background of workhouses, jails, execution yards, thieves' kitchens and cemeteries. His readers could depend on him to bring in the theme of maiden virtue rudely strumpeted as often as possible. The rake's progress of one daughter of the poor began when she 'sold her face'—that is, allowed masks to be made from it, even though these were for the modelling of Madonnas in Catholic chapels. She next sold her likeness to an artist; then her bosom to a sculptor (he is pictured poised over her naked torso with a pair of callipers); and finally her whole form to a photographer (French). At a later stage her wealthy protector asked her why she was *distraite* in his house. The reason was that it contained reminders of most of the steps in her downfall: a plaster of paris Diana in a staircase recess was the work of the man who had bought her face; a portrait of Venus rising from the waves was the work of the artist who had bought her likeness; and a female bust was the work of the man who had bought her bosom. As for her virtue, she reminded him, he himself had bought that. But what, asked Mr. Reynolds, was the girl's alternative to selling herself piecemeal? To work for a farthing and a half an hour at embroidering flowers, or to earn twopence-half-penny a time stitching 'dissecting trousers' for sale to anatomy students.

When his indignation grew too much for him Reynolds would reproduce workhouse dietary tables or introduce diagrams of this kind:

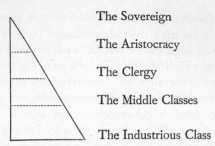

The Sovereign

The Aristocracy

The Clergy

The Middle Classes

The Industrious Class

Declared the author:

The lowest step in the ladder is occupied by the class which is the most numerous, the most useful, and which ought to be the most influential.

The average annual incomes of the individuals of each class are as follows:

Sovereign £500,000
The Member of the Aristocracy £30,000
The Priest £7,500
The Member of the Middle Class £300
The Member of the Industrious Class £20

Is this reasonable? Is this just? Is this even consistent with common sense?

It was New Year's Day, 1839.

The rich man sat down to a table crowded with every luxury; the pauper in the workhouse had not enough to eat. The contrast may be represented:

Turtle, venison, turkey, hare, pheasant, perigord pie, plum pudding, mince pies, jellies, blanc-mange, trifles, preserves, cakes, fruits of all kinds, wines of every description.	half-pound bread, four ozs. bacon half-pound potatoes, one and a half-pints of gruel.

And it was New Year's Day, 1839. But to proceed. . . .

And to give him credit, when he did proceed Reynolds left few dull passages, though sometimes half a column was taken up with a glossary of thieves' slang. He also persuaded his artist to provide in addition to the customary illustration every eight pages, incidental illustrations showing card sharpers' sleight of hand and the secrets of dice manipulation. No one could say that Reynolds did not give value for money.

His output was tremendous. Once, fired perhaps by the feats of Mr. Rymer, he took on, and won, a bet that he would write four romances each involving an eight-page weekly instalment, simultaneously. He was never averse to chronicling the woes of erring womankind; typical works from his pen were *Pope Joan*, *Lives of the Harem*, and *Mary Price, or the Memoirs of a Servant Maid*.

Statistics about the sales of early 'penny dreadfuls' are hard to come by, but there is no doubt that these ill-printed sheets formed the basis of many a publisher's fortune. The successful romances went on for years, then after an interval were republished under the same or different titles, or were appropriated by rivals and purged or made bloodier according to taste. Penny parts were rarely dated, and not all bore a publisher's imprint. It was a common custom, in launching a new 'penny dreadful,' to announce 'Numbers Two and Three Given Away With Number One,' or to present the opening instalment with the last number of a completed story, to ensure that no reader dropped out. Often 'beautiful chromo pictures' were given away open-handedly during the early chapters, then more frugally as the story caught on. Some publishing houses made a habit of presenting with alternate issues sets of scenes and cut-out characters for use in toy theatres—the 'penny plain, two-pence coloured' models beloved by R. L. Stevenson—along with an offer of a book of words, price one penny.

According to Thomas Catling in *My Life's Pilgrimage* the practice in Lloyd's Salisbury Square offices was to plan each story eight weeks in advance. For each instalment of eight book-size pages the author received ten shillings. It was small wonder, in view of these sweated rates, that other writers found it easier and more profitable to plagiarise stories from across the Atlantic. If contemporary evidence is to be believed, their working day was spent, not disagreeably, in eliminating Americanisms, changing Saratoga to Brighton, Senator to Duke and 'brown-stone mansion on Fifth Avenue' to 'stately edifice in Belgravia.' It was a two-way traffic, for the Americans were pirating British publications at the same time.[1]

The task of editing and proof-reading 'penny dreadfuls' would appear to have been discharged light-heartedly. There was no attempt to make an instalment end at a logical pause in the narrative. Nor was there any attempt to build up a climax, in order to stimulate the reader to buy the next number. Possibly such a device would have been considered meretricious by the peculiar standards of the time; it is more likely that editor and author just could not be bothered. As it was, an instalment frequently ended in the middle of a sentence of dull explanation, and there was no 'Summary of what has gone before' in the next instalment. It was by no means rare for the illustrations to refer to a previous part, or to a future part; occasionally they bore no relation to the story whatever. Spelling mistakes were nearly as copious as grammatical mistakes, and they were legion. Few of the writers of penny parts seemed to be happy about their moods or tenses. Any entry into the field of the conditional or the subjunctive was usually doomed to failure. Gradually extreme simplicity of style came to be cultivated in the 'penny dreadful'—that *pizzicato*, short-sentence style of which a glimpse has already been seen in the extract from *The Darling of Our Crew*. The old school of writers despised this literary adulteration, pointing out that some columns of narrative contained more white space than black. Each paragraph consisted of but a single sentence, and five out of six sentences were strangled at birth. Quite a number of sentences, indeed, contained one noun, one verb and nothing more. Sometimes they did not contain even a verb. All affectations like colons and semi-colons were ruthlessly purged, but exclamation marks were used profusely. Simplification—presumably for the benefit

---

[1] The *Quarterly Review* (1890) describes how an English author complained that he had found on an English bookstall a plagiarized version of one of his books. It turned out that his original work had been pirated in America. This in turn had been pirated in Britain, and 'translated' back into English (though not quite the same English as the original) by a firm which was ignorant of its English origin. This firm, however, was able to escape the consequences by showing that the plot had originally been lifted from a German source.

Nearly sixty years later, on November 28, 1947, Mr. Skeffington-Lodge complained in Parliament that British magazines were using American fiction and changing Detroit to Birmingham, Central Park to St. James's Park, and so on.

THE YOUNG APPRENTICE
OR THE WATCHWORDS OF OLD LONDON

"NELLY STARTED BACK IN HORROR."

"Well, Max," he said, "you must go your way. My daughter can never wed one who is so utterly an enemy to his king and his country also. Return to me in a week, and let me hear that your ideas are changed. Otherwise, Nelly can never be more to you than she is."

"May I not bid her farewell?" asked Max, sorrowfully.

Typical title page to a popular Victorian 'penny dreadful'

C

of the only-just-literate public and not (as some averred) for the convenience of only-just-literate authors—was carried to a pitch never seen before or since. Two possibilities cannot be ruled out: that the short sentence style was a deliberate economy of effort by writers earning considerably less than a penny a line; and that sometimes the extreme brevity of the paragraphs may have been a desperate editorial device to spin out copy which had fallen short of the space allotted.

Here is a characteristic short-weight passage from *The Young Apprentice or, The Watchwords of Old London:*

She could see every now and then glimpses of the road and the solitary windmill, whose phantom-like sails moved slowly some quarter of a mile away.
This was all.
No human being seemed here.
Not even a wild animal disturbed the stillness by leaping from its lair.
Yet presently, as I have said, footsteps seemed following her.
She stopped and listened.
All was still.
Then again she advanced.
The steps went on once more.
She became alarmed.
Should she go back?
Or should she hide herself?
The latter idea she soon dismissed.
It would be useless.
If followed in the way she imagined, the one who followed could see her and would find her at once.
So she hurried on more quickly.
'I shall soon see Max,' she thought, 'and he will protect me.'
Suddenly she started back in horror.
A man was hanging from the tree.
It was the Alsatian.
She shrieked aloud.

With all their editorial infelicities the 'penny dreadfuls' prospered. Some, like *Tyburn Dick*, came out twice a week, on Tuesdays and Fridays. They carried no advertisements, save of romances published by the same house, so that a healthy circulation was essential for profit-making. A flagging story would be knocked on the head, without compunction, no matter how far the plot had progressed; a successful one had to be kept going at all costs. The author might have made his plans to finish the story in, say, a score of instalments, but would find himself forced to spin it out for fifty, or a hundred.

Thomas Catling has a story of one of Lloyd's woman writers who unexpectedly sent in the last instalment of a serial which had looked like running for a long time to come. Lloyd sent round a trusted representative to find out what was the trouble. The answer was that the lady was imminently expecting a baby. Tactfully, they persuaded her to write as much as possible in the fortnight which remained. A few chapters came in, then the supply stopped abruptly. As the printers' deadline grew uncomfortably close Lloyd put one of his own writers on the job of improvising an instalment. This conscienceless deputy skimmed through the previous chapter without bothering to read what had gone before, and dashed off enough copy to placate the printer. When the authoress was in a position to sit up she grew most indignant over the interpolation; but on being pressed to supply twelve more chapters her displeasure abated.[1] (Clare Leighton in her book *Tempestuous Petticoat* tells how the *accouchements* of her mother, Marie Connor Leighton, who wrote 'powerful' serials for North-cliffe, caused dismay among her editors. Northcliffe did not share their fears, asserting that not even triplets would prevent Mrs. Leighton from completing her instalments.)

Many stories have accumulated about Lloyd. In the course of a restless youth George Augustus Sala was apprenticed for a short spell to a Mr. Calvert, who cut—'or rather chopped'—the illustrations for Lloyd's penny publications. Sala in his *Life and Adventures* claims to have received from Lloyd a letter asking for more blood—much more blood, spouting blood in fact, and more prominent eyes. Illustrations, supposedly the work of Sala, from

---

[1] There is a delightful story, attributed to more than one publishing house, of the serial writer who disappears in the middle of a story. As he shows no sign of turning up, it is decided to carry on without him. Unfortunately he has left his hero bound to a stake, with lions circling him, and an avalanche about to fall for good measure (or some such situation). Relays of writers try to think of a way out, and give it up. Then at the eleventh hour the missing author returns. He takes the briefest look at the previous instalment and then, without a moment's hesitation, writes: 'With one bound Jack was free.'

The Heads of the Headless suggest that he did his best to follow instructions.

Lloyd's romances were among those sternly criticized by a fellow publisher, Charles Knight, in *Passages of a Working Life* (1865). Knight spoke of the mortification inspired by much of the literature of the 'forties in 'those who, like myself, had formed an over-sanguine estimate of the benefit that was likely to result from the general diffusion of the ability to read.' He went on to cite 'manufactories . . . where large bodies of children are employed to arrange types, at the wages of shirt makers, from copy furnished by the most ignorant, at the wages of scavengers.' It is not clear just whose sweat-shops these were. Certainly Knight's charge of 'diffusing a moral miasma through the land' would be hard to substantiate against Lloyd, who was by no means without his standards. In one of his journals Lloyd claimed that all his stories went to show that 'the wild turbulence of vice' could bring 'nothing but evil fruits and deep vexation of spirit.' And his publications in no way contributed to the outcry which produced the Obscene Publications Bill in the 'fifties.

In later life, when he had acquired *The Daily Chronicle* and was a publisher of power and prosperity, Lloyd preferred not to be reminded of the penny parts which he put out in the 'forties. He lived to be a member of the Political Committee of the Reform Club, a citizen of the utmost respectability. When he died the newspapers forebore to dwell on his early publishing activities. If the obituarist of *The Times* knew that this worthy old gentleman was the first sponsor of Sweeney Todd he held his peace.

CHAPTER II

THE DEMON BARBER

A LEADER WRITER in *The Times Literary Supplement* has advanced the interesting theory that it was the astonishing popularity of the Sweeney Todd legend in early and mid-Victorian times that caused a good old English word to lapse into disrepute among respectable people. In the late 'nineties when the public 'sacrificed almost anything to be genteel,' Sweeney Todd 'both on the stage and in print was considered so vulgar the word "barber" was considered vulgar too.' Hence arrived the word 'hairdresser.'

Probably a psychologist could be found to assert that the macabre relish with which successive generations have devoured the stories, stage plays and even radio plays and films of Sweeney Todd, the Demon Barber, springs from a desire deep down in every man's heart to know what his neighbour tastes like. Whatever the reason, dealers in 'bloods' to-day know that in Sweeney Todd they have one of their best-selling lines, and raise their prices accordingly.

Mr. Tod Slaughter, who played the part of the barber in a stage tour of the British Zone of Germany in 1947, is reported to have ascribed a German origin to the legend of Sweeney Todd (incidentally the Germans seem to have been a little hurt at the British troops' irreverent participation in the performance: they thought this a poor way to treat a great classic). Others have claimed that

Sweeney Todd was modelled on the infamous Sawney Bean, whose trial in the thirteenth century provides one of the more gruesome titbits in the annals of Scottish crime. But the bulk of the evidence suggests that the story of Sweeney Todd was imported from France.

The historian can take his pick of two French Figaros, both Parisians. One supposedly flourished in the fourteenth century in the Rue des Marmouzets. According to *Les Rues de Paris* (1844): 'Le temps n'effacera pas le souvenir du patissier homicide qui sert encore d'épouvantail aux petits enfants de la Rue des Marmouzets.' The better-documented of these monsters—his record is detailed in Fouché's *Archives of the Police*—operated in a barber's shop in the Rue de la Harpe, Paris, in the first flush of Liberty, Equality and Fraternity. One day two hurried travellers, accompanied by a dog, arrived at the *perruquier's*, and asked to be shaved. While one sat in the chair the other slipped round the corner to make some inquiry, only to find when he returned that his friend had disappeared. According to the barber the traveller had paid his money and left as soon as he had been shaved. This seemed odd, but odder still was the presence and behaviour of the dog outside, impatiently awaiting the reappearance of its master. Presently the dog began to shiver and howl and no entreaties could move it from the spot. The suspicions of the second traveller were aroused. He rallied a crowd, told his story and led them in an assault on the now-locked shop. When the door was breached the dog flew at the barber's throat and nearly killed him. Then he nosed his way to the basement, where he sniffed around and set up an anguished howl. In the basement wall was found an aperture leading to the next house, and in the adjacent basement was found the body of the missing traveller. The owner of the building was a pie-maker, whose wares were the most-sought-after in Paris. Then neighbours remembered that they had never seen meat going into the shop. A search revealed as many as 300 skulls on the premises. And a search of the barber's disclosed the casket of pearls which had been in the possession of the unfortunate traveller.

For their part in this odious trade the barber and the pie-maker were executed on the rack, and the law directed that the property should be pulled down and the site left vacant evermore as a reminder of great wickedness.

Newspapers and magazines on both sides of the Channel made much of this story, but gradually the excitement died down. One who may well have read and remembered the story was Thomas Peckett Prest, the wayward virtuoso of Salisbury Square. Whether this report formed the direct inspiration of Sweeney Todd will never be known, for Prest was almost certainly acquainted with the story of Sawney Bean, and has in fact been credited with the authorship of *Sawney Bean, the Man-Eater of Midlothian*.

At all events Prest took the theme of the barber and the pie shop, selected Fleet Street for his setting, and had little difficulty in selling the story to Edward Lloyd, who published it about 1840 under the strangely restrained title *The String of Pearls (A Romance)*.[1] It was an excellent story, in the wordy fashion of its time, and the suspense was well kept. To the unsuspecting readers of that day the confirmation of their mounting suspicions must have come as a first-class shock. So far as is known no one attacked the publishers on the ground that the story was likely to drive unbalanced persons to practise cannibalism.

Two years later a stage version of Sweeney Todd by George Dibdin Pitt was being produced at the Britannia Saloon, Hoxton. It was a theme which was readily adapted to the theatre, and stage carpenters were to be busy for the next hundred years constructing disappearing chairs. In 1846 the story was again run by Lloyd in his *People's Periodical and Family Library*, a weekly magazine which contained, *inter alia*, articles entitled 'Confessions of a Deformed Lunatic' and 'The Madhouse of Palermo.' Despite the extreme thinness of the paper and the trying type-face the story sent new joyous waves of horripilation through the respectable families who read it.

The String of Pearls set the general pattern for all Sweeney Todd stories. Todd usually had a terrified assistant whom he ill-used, and sent out of the shop on some errand when a likely customer was about to be despatched. The chair was dropped through

---

[1] Oddly enough a pie shop used to flourish in the quarter where Prest located his story, in spite of the unfortunate association.

the floor by the pulling of a bolt in a back room. Victims were usually strangers to the town, wealthy drovers who boasted of their profits at market, or seafarers back from, or setting out on, long voyages. The proprietor of the pie shop was always a woman, and the actual pie-maker was a wretch imprisoned in the basement. There was commonly a hat found hanging in the shop after the customer had departed, and of course a dog which sat outside the shop and howled. A curious point in Prest's version was that while this dog turned 'with loathing' from bits of pie thrown to it, a newly bereaved widow showed no instinctive dislike to a pie containing portions of her late partner in marriage.

A grim *double entendre* was a feature of Prest's narrative, and was copied, not always so successfully, by those who later took over the torch. The barber would assure his customers that there was not a shop in London which could polish off a customer as quickly; or he would advise a waiting customer to go round the corner to watch the animated clock of St. Dunstan's striking the hour 'while I finish this gentleman.' Once he extracted himself from a tedious discussion by saying 'I have another subject to dissect.' Not always was the double talk deliberate on the speaker's part, however. When the boy Tobias, having newly applied for the job, was advised not to 'repeat a word of what passes in this shop, or dare to make any supposition, or draw any conclusion from anything you see or hear, or fancy you see or hear,' he replied: 'Yes, sir, I won't say anything. I wish, sir, as I may be made into veal pies at Lovett's in Bell Yard if I as much as says a word.' It was not surprising that Sweeney Todd looked at him for a minute or two in silence. On another occasion an apprentice eating one of Mrs. Lovett's pies exclaimed to his friend, 'Lord bless ye, I'd eat my mother if she was a pork chop!'

The artist who illustrated 'The String of Pearls' in the *People's Periodical* hardly did justice to the author's description:

The barber himself was a long low-jointed, ill-put-together sort of fellow, with an immense mouth, and such huge hands and feet that he was, in his way, quite a natural curiosity; and what was more wonderful considering his trade, there never was such a head of hair as Sweeney Todd's. We know not what to compare it to; probably it came close to what one may suppose to be the appearance of a thick-set hedge in which a quantity of small wire had got entangled. In truth it was a most terrific head of hair; and as Sweeney Todd kept all his combs in it—some people said his scissors likewise—when he put his head out of the shop door to see what sort of weather it was he might have been mistaken for some Indian warrior with a very remarkable head-dress.

Later it appeared that he 'squinted a little to add to his charms,' and his short, hyena-like laugh (described as a 'cachinatory effusion') was such that 'people had been known to look up to the ceiling, then on the floor and all around them, to know from whence it had come, scarcely supposing it possible that it proceeded from mortal lips.'

Prest never lost an opportunity of discoursing on the merits of Mrs. Lovett's pies. The arrival of each fresh batch from the bakehouse was the signal for a near-riot in Bell's Yard. Lawyers and their clerks and apprentices were the principal consumers.

And well did they deserve their reputation, those delicious pies! There was about them a flavour never surpassed and rarely equalled; the paste was of the most delicate construction and impregnated with the aroma of a delicious gravy that defied description. Then the small portions of meat which they contained were so tender, and the fat and lean so artistically mixed up that to eat one of Lovett's pies was such a provocative to eat another that many persons who came to lunch stayed to dine, wasting more than an hour perhaps of precious time and endangering (who knows to the contrary?) the success of some law-suit thereby.

Although he had been promised that his throat would be slit from ear to ear if he did not mind his own business, the boy Tobias could not restrain his curiosity. It was strange that a customer should depart and leave his hat, and not come back for it. And then there was the mystery of why the barber's chair was securely screwed to the floor. One day he broke into Sweeney Todd's private apartments. Here he found a large number of walking-sticks, more than a hundred umbrellas, a collection of swords and some pairs of shoes, and finally, a large desk stuffed with jewellery. His unlawful entry was detected; but instead of cutting the boy's throat the barber decided to have him shut away in the madhouse at Peckham Rye, knowing that if the lad began to voice his suspicions of what went on in the barber's shop his statements would be accepted as proof of insanity. The madhouse keeper was an understanding fellow and knew that Sweeney Todd would not want to pay the expenses of Tobias's incarceration indefinitely. A previous lad whom Todd had committed to his care for a year died conveniently at the end of the paid-up period.

Now the author found something else on which to let his fancy roam—the frightful stench which welled up from the gratings of near-by St. Dunstan's.

About this time and while these incidents of our most strange and eventful narrative were taking place, the pious frequenters of old St. Dunstan's began to perceive a strange and most abominable odour throughout the sacred edifice.

It was in vain that old women who came to hear the sermons, although they were too deaf to catch a third part of them, brought smelling bottles and other means of stifling their noses; still the dreadful charnel-house sort of smell would make itself most painfully and most disagreeably apparent.

As for the beadle, whose job it was to cuff small boys who dared to look at the bishop, he used to go about with a key in one hand and a vinegar cloth in the other, as was the fashion during the Great Plague.

The author had a streak of irreverence in him, and really enjoyed describing the effects of the fearful stench at St. Dunstan's. He told of the day when the bishop arrived to take confirmation classes and was so overwhelmed by the odour that 'the people found themselves confirmed almost before they knew where they were.' The bishop then stalked out to his carriage, ignoring the cold collation which had been set out for him (and which, for once, did not contain any of Mrs. Lovett's pies). At this stage the church authorities decided, a little belatedly, to explore their mephitic vaults in an effort to trace the nuisance. It could not have been caused by the corpses in their racks, they decided, because these had been dead too long to vex the atmosphere.

Meanwhile a humble pieman was becoming dissatisfied with his conditions of labour in Mrs. Lovett's underground bakehouse. It had seemed like a good job at first—he was allowed to eat unlimited quantities of pies, which he did until he was glutted. But he was not allowed to leave his underground chamber. He even had to sleep there. And while he slept after his labours a fresh supply of meat would arrive on the shelves at the other end of the room, ready for the next day's bake.

This mysterious arrival of the meat puzzled the pieman. He began to search the far end of the vault. Lightly pencilled on the wall was this disturbing message:

'Whatever unhappy wretch reads these lines may bid adieu to the world and all hope, for he is a doomed man! He will never emerge from these vaults with life, for there is a secret connected with them so awful and so hideous that to write it makes one's blood curdle and the flesh to creep upon your bones. The secret is this—and you may be assured, whoever is reading these lines, that I write the truth, and that it is impossible to make the awful truth worse by exaggeration, as it would be by a candle at midday to attempt to add any lustre to the sunbeams.'

Here, most unfortunately, the writing broke off.

If the unknown author had thought less of his literary style and more of his duty to society he might have been able to get his message across. As it was the communiqué broke off with an ominous scrawl which suggested that the author had been forcibly interrupted. While pondering the possible implications of this warning, the pieman noticed a clean sheet of paper on the floor. It bore a written message:

You are getting dissatisfied, and therefore it becomes necessary to explain to you your real position, which is simply this: you are a prisoner and were such from the first moment that you set foot where you now are . . . it is sufficient to inform you that so long as you continue to make pies you will be safe, but if you refuse, then the first time you are caught sleeping your throat will be cut.

Then, as if to drive the message right home, the trapdoor in the roof opened and Sweeney Todd's evil face appeared.

'Make pies,' advised Todd. 'Eat them and be happy. How many a man would envy your position—withdrawn from the struggles of existence, amply provided with board and lodging, and engaged in a pleasant and delightful occupation; it is astonishing how you can be dissatisfied.'

But not all these warnings could keep the prisoner from trying to find out where the supplies of meat came from. With the aid of an iron bar he forced the hidden communicating hatch at the end of the vault and stepped through, bearing a torch. There he found his answer.

With a cry of horror he fell backwards, extinguishing the torch in his fall, and he lay for fully a quarter of an hour insensible upon the floor. What dreadful sight had he seen that had so chilled his young blood and frozen up the springs of life?

By now Sweeney Todd, who had spent such of his time as was not passed in slaying and dissecting in trying to sell the string of pearls which gives the story its name, had made enough money to retire, and was preparing to poison Mrs. Lovett in order that she should be in no position to betray him. But the net was closing in.

In reply to the notice in his window after Tobias's departure— 'Wanted, a lad; one of strong religious principles preferred. Apply within'—he received an application from a strikingly good-looking youth, whom he engaged. This was Johanna, the heroine of the story, who had volunteered to play an undercover role in an endeavour to find out what had happened to her seafaring lover, missing after a visit to Sweeney Todd's. Two gentlemen of the town had also undertaken to visit Todd's shop as customers. These were exciting hours for Johanna—and for the reader. One thing which gave Johanna food for thought was that a gash in the arm of the chair caused by her carelessness with a razor had vanished completely a few minutes after her return to the shop from an errand.

The *dénouement* was as exciting as could be hoped. One of Johanna's gentlemen was seated in the chair, the other was concealed in a cupboard. Johanna herself, sent on another errand, was watching obliquely through the window. After the usual double-talk the barber made his excuses to go to the back shop. Smartly, and none too soon, the intended victim jumped out of the chair. With a clank and a thud the chair on its trapdoor dropped through the floor and a duplicate swung up in its place. The 'victim' sat down in the seat again. When Todd reappeared he went rigid with fright, thinking that the dead man had returned to confront him. At that point he was arrested.

The climax in Bell's yard was equally satisfactory. A fresh batch of pies was due up at nine o'clock.

One, two, three, four, five, six, seven, eight, nine! Yes, it was nine at last. It strikes by old St. Dunstan's Church clock, and in weaker strains the chronometrical machine at the pie shop echoes the sound. What excitement there is now to get at the pies when they shall come! Mrs. Lovett lets down the square moveable platform that goes on pullies into the cellar; some machinery which only requires a handle being turned brings up a hundred pies on a tray. These are eagerly seized by parties who have previously paid, and such a smacking of lips ensues as was never known. Down goes the platform for the next hundred and a gentleman says:

'Let me work the handle, Mrs. Lovett, if you please. It is too much for you, I am sure.'

'Sir, you are very kind, but I never allow anybody on this side of the counter but my own people, sir. I can turn the handle myself, sir, if you please, with the assistance of this girl. Keep your distance, sir. Nobody wants your help.'

How the waggish young lawyers' clerks laughed as they smacked their lips and sucked in all the golopshious gravy of the pies, which by-the-way appeared to be all delicious veal that time, and Mrs. Lovett worked the handle of the machine all the more vigorously that she was a little angered with the officious stranger. What an unusual trouble it seemed to be to wind up those forthcoming hundred pies! How she toiled and how the people waited, but at length there came up the savoury steam and then the tops of the pies were visible.

They came up upon a large tray about six feet square, and at that moment Mrs. Lovett ceased turning the handle and let a catch fall that prevented the platform receding again, to the astonishment and terror of everyone away flew all the pies, tray and all, and a man who was lying crouched in an exceedingly flat state under the tray sprang to his feet.

Mrs. Lovett shrieked, as well she might, and then she stood trembling and looking as pale as death itself. It was the young cook from the cellar who had adopted this mode of escape.

The throng of persons in the shop looked petrified, and after Mrs. Lovett's shriek there was an awful silence for about a minute and then the young man who officiated as cook spoke.

'Ladies and gentlemen, I fear that what I am going to say will spoil your appetites; but truth is beautiful at all times, and I have to state that Mrs. Lovett's pies are made of *human flesh!*'

      *   *   *   *

How the throng of persons recoiled—what a roar of agony and dismay there was! How frightfully sick about forty lawyers' clerks became all at once, and how they spat out the gelatinous clinging portions of the rich pies they had been devouring. . . .

The exclamations of the consumers, once they could find tongue, were strangely anti-climactic, consisting of 'Good gracious!' 'Oh, the pies!' and 'Confound it!'

Mrs. Lovett collapsed and died from the mingled effects of shock and the poison with which Sweeney Todd had already laced her brandy. The barber himself was removed to Newgate and in due course hanged. By a happy coincidence the pieman turned out to be Johanna's missing lover.

Concluded the author:

The youths who visited Lovett's pie shop and there luxuriated upon those delicacies are youths no longer. Indeed the grave has closed over all but one and he is very, very old, but even now as he thinks of how many pies he ate and how he enjoyed the flavour of the 'veal' he shudders and has to take a drop of brandy.

Beneath the old church of St. Dunstan's were found the heads and bones of Todd's victims. As little as possible was said by the authorities about it, but it was supposed that some hundreds of persons must have perished in the frightful manner we have detailed.

It is unnecessary to follow Sweeney Todd through all the vicissitudes of penny publication. A generation after Edward Lloyd had launched him, Charles Fox took over and gave the barber a new run under the best-known title—'Sweeney Todd, the Demon Barber of Fleet Street.' The artist portrayed Todd knife in hand descending the cellar steps with an expression of unparalleled villainy. Smaller pictures showed him chasing away the dog with his master's hat, and offering the string of pearls to a dealer. And, of course, there was a view of an apprentice buying pies.

Sweeney Todd also made appearances in quite unexpected quarters. In 1883 a story called 'The Link Boy of Old London' began in Fox's *Boy's Standard*. After a few chapters of old-fashioned Gothic, with a highwayman or two for good measure, the Demon Barber made his appearance. There were certain variations. Instead of the victims falling on to their heads twenty feet below the trap-door, as in Prest's story, this author had them falling on to iron spikes. A suspicious constable was introduced. Failing to get any evidence on Todd he would go round the corner and solace himself with half a dozen pies from Mrs. Darkman. Instead of having his assistant put away in a madhouse, the Barber knifed him in the back after a particularly crimson battle with two customers.

Wiping his hands at the end, Todd observed, 'Well, well, Mrs. Darkman can't complain of the supply to-night.'

This barber was sufficient of a sentimentalist to fall in love with the wife of one of his customers. He dispatched the husband in the usual way, but knowing that he could not marry the widow unless she had proof of her husband's death he forebore to have the corpse made into pies and arranged for it to be discovered mutilated in the street.

In this version Todd was finally spitted through by a constable in a fight in the cellars of his shop. Mrs. Darkman died by poison. 'A good riddance of two wretches,' said the head officer, 'for there is no death devised by law except burning which is bad enough for them.'

By way of postscript it should be put on record that at least one publisher in the squeamish times we live in has issued the story of Sweeney Todd disinfected of any dubious odour of cannibalism. The cover of the Mellifont Press *Sweeney Todd* (1936) was a lurid affair in colour, showing a victim being precipitated through the trap-door; but only in one shocked sentence near the end was there any suggestion of dirty work below stairs:

It was never made quite clear how Todd got rid of the bodies of his various victims, the men whom he had murdered and robbed. There was one horrible rumour which grew into a legend in the neighbourhood that Mrs. Lovett's pie shop had disposed of them, but such a thing is too terrible to contemplate.

A good companion to this work would have been the story of Dracula with all references to blood-sucking omitted.

CHAPTER III

ROGUES AND VAGABONDS

AMONG THE VICTORIAN 'penny dreadfuls' which earned the greatest condemnation and the greatest circulation were those which invested with knightly qualities the knaves of the *Newgate Calendar, or Malefactors' Bloody Register:* Highwaymen, jail-breakers, house-breakers, all the incorrigible free-lances who haunted the thieves' kitchens of the Great Wen and ended their days at Tyburn with the bells of St. Sepulchre's tolling in their ears, if they still had any ears.

James Catnach, of Monmouth Court, found an ever-expanding public in the years following Waterloo for his 'last sorrowful lamentations' of criminals, and is credited with selling more than a million copies of Corder's confession in the Red Barn murder. To him is due in no small degree the consuming curiosity of that generation in the exploits of criminals. Only a short remove from Catnach's highly coloured confessions were the penny romances of highwaymen which were to run right through from the 'forties to the 'nineties.

In a day when masked raiders no longer ranged Finchley and Hammersmith the public decided that it wanted its highwaymen depicted, if not as out-and-out heroes, then as dashing rogues with a Robin Hood streak in them. If Rob Roy, a pioneer of what a later age has called the 'protection racket,' could be passed off as a heroic chieftain, there seemed no reason why gentlemanly and gallant instincts should not be attributed to his contemporary, Dick Turpin.

Wage slaves had no intention of spending their scanty leisure reading about wage slaves. Their spirit craved more powerful stimulus. They wanted to read about fiery individualists, men of spirit who defied harsh laws and oppressive officialdom, even though they finished at the end of a hempen rope. The public were prepared to be especially tolerant towards any malefactors who could be shown to have been forced into wrong-doing through deprivation of parents, miscarriages of justice, or the activities of oppressive guardians, grinding employers, rascally landlords and lecherous squires. If their hero put himself on the wrong side of the law in order to fight organized wickedness masquerading as virtue, the issue—as far as the public was concerned—was still between good and bad. The author of Hogarth House's *The Blue Dwarf* (*c.* 1870)—some chapters of which enjoyed the distinction of being reprinted as a social document in *Pilot Papers* (March 1947)—disposed of the moral and ethical problems involved as follows:

The sum realized by some highwaymen in those days was something fabulous. The money spent in riot and debauchery in a week would often have provided for fifty families.

'Light come light go' had always been the motto of those whose money came to them in a nefarious way.

But many modern ways of making money are infinitely more nefarious than taking it by force.

The cheating done by lawyers and brokers whose clients trust them, the hundred and one ways of levying blackmail by men in power and with influence in any place of trust, the disgraceful sweating exercised in professions where such mean tricks were never supposed to have been heard of, are infinitely more despicable than highway robbery.

At all events, the man risked his neck, and was always amenable to the laws of his country.

But for the mean, crawling thieves we speak of there is no punishment —not even that of their consciences, for they have none.

There were scores of highwayman stories, in both penny and halfpenny parts: *Dick Turpin, Tom Turpin, Captain MacHeath, Captain Midnight, Moonlight Jack, Gentleman Jack, Black Hawk, Black Wolf, Black Highwayman, Sixteen-String Jack, Turnpike*

D

Dick and *Tyburn Dick*, to name but a few; and, on the distaff side, *May Turpin*, *Starlight Nell* and *Nan Darrell*. Consistently the most favoured character was Dick Turpin. Any similarity between the facts of his life and the fancies of his chroniclers was purely coincidental; and the liberties the authors took with the facts of Turpin's career (even his schooldays became a theme for high-flown adventure) were as nothing compared with the liberties they took with Time and Space. Certain writers would distract attention from a blatant impossibility in their narrative by scoffing at some critic's unfamiliarity with one of the lesser-known versions of the *Newgate Calendar*, or by pointing out a trifling defect in the work of a late-starting imitator; thus giving the impression that they themselves were conscientious masters of detail.

The industrious author of *The Blue Dwarf* made Turpin the faithful tool of his terrifying blue-spotted homunculus, Sapathwa. The Dwarf was supposedly the heir to ancient estates, but was prevented by his revolting appearance from assuming his inheritance. He and the loyal highwayman used to rescue each other from calamity in turn. After one narrow squeak the Dwarf gave this instruction to Turpin and Tom King ('the modern Damon and Pythias,' as the author liked to call them):

'Hold yourselves in readiness within ten days to leave the country. We must go no matter where, so we be out of their reach—Scotland, Ireland, even America, if need be.'

And go they did. The author of *The Blue Dwarf* had to throw in not only Scots clansmen, Irish banditti and Red Indians, but a great deal else before his tale of Turpin had run its course.

Perhaps it was not strictly necessary in these highwayman stories to show Runners and Dragoons as so often corruptible, dull-witted and cowardly, the occupants of stage coaches as invariably pompous and crapulous, and to describe the robbers as 'our gallant and adventurous friends,' or to give them fine-sounding names like Victor St. George, Gallant Tom, Dashing Ralph or Devil Duke. Highwaymen were always attentive to their horses and womenfolk, and generous to their ostlers, as well they might be. The *Quarterly Review* complained that they always got the pick of the women—'lovely and persecuted damsels whose

The Blue Dwarf to the rescue . . .

physical charms and voluptuous embraces are dilated upon with exceeding unction.' And again: '. . . their mistresses are queens of beauty and romance, whose venal caresses are the rightful guerdon of skill, daring and dash.' In *Tyburn Dick*, however, the heroine was a woman of singular modesty, even though at one stage she dressed as a man. In this garb she withstood a protracted battle with an evil adversary, and would probably have won had not her tunic become unfastened and 'exposed to the fiery gaze of the brutal captor her beautiful white, heaving breast.' The shame was too much. All the fight went out of her and she crumpled on the spot.

According to *The Blue Dwarf* Dick Turpin and his crony Tom King were 'excellent Protestants,' with a healthy contempt for the frog-eating papists of France. In this story a certain moral laxity was permitted to Turpin, as the following extract from Chapter 113 will show:

Having a couple of days before them and ample funds at their disposal, they determined to put on their most fashionable dresses, and, favoured by a friend, to visit the 'Young Cocoa Nutt' on one of its grand nights when ladies were admitted.

Whatever the rank of the persons attending this club, they were men of tainted character, and some of them as anxious to avoid the ken of the Runners as Dick and Tom.

Several of those frequenting the place were under obligations to the high tobies, who had often assisted them liberally with cash, to get the unquestioned *entrée* of places frequented by themselves.

It was a lady's night—when a queen of the then *demi-monde* would be present; flaunting molls, Dick called them. But Dick and Tom were both partial to female society.

For a family man, Dick was particularly lax in his observances.

But then he was away from home, and playing the bachelor.

The club was elegantly furnished, and in every way made attractive. There was a well fitted-up ante-chamber, looking out on one of the parks, with pictures, counter for refreshments, and every convenience.

Beyond this was a very well-appointed supper room, where every delicacy of the season was provided gratis.

Wine was choice, varied and served without stint.

They went straight to the supper room, and, sitting down, had themselves served speedily. The waiters knew them, and knew them to be liberal. They got the best of everything and wines in abundance.

As soon as they were satisfied, they rose and went into *the* room, where they found everybody either hard at work or looking on.

Dick and Tom picked out a couple of flaunting molls, all furbelows and laces, and began a regular flirtation with them.

In this way and in playing, a very jolly evening was spent; then they rose, and in company with their inamoratas, and with several other persons of both sexes prepared to retire.

Suddenly a bell rang, and it was known that there was a raid. . . .

The biggest monument to Turpin was that produced by Edward Viles, whose *Black Bess, or The Knight of the Road*, published by E. Harrison of Salisbury Court, ran to 254 weekly parts, a total of 2,028 pages—believed to be the longest 'penny dreadful' by one author on record. The total number of words, allowing for illustrations, is something like two and a half million.

On the title page of the bound work, published in 1868, is a quotation from Henry Fielding's *Tom Jones*:

'Some of the author's friends cry'd—"Look'ee, the man is a villain; but it is Nature for all that." And all the young critics of the age, the clerks, apprentices, etc., called it low and fell agroaning.'

Supporting this is a defensive preface:

The author of *Black Bess*, or *The Knight of the Road*, has one request to make:

It is that those who have, unread, condemned the present work will take the trouble to peruse it. And an entire change of opinion will be the result, because in no place will vice be commended or virtue sneered at; nor will any pandering to sensuality, suggestion of impure thoughts or direct encouragement of crime be discovered; neither are there details of seduction, bigamy, adultery and domestic poisoning, such as are indispensable ingredients of our popular three-volume novels. On the contrary, the work will be found full of exciting personal adventures such as can never be re-enacted until the railways are swept away and the stage coaches replaced on our highways—until, in fine, the present state of things is changed to what it was a century and a half ago. If anyone is weak-minded enough to be carried away by the idea that a highwayman's career as depicted in these pages can be equalled in reality at the present day he must be imbecile indeed. Let not the 'Life of Robin Hood' fall into the hands of such a one, or, sure as fate, Sherwood Forest would be his destination, with bow and arrows for his stock in trade.

There were four heroes in *Black Bess*: Dick Turpin, Claude Duval, Tom King and Jack Rann (Sixteen-String Jack); or five

including the horse. Critics who point out that Turpin lived from
1706 to 1739 and Duval from 1643 to 1670 are informed by the
author that 'the Claude Duval of whom we are about to speak
was not the one who came to an ignominious end in the reign of
the second Charles, but his nephew. The two have often been
ignorantly confounded.' The author does not appear to have
considered it necessary to explain how Turpin came to rescue the
Young Pretender at Culloden in 1746.

At least Viles kept his hero within these islands. The story opened
with Turpin, single-handed, robbing the stage coach containing
London's Lord Mayor, who was clutching to his fat belly a massive
silver cup on which were 'set forth at length the supposititious
talents of Lord Mayor Funge. Such was his euphonious appellation.
Ezekiel Funge.' In the remaining 1,135 chapters Turpin spent
his time shaking off bloodhounds and police spies, rescuing op-
pressed damsels, cutting down the bodies of his less fortunate
comrades, exploring haunted houses, escaping from Newgate,
following the Pretender and resuscitating Claude Duval, who was
for ever being picked up 'dead' after some bloody encounter and
escaping live burial at the last minute. Among the highlights were
a battle on the deck of a smuggler's vessel, an encounter with
dragoons amid the monoliths of Stonehenge, and Dick's marriage to
Maud Gouldman, performed under duress by a kidnapped parson
standing on a powder barrel with a train of explosive running to it.

Long before the end Turpin knew he was a doomed man. He
mourned at the death-bed of his wife, and he mourned at the death-
bed of Black Bess. The horse he buried personally at dead of night—
a feat which can be appreciated only by someone who has tried
to bury a horse single-handed. Then came his final capture and
trial, at which the judge found him 'guilty of innumerable crimes
all of which are punishable by death . . . may Heaven extend
that forgiveness towards you which the Law will not allow us to
show on earth.'

There was an illustration depicting Turpin on the scaffold,
but the text showed a certain reticence:

It would be too painful to linger over the last moments of the hero
whose career we have followed for so long with such deep interest.

Viles's Turpin was drugged before execution to prevent him making a last-minute attempt at escape. But he was able to deprive the executioner of the pleasure of pushing him off the ladder, electing to jump of his own free will.

The 2,028th page was the only short-weight page of them all; it contained seven-eighths blank space. With the penultimate instalment came the announcement:

OBSERVE! With next week's number, No. 254, will be given away No. 1 of *The Black Highwayman*, being the second series of *Black Bess*.

Edward Viles had not yet shot his bolt.

Nor had his conscientious illustrator, who had seen Turpin through all his scrapes (frequently, and perhaps deliberately, anticipating the event by several chapters), with an occasional large folding picture thrown in. But *Black Bess* did not depend on give-aways; it earned its 'unexampled favour' on its own merits.

The veneration for Turpin died hard. After the twentieth century had dawned the Aldine Company started, almost simultaneously, a Dick Turpin Library and a Claude Duval Library. The former was the more popular and ran for several years. No useful purpose was to be served at this late stage by bringing Turpin back to the Great North Road. He was left free to pace the deck of *The Flying Foam* and to consort with his pirate queens.

Not even Alfred Harmsworth, who vowed to have no rogues as heroes in his boys' papers, was able to exclude highwaymen. Claude Duval was to be found—albeit on his best behaviour—in one of the earlier numbers of *Pluck* and in the last numbers of *The Boys' Friend*. The first issue of the *Penny Wonder* (1912) featured a high-pressure serial, 'Lady Turpin,' sub-titled 'The powerful story of Galloping Gloria Gale, the modern Highwaywoman, and her black mare Midnight.' Gloria held up, successively and successfully, the Royal Mail (to recover a letter), the coach containing the magistrate who was due to try her lover, and the Black Maria (to recover an innocent victim). She escaped from the centre of a monolithic ring, behind every stone of which was an armed policeman. (Thirty years later the film *The Wicked Lady* was to feature a highwaywoman no whit less beautiful and spirited, though with less noble motives.) In 1913 *Pluck*, perhaps as a counterblast to all the serials prophesying war, announced that a story of Dick Turpin, the famous knight of the road, would run weekly until further notice. And as soon as the war was over, George Newnes began to reprint many of the Aldine Turpin stories.

There were some critics who were prepared to wink at the romanticizing of highwaymen of a bygone age but who strongly deplored the sympathies lavished on such ruffians as Jack Sheppard, the robber and jail-breaker, and Charles Peace, the burglar. Plain robbery and burglary were too easy to imitate, they felt.

This trend in publishing reduced certain writers in the *Edinburgh Review* and *Quarterly Review* to a state of near-apoplexy. 'If Fagin the Jew, Baron Munchausen and Jack Sheppard had set up work as joint editors of a Thieves Library they could well have been proud of the whole series now before us,' wrote the *Edinburgh Review's* critic in 1887.

Even Bill Sykes, if driven to pen and ink, can sign his name; and any one of his numerous offspring can read with fluency the weekly Police News or the last edition of the Newgate Calendar, and criticize the details of the latest burglary, outrage or murder with the flippant ease of a connoisseur of crime. Murder as one of the fine arts is not too much for him; his library is both extensive and varied, and to be had at the rate of a penny a volume. It is to be found anywhere and everywhere throughout the whole domain of poverty, dirt, hunger and crime. It tempts him under a hundred different and seductive titles alike in country and in town. Every alley and foul court in Babylon reeks with it, and the remotest hamlet can no more escape from some sign of it than from the ubiquitous placard of the last new transparent patent soap.

One of the stories dissected by the *Edinburgh Review* was entitled *Joanna Polenipper, Female Horse Stealer, Footpad, Smuggler, Prison Breaker and Murderer*. The critic's indignation was divided between the style of writing—'Bombastic rant, high-flown rhodomontade and the flattest fustian flow from the lips of all speakers alike'—and the inadequate retribution visited upon Joanna for the havoc she made of the Decalogue, as indicated at the end of the story:

Joanna was transported for her crimes, retrieved her character in Australia, married a rich settler and lived for many years respected and beloved by all who knew her.

The *Quarterly Review's* assault, possibly written by the same person, occurred three years later. This journal, which had savaged Keats and called Dickens vulgar, had already wrinkled a fastidious nose over the domestic romances and tales of high life published in mid-nineteenth century, exclaiming incredulously, as it said every normal person must be tempted to exclaim on first dipping into one of these works, *Quis leget haec?*

Despite the advance of education, complained the *Quarterly Review* in 1890, such works as *Joskin the Body Snatcher* were still there to 'dispute the favour of the poorer class of readers with translations of the improving romances of MM. Zola and Paul de Kock. . . . In a lane not far from Fleet Street is a complete factory of the literature of rascaldom—a literature which has done much to people our prisons, our reformatories and our Colonies with scapegraces and n'er-do-wells.'

Spring-Heeled-Jack was the first item on the critic's list. It was typical, he said, of highwayman literature in which 'spirited lads' were encouraged to resist 'tyrants' of the law, handicapped by a 'paternal' government which would not let every man carry arms to defend himself. The moral tone of highwayman and pirate stories—particularly instanced was *Three-Fingered Jack, the Terror of the Antilles*—was simply deplorable.

Lawlessness and violence are the subjects of the writers' fondest admiration, and the severer matter is pleasingly seasoned with love scenes of the 'luscious' kind, which are almost as offensive in their way as the performances of certain young lady novelists of higher rank.

Others which came in for scathing mention were *Sweeney Todd* and *Broad-Arrow Jack*, and various 'shabby American importations.' Later the critic, cooling off a little, claimed to have private knowledge of the authors of many of these penny publications— 'not as a rule very distinguished members of the Republic of Letters, though in some few instances their antecedents are better than might be expected.' One, it appears, was a beneficed clergyman who had cast off his cloth. Another, who translated 'dubious

French novels' on weekdays, actually officiated on Sundays at
'some sort of Dissenting Chapel.' But most laughable, in the
critic's view, was the case of a friend whose maid had a father
who wrote novels from ten to four for a cheap publisher. Still more
ludicrous was the experience of a lady whose cook, taxed with
dilatoriness in the preparation of meals, explained that she was
busy in the kitchen writing novels.

Other cooks, of course, were busy in the kitchen reading novels.
And they, in company with the footmen, the pot boys and pit
boys, the errand boys and apprentices, were not going to be cheated
out of their Dick Turpins and Jack Sheppards. Respect for property
was a Victorian tradition. But if one had no property and small
prospect of ever having any it was a welcome exercise to read of
a 'have-not' with near-supernatural characteristics successfully
preying upon the 'haves.' Those who most bitterly criticized the
vogue for Jack Sheppard never had the wit to see that in lurid
fiction of this kind the masses were being given a harmless safety
valve.

There is no doubt that Jack Sheppard earned a great meed of
sympathy because he was consistently matched against the infamous Jonathan Wild. Opposed to this self-styled Thief-Taker,
who was himself an organizer of thieves, receiver, blackmailer,
brothel-keeper and murderer—probably the blackest rogue
England has produced—any adversary was apt to look like the
embodiment of justice in arms, a daring knight-errant fighting
against a corrupt confederacy of crime.

The *Dictionary of National Biography* says that Sheppard
was born in Stepney in 1702, a year before his father died. He
was brought up in a workhouse, apprenticed to a chair-mender
who ill-treated him, then befriended by a draper whom he later
robbed. He fell under the influence of Bess Lyon, or Edgeworth
Bess, who encouraged him to steal. So successful were his lone-
hand exploits that Jonathan Wild felt impelled to take action against
him. Prisons could not hold Jack Sheppard, however. He escaped
from St. Giles' Roundhouse, the New Prison, and finally from the
condemned cell at Newgate, an operation which involved mounting
a blocked chimney, breaking open several doors, climbing to the

leads and lowering himself by a blanket rope to the ground. He
went into hiding but later drove past Newgate wearing stolen
finery in an open coach. Then he drank himself silly and was
recaptured. His execution in 1724, at the age of twenty-two, is
said—improbably—to have drawn a crowd of 200,000 people
(twice as many as can be packed into Wembley Stadium). Troops
were called out to control the crowds and to quell the riot which
broke out over the disposal of his corpse. The *D.N.B.* records how
chapmen rang his exploits in every street, how the clergy, ever
alive to the value of topical metaphor, urged the faithful to emulate
Sheppard in a spiritual sense by ascending the chimney of hope
to the leads of divine meditation. In his studio Sir James Thornhill,
leading portraitist of the day, put the finishing touches to the
picture of Sheppard he had painted in the condemned cell. Daniel
Defoe was only one of many famous authors to chronicle the
feats of the jail-breaker. Books about Sheppard were published
in Amsterdam, Leipzig and Sydney. More than 100 years afterwards Harrison Ainsworth wrote his well-known life of Sheppard in *Bentley's Magazine*. It was only when cheap publishers
in Victorian times dared to put out halfpenny and penny instalments of the life (more or less) of Jack Sheppard that any serious
complaints were made about the danger to public morals.

One version of Jack Sheppard's adventures, published by
J. and H. Purkess of Dean Street, Soho, described how Sheppard
parted from his ally Skyblue because this impatient character in
the course of a jointly conducted robbery had plunged his knife
into a tiresome old woman. Later Jack was not above accepting
a smuggled file from Skyblue. This story had him respectably
married to Edgeworth Bess, with whom he shared the same room
in the New Prison. His escape involved not only the usual sawing
and filing but the lowering of both himself and Edgeworth Bess
over various high walls on a rope largely made of Edgeworth
Bess's underclothing. The modern jail-breaker can rely on no such
adventitious aid from his female accomplice.

A twopenny and rather better spelled life of Jack Sheppard—
though not necessarily any more reliable—by 'Blueskin' was
published by Glover, of Water Lane, Fleet Street. It was entitled

'The Illustrated Library of Romance: Life of Jack Sheppard the Housebreaker; being a faithful account of his birth, parentage and education, with full particulars of his career from his First Theft down to his Execution at Tyburn; interspersed with interesting anecdotes of his AMOUR WITH EDGEWORTH BESS; and particular descriptions of his CELEBRATED ESCAPES.' A 'splendid lithographic drawing' was given away with each number. This version had a meant-to-be-harrowing description of how Sheppard overheard in a tavern that his mother had died of shock and shame, and gave himself away at the funeral by his inordinate professions of remorse.

Less ready to ascribe worthy motives to Jack Sheppard was the author of *The Rogues of Old London* in the Aldine Boys' Library (1911). He did, however, give the jail-breaker the honorary military rank usually reserved for highwaymen. Captain Sheppard was introduced making his way through the alleys of Covent Garden, where the Mohocks[1] danced fandangos on the bodies of innocent citizens, to the house where he had undertaken to dispose of an unwanted heir. A baronet had commissioned him at the modest fee of a hundred guineas. 'The money was the main point. What villainy he had to execute he did not care much.'

When he saw the pathetic victim Sheppard chose not to murder him, deciding a little belatedly that the baronet must have been prompted by an ignoble motive

In this story Sheppard was prosperously teamed up with the ex-coachman Jack Rann, better known as Sixteen-String Jack, 'the noble-hearted highwayman.'[2] Another picturesquely named character in the story was Half-Hanged Smith. When Sheppard was finally strung up at Tyburn Jack Rann was there to leap from the crowd and cut him down. But before he could carry off the body Jonathan Wild fired a bullet into Sheppard's spine. All

---

[1] Gangs of street ruffians.

[2] There are varying explanations of the name 'Sixteen-String Jack.' The Aldine story referred to above describes how Jack Rann, dismissed from his job as coachman and not yet a highwayman, says to his employer: 'There's only one favour I'd like to ask, my lord. When I take off your lordship's livery I hope at any rate you will let me keep my bows of sixteen strings.' J. G. Rowe, in *Chambers's Journal* (1942), says Rann wore breeches with eight strings at each knee to record the number of his acquittals.

that Rann could do was to see that his comrade was decently interred at Willesden. The crowd was soon to see Jonathan Wild hanged too, to say nothing of Jack Rann. The only moralizing this author allowed himself was when he encouraged those whom Sheppard had befriended to wonder 'would it have been the same had Jack Sheppard known a good man's guiding care.' Even the Harmsworth *Boys' Friend*—sworn to carry only pure, healthy literature—published a serial, 'The Idle Apprentice' (1905), which revelled from week to week in the 'strange yet wonderful, mis-spent career' of Jack Sheppard. In the last chapter Jack was borne to Tyburn, but the execution was not described. It was made clear, too, that Jack before his death had undergone a spiritual reformation—'he might die a felon's death but it would be the new Jack not the old one that would die.'

In August 1947 the B.B.C. devoted three-quarters of an hour of their Home Programme to a play on the life of Jack Sheppard. It was entitled *The Bowl of St. Giles*, after the bowl of liquor which, traditionally, every condemned man en route to Tyburn was entitled to claim at St. Giles. In this version Sheppard was arrested at his mother's funeral before he had time to protest his grief. The last-minute attempt to cut him down from the gallows was made by Blueskin, both men being shot by Wild. But the climax was lacking in drama. Instead of a near-riot by 200,000 people the finale sounded more like half a dozen men brawling in a cellar.

This version, like many others, claimed that Jonathan Wild had caused Jack's father to be hanged and was determined to see the son strung up at Tyburn too.

Charles Peace, most successful burglar of Victorian times, hardly rivalled Sheppard in popularity, but he had his admiring public. For the benefit of later generations it may be recalled that Peace, who started in crime as a Manchester porch robber, shot a policeman and confessed only just in time to save another man from the gallows. Later he shot another man, and then disappeared. Not for a long time did anyone suspect that the respectable Mr. Thompson of Evelina Road, Peckham, was Charles Peace, or that he was carrying out lucrative burglaries almost every night. Eventually he was hanged for the second murder.

One of the 'penny dreadfuls' which took Peace for hero, *Charles Peace, or the Adventures of a Notorious Burglar*, is a literary curiosity by virtue of the columns of staggering irrelevancies with which the author eked it out. For thousands of words on end Charles Peace was never mentioned; then, in an effort to be disarming, the author would say: 'We must now return to our hero, who probably many of our readers may think has been left too long unnoticed.'

A typical example of padding—and of fine confused writing— is seen in this description of Miss Jamblin waiting in vain for her murdered brother to return:

She watched and waited—waited anxiously. Something whispered to her what was to happen next.

There are times when a quick succession of 'next' is found merely soothing; but there are times of reactionary languor when there is not left force enough to watch when that which we attend to is the rhythm only.

Thus we may find the ticking of a clock nothing—indeed, to mention this is commonplace.

But what a dreadful effect may be produced on the mind by the sudden cessation of the ticking of the clock when once a certain experience has to be gone through!

Who that has counted the beatings of a pulse or listened to the flutterings of a breath, watching for the next and the next and the next, and coming at last to the one that has no next, can bear without agony to hear a watch or a clock stop ticking, or to hear any rhythmical sound cease suddenly?

One of the most horrible moments in my life was a moment in which the rhythmical noise of a common saw, heard over the parapet of a bridge in London, stopped suddenly when I was listening for it. In the distance the sound was softened; it had a sough with it which reminded me very painfully of the sound of human breath, but when it ceased I thought I could hear no more in this world and longed to be at that moment taken away.

Of course the emotion of that moment was imparted from my recollection of a moment of which it was the symbol, but I think the cessation of something with a beat in it has always a terror for me.

'Can you draw an inference?' said Coleridge to the clown. 'Yes, sir,' said the clown, 'a cartload of them.'

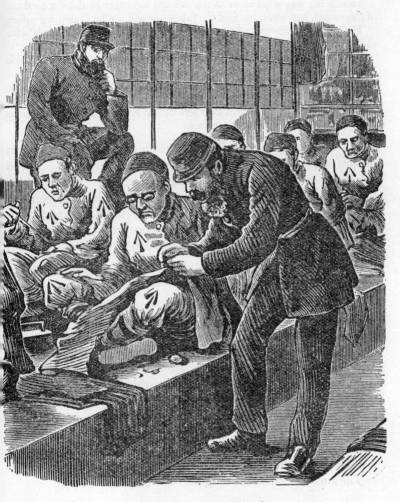

Charlie Peace in the tailor's shop

That is the way with most of us. We are too eager to draw a cartload of inferences, and when we find the inference will not be drawn we suffer.

There is a peculiarity about the next thing, remember—that it is sure to happen, and what a blessing there is in certainty!

We know the difficulty of holding in check our tyrannical habitual mode of passing on.

Every second of time in our experience throws out a pontoon bridge to the next.

We live by a clock that has two sets of hands on the dial plate. One is right and the other is always too fast.

The author of *Charles Peace* was incapable of mentioning an inquest without discussing at great length whether inquests served a useful purpose or not, and the behaviour of people who attended them. He could not mention a jail without describing the operation of a treadmill, which 'must be terrible work for a fat man. It is possible for such a one to lose three stone in as many months.' At the end of one such lengthy digression he naively explained:

Happily for Peace he was spared this dreadful infliction, as the jail in which he was confined did not at that time contain a treadmill. . . .

But that digression was trifling compared to the one which occurred in Chapter LIX, entitled 'Mysterious Murders.' The author described the vain search for the man who had slain the brother of Miss Jamblin, and then went on to say that it was most extraordinary how many crimes of this kind went undetected. As proof he cited for the next 3,600 words a series of notorious unsolved crimes, including murders (mostly of prostitutes) by mutilation, dismemberment, garrotting, throat-slitting and clubbing. Many of the facts were taken from newspaper reports of inquests and were scarcely paraphrased. Other passages read like rehashed editorials denouncing the wickedness of the age.

The author finished his long digression with:

Some alteration in the mode of administering justice will have to be made, as we are going on at present. The evil is beginning to assume gigantic proportions, and nobody's life will be safe.

He then persuaded himself to tackle the next chapter of the narrative, in which again there was not the slightest reference to Charles Peace.

Soon he steered the story round to a mention of witchcraft, which gave him an excuse to recapitulate the historic cases of witch-hunting in England and elsewhere; not omitting references to capsie-claws, pilliewinks and torture-boots. This occupied the author, if not the reader, for 2,400 words.

In the next chapter, describing the last hours of a condemned man (not Charles Peace), he discussed for 1,300 words whether capital punishment was a good thing or not, and decided that it was. He did at least mention Peace in passing:

Peace often declared that he never took human life if there was any means left open for him to escape without having recourse to such a dreadful alternative.

He was, perhaps, the most reckless scoundrel of modern times, but 'fired wide,' as he termed it, to frighten his pursuer, whose life he had no desire to take.

The hanging of the malefactor, in the next chapter, inspired 1,100 words of discussion on the best method of dispatching a condemned man; with notes on strangling as practised by 'our estimable ally, the Turk, and despotic Russia,' the Spanish garrotte, the German sword, the French guillotine and the Jack Ketch technique in which the hangman perched astride the suspended victim's shoulders to ensure the breaking of his neck. The next chapter, promisingly entitled 'Charles Peace Leaves Dartmoor,' described chiefly the unsatisfactory treatment of discharged prisoners, and deplored the stupidity of handcuffing men on their way to discharge.

The author was really a leader writer *manqué*; it is clear that he preferred airing his views and knowledge to telling a story which he must have realized was stale.

Sheppard and his cronies inspired a variety of fictional characters who traded on their names.[1] Most notorious of them all was Charley Wag, described variously as 'the new Jack Sheppard' and 'the Boy Burglar,' whose adventures appeared about 1860. The authorship is in some doubt. In Montague Summers' *A Gothic Bibliography* the work is ascribed to Sala. According to the publishers,

---

[1] Cartouche, the legendary French criminal, was introduced to English readers as 'the French Jack Sheppard.'

E

the writer of this least defensible of 'penny dreadfuls' had spent two years collecting background material, and his 'intensely exciting real-life romance' was not a product of the 'wild imaginings of the novelist's brain,' but a story rendered 'in stern truthful language by one who has studied in all its blackest enormity the doings of secret crime.' It is more probable that the writer had spent his two years studying G. W. M. Reynolds. He reproduced in his narrative the same familiar dietary tables from workhouses and incorporated admiring references to the *Mysteries of the Court*, one of his characters claiming that aristocrats were in the habit of borrowing the penny parts from their footmen. It is always possible that *Charley Wag* was the work of Reynolds himself, but it has a more pronounced tongue-in-cheek quality than the run of Reynolds' writing.

The creator of Charley Wag seems to have derived great pleasure from shocking the righteous, mixing sex, scandal and a crude form of socialism freely. 'A thoroughly depraved, unprincipled, godless, servile, blasphemous, lecherous old wretch' was his description of an aristocrat introduced as an ex-Premier of England. This skinny old goblin was said to bathe daily in beef tea to strengthen his satyr's appetites, with a bath of rosewater afterwards as a freshener. He dined with six demireps and took pleasure in seducing virtuous country spitcats.

A magistrate who entered the story was said to give (like most of his kind) 'a daily recurring exhibition of besotted ignorance, sickening vulgarity and bad taste.' Clergymen turned out to be Tarquins one and all. This obviously proved too much for many readers. The author tackled protests as they came:

I left Lucinda in very bad company, although that company was chiefly composed of reverend gentlemen.

Since I had the misfortune in a luckless moment to introduce these clerical parties into my story a terrific volley of letters from unknown correspondents has been fired at my offended head.

It seems, if I am to believe these ladies and gentlemen, that there really are no naughty parsons in existence, and even if there were it is not the proper thing to represent them in their natural colours. There are a great many people in the world who do not like to hear the truth, and a great many who do not like truth to be told. . . .

The author went on to protest that while he portrayed wickedness he did not encourage his young readers to practise the sins
he showed up. If they did so, all they could expect was tears and
anguish, and the Devil's pitchfork.

Always, however, he declined to give his readers any hint
whether the boy Charley was to be 'comfortably hanged' or made
a Lord Mayor of London. 'You do not imagine I am going to tell
you what it is to be, do you?'

As an unwanted babe, Charley was thrown into the Thames
in the first sentence of the story. His mother, retreating up Villiers
Street, remarked a little prematurely, 'There goes the record of
my sin and folly.' Charley was rescued, offered to the workhouse
of Saint-Starver-cum-Bag-o'-Bones and rejected, and then left on
the doorstep of—inevitably—an elderly spinster. He grew up
high-spirited and uncontrollable, a cigar smoker at thirteen.

The author undeniably had a weak place for Charley:

He is pugnacious, great at punching heads and bunging up eyes, and
gave the youth of Slogger's Alley one of those heavy taps upon the nasal
organ which is, I believe, in the language of the prize ring denominated
a 'smeller.'

Add to this, he is a regular rascal where a pretty girl is concerned.

Half a dozen times at least I have begun a sentence in which I was
going to dress the young gentleman's jacket. I have a small collection
of moral remarks about things in general, all nicely cut and dried, and
when I am at a loss to fill my chapter I stick one or two in to make my
incidents go a little further. You do not blame me, do you? We all have
little tricks. Have we not, brother tradesmen?

I will not upon this occasion inflict upon you any of the moral philosophy
to which I have referred. I am at a loss to tell what I ought to say about
a young fellow who is too general in his love-making. Why are so many
of you young ladies so pretty? It is very hard to choose among you.
I should feel much obliged if one out of my thousands of fair readers
would write and tell me what she thinks of Master Charley's conduct,
and I could put her opinion into the next part.

It was the insincerity of these protestations which doubtless
infuriated the 'unco guid.' But the first number had sold 40,000
copies and the author of *Charley Wag* thumbed his nose at Society
as cheerfully as Charley thumbed his at the magistrate. A provocative cover showed the boy burglar fleeing confidently down

the street with a stolen goose and two bottles of rum. His dog scampering beside him was also in possession of a stolen goose. In the background a policeman brandished a truncheon. A notice on the wall offered £500 for the apprehension of Charley Wag.

From small-scale crimes the boy burglar worked his way up till very soon he was breaking into the Bank of England. Justice, panting, caught up with him from time to time but incarceration often had its compensations—such as flocks of frangipani-scented French ladies coming to gaze enraptured on him. And soon he was back at the old round of breaking into bank and boudoir.

The fate which the author had in store for Charley Wag proved to be an uncommonly lenient one—more lenient even than that meted out to Joanna Polenipper. He was arrested for murder but was pardoned through the intercession of his mother, who was, of course, a duchess. Fortunately he had the grace to retire from the Park Lane high life which he was then adorning and to spend the remainder of his days abroad in strict retirement. Less fortunate was his mother, the duchess, who was strangled by her mad husband in a charnel house.

A 'penny dreadful' difficult to classify was *Spring-Heeled Jack, the Terror of London.* There are many theories as to who was the original Spring-Heeled Jack; some say he was an ingenious ruffian with mechanical springs in the heels of his boots who terrified the women of a South Coast resort, others claim that he was an eccentric nobleman. The dictionary declines to commit itself. Its definition of Spring-Heeled Jack runs:

A name given to a person who from his great activity in running or jumping, especially in order to rob or frighten people, was supposed to have springs in the heels of his boots. *dial.* a highwayman.

The Spring-Heeled Jack of the 'penny dreadfuls' was a sort of supernatural highwayman who had goats' horns growing from his forehead and a long mane of hair down his back. Attached to the backs of his arms were black bat-like wings. There was no question of mechanical springs in the heels of his boots, since he wore no boots; nor, for that matter, did he wear any clothes. As a rule his appearances, which coincided with tremendous thunderstorms, were staged for the petrifaction of evil-doers, titled for preference. For example:

Sir Roland Ashton uttered a cry of horror and started back. . . . As he did so he felt a pair of long, wiry arms encircle his waist, and the next moment his head was dashed violently against the wall.

A thousand jagged lights, more brilliant than the lightning, flashed before Sir Roland's eyes, and as they became greater and died away he lost all consciousness and lapsed into oblivion.

It was impossible for him to tell how long he had remained in this state.

He heard the storm raging, knew that he was drenched to the skin, and chilled to the marrow with cold; but his eyes were dim and hazy, and he could make out no object distinctly.

Suddenly it dawned upon his brain that he must have been removed by some mysterious means from Cypress House.

Where was he?

Independent of the deluge falling from the sky, Sir Roland Ashton could hear a great rushing of water.

The baronet pressed his hand to his throbbing brow, rubbed his eyes, and moved his hands about.

Presently he became convinced that he was in a boat, and as his vision cleared a little he saw a peculiarly shaped white object sitting opposite him.

Sir Roland with a great effort forced himself into a sitting posture.

Then what the baronet had dreaded had become a reality.

He was in a boat, which had been anchored by a pole in the middle of a lake.

The lightning flashed and the thunder rolled furiously overhead, and Heaven and earth seemed to have come together.

But it was not the storm or his position in the boat that terrified Sir Roland Ashton.

It was not danger from the conflicting elements that caused him to yell out an exclamation of horror, to leap to his feet, and then to sink crouching like a wild animal at bay under the bows of the boat: for Spring-Heeled Jack, ghastly and mocking, sat in the stern, pointing with extended hands and arms at the baronet.

Squatting cross-legged, and seemingly finding enjoyment in the very fury of the storm, the weird being laughed until the sound of his voice rose above the crashing thunder.

Suddenly he ceased this wild and terrible mirth, but his attitude remained unchanged.

'Sir Roland,' he said, 'this is a merry night for us to meet.'

The baronet could not speak.

His tongue clave to the roof of his mouth, and a strange feeling came over him, as if he were already numbered with the dead.

Spring-Heeled Jack laboured under the Gothic hangover. Jacob Butler, trapped in a cellar, began to fancy that the cellar was growing smaller.

He had heard and read of the old German tortures.

As swift as a flash of lightning the story of the Chamber of the Seven Windows rushed into his brain.

A man was placed in the room, and each morning he missed a window, until he stood in a kind of huge coffin, which suddenly closed in upon him and crushed him to death.

Could such things exist in England, the land of the brave and the free?

This hideous piece of mechanism so terrified Jacob Butler that he reeled to and fro like a reed blown before the wind.

'Murder—most horrible!' he shrieked. 'It is impossible that they are such fiends to take life in this way. Oh, help—mercy! Help!'

There was no sound but of the masonry, as it was slowly moved again by some powerful agency.

The Aldine Publishing Company, whose motto was 'Try anything once,' started a Spring-Heeled Jack Library as late as 1904, but not even horrific covers could make it prosper. The young generation was growing just that little bit more sophisticated.

CHAPTER IV

BRAVEALLS AND FEARNOTS

THE 'PENNY DREADFUL' industry which Edward Lloyd grew too proud to carry on was not allowed to languish. Other publishers saw in it the first rung on the climb to wealth. Gradually, as the 'fifties progressed, 'penny dreadfuls' came to be aimed more specifically at the juvenile market. There was a crop of stories about boy apprentices, link boys, call boys, trace boys, boy gipsies, boy sailors, boy soldiers, and boy crusoes. Needless to say, those who remained obstinately convinced that a boy was a creature to be sent up a chimney or down a mine continued to deplore this unnecessary widening of the horizons of youth.

Charley Wag, the Boy Burglar (discussed in the preceding chapter) was the most notorious of a batch of 'Wild Boys' romances. These included *The Wild Boys of Paris, or The Secrets of the Vaults of Death; The Wild Boys of London* (which was to achieve the rare distinction of being suppressed by the police in the 'seventies); *The Poor Boys of London, or a Life Story for the People*, which described boys being driven by evil surroundings into crime; and *The Boys of London and New York*, printed rather surprisingly in Wigan. Even the transatlantic influence did not succeed in ousting from the pages of this publication pictures of witches in red ponchos and Welsh hats, complete with attendant vipers, toads and bats. Then there were such Wag-and-water characters as those to be found in *Cheeky Charlie, or What a Boy Can Do*, and *Willie Wideawake, or the Wonderful Wanderings of a Wilful Wight*. More acceptable to adult critics were tales like Hogarth House's *Charity Joe, or From Street Boy to Lord Mayor*. Not that the highly productive Hogarth House could claim that its boy heroes were always fired by such laudable civic ambition. The smooth-cheeked hero of *Young Will Watch, the Smuggler King* would leave his devoted mother and adoring sister—'a fair and fragile flower of delicate perfume'—to swagger into a nearby cavern where he would be extravagantly hailed as leader and toasted by a gang of rakehelly cut-throats.

One of the publishers of full-blooded 'penny dreadfuls' in mid-century was Edwin J. Brett. In the 'sixties he decided on a change of policy. It may be that, like Lloyd, he had merely become a publisher of penny parts in order to amass working capital for bigger enterprises. At all events in 1866 he published the first number of his famous weekly magazine, *Boys of England*, in which Jack Harkaway first saw the light. It was to run until 1899, absorbing many shorter-lived publications. 'Our aim is to enthral you by wild and wonderful but healthy fiction,' said the first number, promising that the journal would be a 'hearty, free and trusty companion.' Later issues carried this boast under the title:

'Subscribed to by H.R.H. Prince Arthur, the Prince Imperial of France[1] and Count William Bernstorff.'

The *Quarterly Review*, which missed nothing, professed to be at a loss to understand why these gentlemen should give the journal their patronage. It was an improvement over 'penny dreadfuls' admittedly; but, with insufferable smugness, the *Review* added: 'It may be doubted whether the time spent over [such journals] would not be infinitely more usefully employed in cricket and football or some lighter games.'

At once there followed a fierce competition—none the less fierce for being on occasions farcical—with W. L. Emmett, who had also published full-blooded penny dreadfuls. Emmett's counter to *Boys of England* was the *Young Gentleman's Journal*, first published in 1867. Brett retorted in the next year with *Young Men*

---

[1] Then an exile in England.

of Great Britain, and the same year Emmett capped this with
Young Gentlemen of Britain. The climax came when on the same
day in 1872 Brett issued *Rovers of the Sea*, and Emmett put out
Rovers' Log. In his unduly reticent *History of Old Boys' Books*,
which records the Brett–Emmett rivalry, Ralph Rollington[1] gives
no clue as to how this unfortunate 'double' occurred.

It is not surprising that there was no love lost between the
two firms. One of the Emmett family—there were five of them—
got Brett on the raw by making fun of his collection of arms and
armour. Brett was left to find satisfaction in the fact that his
periodicals were usually the more successful. Both houses put out
numerous other titles like *Sons of Britannia*, *The Young Briton*,
The Young Englishman (Emmett) and *Boys of the Empire* (Brett)
which the youth of the day must have found almost impossible
to distinguish one from the other. Brett also had a *Boy's Comic
Journal*, which was noticeably more sensational than comic.

In his own good time Charles Fox, another 'penny dreadful'
impresario, who took over many of Lloyd's titles, including
Sweeney Todd, decided to bring out a boys' magazine. His *Boys'
Standard*, raised in 1875, ran for twenty years and enjoyed a
circulation comparable to that of *Boys of England*. Fox also put
out a *Boy's Champion* and a *Boy's Leisure Hour*. Other publishers
in the boys' magazine field were Ralph Rollington (*Boys' World*,
Our Boys' Paper, *Boys' Pocket Library*); S. Dacre Clarke (Guy
Rayner) whose *Bad Boys' Paper* was one of a long string of fail-
ures; and James Henderson (*Young Folks' Budget* and *Nuggets*)
who accepted from one R. L. Stevenson a manuscript unpromis-
ingly called 'The Sea Cook' and ran it as a serial entitled 'Treasure
Island.' In the late 'eighties the Aldine Publishing Company,
under Charles Perry Brown, entered the lists. Over the next
forty years or so it was to put out a profusion of 'libraries' on every
subject from highwaymen to horse-racing. In its early years—
which were its best years—it specialized in reprints of successful
American stories, notably those featuring Frank Reade (Chapter X)
and Buffalo Bill and Deadwood Dick (Chapter XV).

---

[1] His real name was Allingham—an uncle of Herbert Allingham who wrote
popular serials of prodigious length in the *Jester* and many other boys' journals.

Often the stories in the Brett, Emmett and Fox boys' magazines did not greatly differ from the type of story put out as 'penny dreadfuls.' They were written, as often as not, in the short-breath, short-sentence style. Gothic influences were by no means extinct. The tales were still bloodthirsty to a degree, notably those in Fox's *Boys' Standard* (a typical cover picture of which shows a Spartan holding up the decapitated head of his adversary in the arena). There was a high proportion of historical tales, featuring heroic apprentices or real-life characters ranging from Rob Roy to Taffy ap Morgan, from Guy Fawkes to Drake. Probably the Roundheads versus Cavaliers period was as popular as any; and there were any number of tales about Colonel Blood and the 'bravos of Alsatia,' the swashbuckling rogues who found sanctuary from creditors and other persecutors in their own disreputable corner of the City, where they elected their own 'ruler.'

But there were also tales of ancient Greece and Rome, of the Saxon kings and even of the German and Scandinavian gods. It was the day of hairy, deep-chested characters with names like Zar and Zek, which made for confused reading. One story featured a character called Clek, another character called Clek-Clek, and a third called Clek-clek-clek. No matter what the period of the story all characters tended to talk in that peculiar jargon which is reserved for persons who lived and died before 1800. These historical romances seem to have been genuinely popular. The reaction against historical fiction did not set in until the next century, when the plea that boys 'learned too much history at school' was the usual editorial excuse. It is at least doubtful whether twentieth-century schoolboys were primed with as much history as nineteenth-century schoolboys; but tales of the tilt yard could hardly hope to compete against tales of aerial dog fights. It was Excalibur against the death ray, and the death ray won.

The *Boys' Standard* launched a popular Celestial called Ching-Ching, whose adventures, linked with those of Handsome Harry of the Fighting Belvedere, enjoyed a vogue almost rivalling that for Jack Harkaway. There was no malice, but a great deal of cunning, in Ching-Ching. He was a sort of juvenile Charlie Chan; his antecedents were vague and the wily youth told many improb-

THE BOYS' COMIC JOURNAL

STORIES OF FUN, ADVENTURE, AND ROMANCE

No. 545.—Vol. XXII.]　　　　EDITED BY EDWIN J. BRETT.　　　　[Price One Penny.

"LUTTRELL WAS ABOUT TO REPEAT THE COWARDLY BLOW."

UNMASKED;
OR,
THE DAY OF RECKONING

CHAPTER VI.—(continued.)

THE girl's beautiful blue eyes betrayed no signs of fear as Luttrell entered.

"I am here once more, Alice Melville," he said.

For the week ending AUGUST 19, 1893.

"So I perceive."

"And, as usual, a warm welcome awaits me," he sarcastically added.

"I can have no welcome for the man who,

A companion to Edwin Brett's 'Boys of England'—notably more sensational than comic

able tales of his early days and illustrious forbears in Pekin. He spoke in a pidgin dialect which to the modern reader is rather trying, and must have been still more trying to the proof-reader. Ching-Ching was a fellow of infinite resource and inextinguishable cheerfulness. He would tackle a tramp on the highroad with the same insouciance as he sought to tackle that secret society, based on South America, which was in the happy position of being able to give orders to the Nihilists in Russia, the Socialists in Germany and the Communists in France (the date of this story was 1881). There were several series of Ching-Ching tales, with titles like 'Cheerful Ching-Ching,' 'Daring Ching-Ching,' and 'Wonderful Ching-Ching.' There was even a *Ching-Ching's Own* in 1888.

It was the fashion about this time for heroes to be saddled with names which proclaimed to the world their dash and daring—Ben Braveall, Frank Fearnot, Frank Fearless, Dick Dare, Tom Tearaway and Tom Wildrake; names recalling those of the young heroes and heroines of the chapbooks—Jemmy Studious, Johnny Dawdle, Betsy Algood and Nancy Careful. This tendency was especially marked in school stories which were now becoming a firm fashion. There were schoolboy Ned Nimbles, Tom Torments, Rattlin' Toms and Jolly Jacks by the score. Schoolmasters—handicapped by such names as the Rev. Theophilus Wagjaw, or Mr. Hackchild—were commonly represented as pompous and cretinous. Swishing was the recognized cure for high spirits—every academy had a name like Bircham or Scarum or Stingboys. Beating was taken for granted by all except E. Harcourt Burrage, author of *The Lambs of Littlecote* and *The Island School*, who—judging from this excerpt from an Aldine story in the middle 'nineties—was ahead of his times:

It is to be wondered at that the old style of punishment has been tolerated so long.

Fathers who never laid hands upon their boys at home allowed some cruel brute at school to unmercifully thrash them without expostulating. Custom sanctified the unwarrantable assault.

In these school stories comedy, often self-conscious, laboured and crude, was beginning to assert itself. The height of humour was for a boy to impregnate his trousers with snuff or pepper before a beating. One writer was even able to fill several columns describing how an offender sought to mitigate his punishment by the not very original device of lining his trousers with books.

The boys of one school featured in *Boys of England* had fun at the expense of one of their number with a 'probang' which was described as 'a flat board with a hole in the centre. This was used for forcing between the jaws of a cow who might swallow too large a piece of turnip. The other portion, the ramrod to wit, was then forced down her throat through the little hole in the centre.'

The most celebrated schoolboy characters were: Hogarth House's Tom Wildrake, who, when his classroom adventures were exhausted, was pitchforked into the Indian Mutiny and then packed off to Australia; and the redoubtable Jack Harkaway whose adventures require a chapter to themselves.

CHAPTER V

JACK HARKAWAY

To RUB AN octogenarian the wrong way, try making a disparaging reference to Jack Harkaway. It does not matter whether your octogenarian occupies an armchair in Clubland or a bench at Chelsea's Royal Hospital. There never was a lad like Jack . . . high-spirited, of course, but nothing vicious about him. If only the present generation had been reared on Harkaway, how much manlier they would be for it. And so on.

Now a man who has exceeded the three-score-years-and-ten may be forgiven if fading memory throws a gloss of sentiment over a character as hard-boiled as was this idol of the youth of the 'seventies, 'eighties and 'nineties. For the truth is there are few publishers of juvenile fiction to-day who would care to print unexpurgated some of the episodes in the strenuous career of Jack Harkaway. In *Pilot Papers* (March 1947) Mr. M. Willson Disher quoted the first part of a Harkaway passage describing the torture of a Red Indian brave, and then, sickened by the smell of burning flesh, said:

Honestly, for your sake even more than mine, I think I had better leave off. It is, without exaggeration, dreadful. And there is a great deal more of it. Grand Guignol is soon outdone. How on earth schoolboys could read it without vomiting can only be understood by clinging to a belief that they had acquired the horrid taste gradually. My father, who forbade me to read the harmless Dick Turpins and Robin Hoods of the reign of Edward VII, brought himself up on this hardy diet. I have a still

greater admiration for his stoic ideals of life now I know how they began.
The incidents I have spared you are more trying than anything in the
pages of the most admired of unflinching realists.

For the defence, there is Sir John Hammerton, who, writing of
the boys' stories read by him in his youth (*Books and Myself*)
says: 'It pleases me to think that these stories—notably the Jack
Harkaway series in which a robust humour was an ingredient—
wrought not one per cent of the harm to their boy readers that
the gangster films have done to the boys of the last quarter of a
century.' And George Sampson, well-known for his *Concise
Cambridge History of Literature*, admits in *Seven Essays* that he
devoured Jack Harkaway along with Sweeney Todd and Spring-
Heeled Jack, and comments: 'There was no harm in any of them.'

The creator of Jack Harkaway was Bracebridge Hemyng,
barrister of the Middle Temple, who found that turning out fiction
was vastly more profitable than sitting around waiting for briefs.
He threw all he had into Harkaway—adventure, humour, sentiment, sadism, out-of-the-way knowledge, even a dash of religion.
To what extent Harkaway was read for (or in spite of) the author's
descriptions of torture is anybody's guess. Children nourished on
Grimm's Fairy Tales, with their wealth of decapitation and burning
alive, probably took Harkaway comfortably in their stride. It is
more likely that the Harkaway stories succeeded because the
central character was likeable, fearless and full-blooded, an English
lad with an eye for a practical joke who took the whole world for
his oyster and remained aggressively English. There was nothing
Gothic about the Harkaway stories. There may have been a
strong smell of blood, but not of the charnel-house. There may
have been some uncommonly ruthless characters, like Magog
Brand, who cut off one brigand's head and threw it at another,
but there were no secret, black and midnight hags. Here at last
were stories which were free of the aura of the *Newgate Calendar*.

The Jack Harkaway stories began in 1871 in Edwin J. Brett's
Boys of England, the journal for which newsagents had fought
in the streets when it was first published five years earlier. Promptly
the stories were pirated in America, appearing in *The Boys and
Girls Weekly*. The publisher of this, Frank Leslie, was able to

persuade Hemyng without much difficulty to go over to America where, prolific as ever, he wrote a number of Harkaway romances.

The Harkaway titles (which came out in penny parts as well as in magazines) include:

> Jack Harkaway's Schooldays.
> Jack Harkaway After Schooldays.
> Jack Harkaway at Oxford.
> Jack Harkaway's Adventures Round the World.
> Jack Harkaway in Search of the Mountain of Gold.
> Jack Harkaway in Search of his Father.
> Jack Harkaway Among the Pirates.
> Jack Harkaway on the Prairie.
> Jack Harkaway Out West Among the Indians.
> Jack Harkaway and his Father at the Haunt of the Pirates.
> Jack Harkaway in Australia.
> Jack Harkaway and his Son's Adventures in China.
> Jack Harkaway and his Son's Adventures in Greece.
> Jack Harkaway and his Boy Tinker.
> Jack Harkaway at School in America.
> Jack Harkaway at the Isle of Palms.
> Jack Harkaway in the Transvaal.
> Jack Harkaway's War Scouts.

It is said that there was another Harkaway story, 'Jack Harkaway in Search of Wealth,' which was proofed but never published. From the list it will be seen that there was a Harkaway *père* and a Harkaway *fils*. There were in fact three Harkaways. In Brett's short-lived *Jack Harkaway's Journal for Boys* (1893) appeared Harkaway the Third, 'son of the second of that name and grandson of the first who was now well up in years but still hale and hearty as of yore.' All the Harkaways conformed to the same pattern of behaviour.

The first Harkaway, who studied (after a fashion) at Pomona House School, was a lad of uncertain parentage, which prompted the school bully to chant:

> 'He never had a father
> And he never had a mother
> He never had a sister
> And he never had a brother,
> He was nobody's child.'

The first fight between Harkaway and the bully Hunston was notable insofar as it revealed the author's ignorance of, or contempt for, the Queensberry Rules.

The fight began after Jack had kicked the bully's crony for talking out of turn.

'He [Hunston] made a rush at Jack but failed to hit him, whereupon Jack feinted with his left and struck him in the stomach with his right.

'Oh!' ejaculated Hunston, doubling himself up. Jack followed this advantage by dealing his opponent two heavy blows one after the other in the face, and Hunston rolled over.

Excusably, perhaps, the bully thought he would try some dirt now. He tripped Jack by 'a trick learned at Porto Rico.' Jack quickly recovered, however, and caught Hunston round the neck with his left arm 'in an iron-like grip.'

Then he dealt him blow after blow in the face until he fell from his hold and lay like a log on the ground.

'Bravo, Jack! Well done, Harkaway!'

There was a pause while Hunston was slapped on the back, for he was in danger of choking on a half-swallowed tooth. One of his eyes was closed, the other was of little use. But the fight went on:

Hunston senior now tried what in France is known as the *savate*.

This is a sharp and quick kick in the face which is not allowed in fair English fighting. Unprepared for this, Jack was struck under the chin by the toe of his opponent's boot in a way that made his teeth rattle like castanets, and cut his tongue.

'Shame! Shame!' cried half a dozen voices.

While these belated shouts were still ringing, Hunston tried the *savate* a second time, but Jack caught his upraised foot and made him hop about while he battered him senseless.

Fighting apart, there was little to do at Pomona House School except to rag as graceless a set of pedagogues as ever gathered under one roof. Jack, being a ventriloquist, had a head and shoulders start over the others. By causing Mr. Mole to say 'Frogs!' and 'Waterloo!' to M. Bolivant, the French master, he succeeded in making these excitable gentlemen fight in front of the class.

F

Then the Head, Mr. Crawcour, entered, and the fun really started:

'What is this?' exclaimed Mr. Crawcour. 'Mr. Mole with his fists clenched and M. Bolivant on his back. Disgraceful! How can you expect boys to be orderly when they have such a bad example. Gentlemen, I am ashamed of you!'

'Shut up,' said Jack making his voice come from the senior master.

'Mr. Mole!' exclaimed the Principal in astonishment.

'I said nothing, sir,' replied the senior master. 'My opinion is the place is bewitched; I shall go out, and then perhaps you will get at the bottom of it.'

'It wouldn't be the first time. He's caned a good many.'

This time Jack made Mr. Pumpleton speak.

'Mr. Pumpleton,' said the Principal. 'Did that remark emanate from you?'

'No, sir, it did not, on my honour.'

'Don't believe him,' said Jack.

This time it was Mr. Stonor.

'Mr. Stonor, are you too forgetting yourself? It seems to me I shall have to change my staff.'

'Go it, old cock,' said Jack, making M. Bolivant the speaker this time. . . .

And so on and so on. Jack was detected and punished, but the masters of Pomona School never learned by experience. A few chapters later Jack had them at each other's throats again, by the same means.

When it came to punishment Jack was a realist. A panel of his fellows found him guilty (for the Head was a believer in the jury system), and the sentence was that he be sent to Coventry for a week. Many a young hero of fiction would have preferred a whipping; not this one.

Jack thought he had got off very well as he infinitely preferred the silent system to being soundly birched, and congratulated himself on his good luck.

He knew he had been wrong and had sense enough to know that order could not reign in the school if the boys did not obey their masters.

Another pupil who might have preferred seven days in Coventry was the sneak whom Jack punished by forcing him to eat, raw, a soot-covered carp which had died in the course of a prank with

'I mean to run away,' said Jack Harkaway, 'will you help me?'

a fish bowl, and which Jack had earlier stuffed up the chimney out of harm's way.

Though Jack was a realist in not relishing corporal punishment he nevertheless allowed himself to be birched in front of the school on a framed-up charge rather than tell the truth and incriminate Little Emily, the girl on whom he was 'spoony.' Emily had broken open her money-box, and sent him the money he was accused of stealing.

Those who were brought up on Jack Harkaway doubtless shook their heads over the play *Young Woodley*, regarding it as sloppiness at the best and decadence at the worst. But there was a time when Jack was in grave danger of becoming 'spoony' with his headmaster's wife, who had nursed him through an illness.

She put her arm round his neck and kissed his forehead, while she smoothed back his curly, chestnut hair from his temples.

'How would you like to have me for a mama?' she asked.

'I would rather have you—for—for—'

He hesitated.

'Well, dear, for what? Speak out,' said Mrs. Crawcour in an encouraging tone.

'I was going to say for a sweetheart, ma'am.'

'But you have one. The little girl who sent you the money is your sweetheart, is she not?'

'I like her very much, but not nearly as much as I do you, ma'am. You are so very lovely,' replied Jack.

'Am I lovely?' Mrs. Crawcour repeated, looking at her handsome and majestic figure in the glass with some satisfaction.

The hot blood mounted to Jack's face and made it burn.

'How you blush! Why do you blush so?' she said.

'I don't know, ma'am. It comes to me talking to you, I think.'

'But you cannot have me for a sweetheart. I am your schoolmistress and your master's wife.'

'Still, I may love you quietly and at a distance, ma'am. You cannot help people loving you.'

'You funny boy,' she exclaimed, kissing him again.

However, it was not because of this perilous trend in his affections that Jack had to leave Pomona House. There had been too many pranks, and one of them had led to the school catching fire. It was noteworthy that no pupils thought of trying to extinguish the flames until they were dragooned into so doing. Reverence for the Old School was not yet a feature of schoolboy stories.

It was decided to send Jack to sea. He received the news with equanimity, pausing only at the last to write a couple of letters, the first of which he did not scruple to pen in the fist of the beautiful if foolish Mrs. Crawcour:

To Mr. Burroughs, Undertaker, Lillie Bridge:

Sir, will you oblige me by coming up tomorrow about three o'clock to Pomona House to measure my unfortunate husband for a coffin as, I regret to say, he has died suddenly.

The other was to the editor of the *Hertfordshire Mercury*:

A gentleman residing at Pomona House, Lillie Bridge, feels that he has hitherto been wanting in the divine attribute of charity which should distinguish all mankind and wishes to make amends for his deficiency. Therefore this is to say that he will present every woman who calls on Friday at the above address between the hours of ten and twelve with the sum of half-a-crown.

Jack's life henceforth was one of voyage, shipwreck and travel in strange lands. His friend Harvey accompanied him, and other

characters from Pomona House cropped up on one pretext or
another, including Mr. Mole who had a tea garden left him in
China. It was the fate of the hapless Mr. Mole to lose one limb
after another and to be bastinadoed, stuck with stilettos and
otherwise maltreated in Jack's service. For this he received such
dubious compensations as being awarded a plurality of native
wives. The bully Hunston Jack permitted to be tattooed all over
in bizarre patterns by a tribe of cannibals. This was considered to
be a not unfitting punishment for the trouble he had caused.
After all, he might have suffered the fate of the man whom Jack
watched being eaten alive. Explained Mr. Hemyng:

> The parts of the human body which are esteemed the greatest delicacies
> by these cannibals are first the palms of the hands and then the eyes.
>   When the chief has gratified his choice the others are entitled in turn
> to advance and cut out bits.
>   The savage feast proceeded quickly and the victim's shrieks and moans
> were pitiful to hear. Jack ground his teeth with rage, but on looking to
> his rifle found that he had lost the percussion cap off the nipple and had
> not another with him. Beside, the man might have been a criminal for
> what he knew.
>   It was evident that those men did not eat human flesh for lack of
> animal food.

It was important not to be too sentimental about the fate of
criminals. Jack's friend Harvey had both strong principles and a
strong stomach. When Jack was betrayed into captivity by a native
girl Harvey wanted her put to death. The other natives preferred
to torture her for more information. Harvey was not in favour of
this, but did not feel strongly enough to make an issue of it.

> Nuratella was dragged to another part and her cries were soon heard
> at intervals.
>   She was beaten with bamboos.
>   Fire was placed under her feet.
>   Red-hot stones were applied to various parts of her body and a band
> of twisted reeds was tied so tightly round her forehead that her eyes
> threatened to burst from their sockets.
>   At length her fortitude, great though it was, gave way.

One can guess how differently the heroes of the *Boy's Own Paper*
would have reacted in these circumstances . . .

Mr. Mole's experiences were equally trying. The bastinado had failed to make him 'squeal.'

Suffering actually invested the poor old gentleman, tippler and braggart though he was, with a sort of dignity.

'He holds out well,' said the king of the brigands.

'He would not hold out long, sir,' said one of the men, 'if you gave me full power with him.'

Monastos smiled, in a half-condescending way.

'You would kill him before I had squeezed the information from him.'

'No, captain. What I propose will not cause such pain as what he has but now received, but if he holds out against it, take my head.'

The confident air of the ruffian caught the chief's attention.

'Speak, then,' said he; 'what have you to propose?'

The man drew near the pirate chief and whispered.

'Right,' said the chief, 'we will try the English hound.'

The unfortunate prisoner was then bound hand and foot and stretched upon the ground, and then the brigand Sarandi lay down full length beside him.

The pirates looked on.

Mole was wondering what on earth was to come next, when he felt a sharp pricking sensation at the back of his head.

Sarandi had pulled out a single hair.

This is scarcely as painful as the prick of a pin, and Mr. Mole could only wonder what it was for.

He soon found out.

Hair after hair was drawn from his head, until the whole of his scalp was itching to the most painful degree.

The irritation increased every instant—his head was on fire with it.

He could not touch it with his hands, for he was bound.

The sensations communicated themselves to the rest of his body.

From head to legs he felt one mass of fiery irritation.

Indeed, he subsequently described his sensations as those of a man who has inadvertently swallowed a firework.

And Mr. Mole packed in, prudently deciding to win time by telling a false story.

After the successful wind-up of this adventure Jack came home with Emily. (Hunston, tattooed as he was, had beaten him to the first kiss, and not even her plea that it was like the touch of a snake quite reassured him.) He was prepared now to become a soldier if someone would buy him a commission. But first it was agreed that he should go to a university. He chose Oxford because it was 'more swell than Cambridge.' All too soon he was the object of proctorial interest. He took part in a very spirited battle between Town and Gown, going out of his way to assault one townsman on the sole grounds that he was a bargee. Jack's real trouble at Oxford was that he was always being tricked into gambling with shady types. But he was a disconcerting adversary to cheat at cards. On one occasion he startled the assembly by suddenly pinning his opponent's hand to the table with a table fork. When this was extracted (not without difficulty) a card was found underneath the palm; though bloody, it was recognizable as the ace of clubs.

After losing £500 at dice, Jack called 'double or quits' and lost. This £1,000 debt was due to be paid to Moses Manasses, a Jewish moneylender whose daughter Jack had providently saved from drowning in the Cherwell. In the circumstances it did not seem likely that Jack would be pressed for payment. But there was no gratitude in the Tents of Israel. The moneylender was anxious to marry off his daughter to Jack, who, he claimed, had gone out of his way to encourage the girl by turning over the pages of her music. Some of his friends thought that it would be a good thing for Jack to marry the moneylender's daughter. One of them, knowledgeable in these matters, assured him that she was 'as fine a spoon as there is in Oxford.'

But Jack still cherished an obstinate affection for Emily. She for her part must have been deeply in love with him, otherwise she would hardly have co-operated with him in such episodes as the punishment of one Davis, who had been detected making a pass at her. Jack first had the offender bound hand and foot and rolled him under the sofa where he and Emily were sitting. Davis still showed sufficient spirit to bite Jack in the ankle, for which he was threatened with a kick in the face. But Jack thought of a better punishment:

Jack put his arm round Emily's waist and looking at Davis said—
'You wanted a kiss, just now, from the best girl that ever lived?'
Davis made no answer.
Jack got up and kicked him in the ribs.
'Answer when you are spoken to, or it will be the worse for you,' he exclaimed.

'If I did, what then?' asked Davis, with some of his old independent manner.

'Just this. See me kiss her. That's all, old boy. That's your share.'

Jack drew Emily to him as he spoke and she let her head fall on his breast while he bent down and kissed her as he liked.

When he had done, he said—

'How do you like that? Nice, isn't it?'

Nor was that the end of Davis's (or Emily's) discomfiture. In a lordly way Jack ordered a number of fowls to be killed and plucked, and sent someone else for a barrel of tar. Emily was then obliged to witness the disfiguring of the man who had been rash enough to desire her.

Poor Emily! It was no fun being in love with a Harkaway. It must have been both a disappointment and a relief for her when Jack went on his travels again, though she was often to meet him in the most unlikely places.

Powerfully as he appealed to his readers' spirit of adventure, Bracebridge Hemyng periodically went out of his way to preach old-fashioned prudence. For instance, when Jack had been on the point of running away from school, he said:

His wish was to get away, at all hazards, from the tyranny under which he groaned, and when we remember that he was friendless and persecuted, perhaps some excuse can be made for him.

Let us not be misunderstood.

We are no advocates for running away; boys who run away from school generally turn out scamps in after life.

They show an independence of action and a strong self-will, in which it is very injurious for the young to indulge.

Or could that have been the cautious hand of the publisher Brett, who often in his correspondence columns gave out such advice as:

A boy must have his parents' consent before he enters the merchant service, and no boy with good intentions and hoping to get on in the world would dream of going to sea without the permission of those who have loved him and provided for his comforts from infancy.

There is no doubt, however, that in his more sententious moments Hemyng could lay it on thick. This kind of passage, describ-

*Enter Jack Harkaway: his forcibly tattooed opponent is held to the
ground by Harvey*

ing Harkaway's friendship with a boy dying of tuberculosis, reads
oddly from the same pen which so heartlessly described the choking
of a sneak with a sooty carp, or the frying of a Red Indian:

> Of books he [the sick boy] had a large store, but he did not like travels
> and biographies, unless they related to missionaries and good men.
>
> Fisher's eyes would glisten still more brightly, and an expression of
> almost divine enthusiasm cross his eloquent features, as he listened with
> greedy ears.
>
> 'Ah!' he would say with a sigh, 'that is what I should like to have
> done.'
>
> 'You will be able to do it when you grow up,' said Jack.
>
> Fisher shook his head sadly.
>
> 'Gladly would I give up everything for my Saviour," he answered.
> 'But I fear I shall be called away before long.'
>
> 'Oh, no, you won't. You are ill, and feel weak. You'll soon be strong
> and on your legs again,' Jack said.
>
> 'Do you really think so?' asked the invalid thoughtfully. 'I wish I
> could, and yet I don't know why I should wish it. It is nice to die young,
> Jack—I mean before one has been exposed to any great temptation. It
> is very hard to try and keep steadfast in the faith.'

'The doctor thinks you will get better,' said Jack, passing the back of his hand over his eyes.

'Whether I do or not, I shall never forget you. Will you read to me now? Take the New Testament; open it anywhere, you are sure to find something comforting. It is only when we are ill, Jack, that we know the value of the Bible.'

'Have something more lively,' suggested Jack. 'Robinson Crusoe now.'

'To me there is nothing so interesting as the Bible. You are strong, and well, and perhaps don't think as I do. The boys say you did not know your mother. Oh! Jack, if you had a mother like mine, you would —but you seem pained. Have I said anything to hurt you?'

Any admirers of Harkaway the First, who, twenty years later, chanced to read the adventures of Harkaway the Third, might pardonably, if anachronistically, have said, 'This is where I came in.' Young Jack and his chum arrived at Plato House, which also was served by an over-indulgent Head and by masters over-indulgent in liquor. The boys made their snobbish tutor drunk the first night by pretending to be titled Etonians, but no disciplinary action was taken.

Young Jack took exception to a fellow pupil of foreign appearance.

'You're not a true Englishman,' he said. 'There's a touch of the tar-brush about you which shows you are not a white man.'

Later occurred this dialogue:

'There is some of the bandit blood in you.'

'That is my misfortune, not my fault, even if it is true.'

'Fellows like you require to be kept down and have some of the cur knocked out of them.'

'Do you call me that?'

'Yes, a half-bred Spanish cur,' answered Jack.

The 'gipsy' decided that these were fighting words. They fought. Jack licked him (no kicking this time), but the fellow chose an unfair revenge:

To go behind a man and hit him on the head with a cricket bat, exerting all your strength, was not English.

This the Platonians, as they called themselves, knew full well.

Jack Harkaway had fought a fair fight and won it in a handsome British

manner. Why should he be attacked in this disgraceful manner? And by
a youth who could only boast of half-English blood?

All were inclined to cry, 'Out upon the dastard who has brought this
blood upon the school!'

Presumably it was Harkaway the Third who fought the Boers
in 1899. The stories 'Jack Harkaway in the Transvaal, or Fighting
for the Flag,' and 'Jack Harkaway's War Scouts' appeared in
Up-to-Date Boys, a Brett publication which lasted a little longer
than *Jack Harkaway's Journal for Boys*. Harkaway was a captain
in the Hussars, leading a 'private army' which had a spiritual
affinity with some of the irregular units of World War Two.
He had an exhilarating time, rescuing numerous daughters of the
veldt from death or dishonour, and making Boers chant 'Rule
Britannia' at the point of the sword. His keenest displeasure was
visited upon an unfortunate Frenchman whose part in the war
effort was obscure but whose designs on the fair Gretchen were
all too clear. Annoyed at being interrupted by this impertinent
Hussar, the Frenchman sought to run him through with his sword.
Jack announced that to teach him a lesson he would cut off one
of his ears and give him a flesh wound in the arm.

Harkaway was an expert swordsman.

The weapon flashed twice in the air with the rapidity of lightning.

At the first stroke the Frenchman lost his left ear, which was sliced
off close to the head; the second wounded him in the right arm above
the elbow, and he sank to the ground bewailing his fate.

Jack tore a piece of stuff from his tunic and bound up his wound, but
the little man collapsed and fainted away like a woman.

Gretchen did not faint. She entirely approved of the proceedings,
smiled on Jack and handed him his rifle when he had finished.
They were beautiful but tough, those Harkaway heroines.

Not every authority agrees that Bracebridge Hemyng wrote all
the Harkaway stories. Brett liked to pretend to a proprietorial
right in them, and gave the name of Harkaway House to his
publishing offices in West Harding Street, off Fetter Lane. This
was probably intended as a slap at Hogarth House which also
published a number of Harkaway stories.

Hemyng launched many other characters, such as Hal Harkforward and Tom Tallyho, but it is by Harkaway alone that he is remembered. Indeed, it was as Jack Harkaway that he liked to refer to himself, and as such that many of his friends thought of him. Nor was he the only writer of romances to masquerade as his fictional creation.

CHAPTER VI

NOT SO CALLOW

THE MAGAZINES of Brett, Emmett and Fox did not always commend themselves to the more squeamish Victorian parents. More favoured in middle-class homes were journals like *Chatterbox*, started in 1866 by the Rev. J. Erskine Clarke and sold at a halfpenny in an attempt to undercut the reigning 'penny dreadfuls.' James M. Barrie, who had been an avid consumer of sensational literature in his young days, admits that he was side-tracked on to *Chatterbox*, which broke him of the 'penny dreadful' habit (though not before he had tried to write one or two himself). Then in 1879 came the *Boy's Own Paper*, which was approved by the majority of parents. Was it not published by the Religious Tract Society, and edited by James Macaulay, M.A., M.D.? Did it not carry fiction by clergymen, headmasters, baronets, officers of field rank, titled ladies, the worthy Mr. Ballantyne and other gentlemen with M.A. and F.R.S. after their names? Were not the stories, moreover, written in English, and the drawings executed by persons who had been to art school? This obviously was a journal which could safely be allowed in the home.

Some younger readers were more cautious. Because an author put after his name the letters C.M., M.D., R.N. (as Gordon Stables did), or 'Late Professor and Crown Examiner at Moscow' (like J. F. Hodgetts, author of 'Edric the Norseman'), did that make him any the better story-teller? And who was Lady Broome, that she should pretend to be a boy and write a first-person adventure story? Again, the editor of the *Boy's Own Paper* had a good deal to learn when it came to thinking out a lively title; witness 'Frank Harding; or From Torrid Zones to Regions of Perpetual Snow.' He was partial also to headings like 'For England, Home and Beauty.' In long-windedness of titles, however, he was not unchallenged. The Aldine *Garfield Boys' Journal* (1894) offered a story entitled 'Over the Deep Blue Sea for Freedom, Fame and Fortune.'

The *Boy's Own Paper* may not have been strictly blood-and-thunder, but it was a long way from being milk-and-water. Mr. D. B. Wyndham-Lewis was at pains to point this out recently in *The Tatler*, when rounding on a critic who had described a film as 'almost callow enough for the *Boy's Own Paper.*' Wrote Mr. Wyndham-Lewis:

Callow (unfledged, innocent, inexperienced, downy) is the last epithet we should have applied to that paper, which we remember from our golden infancy to be full of tough, hairy, conquering Nordics plunging through trackless forests and lethal swamps, wrestling with huge apes and enormous cobras, foiling villains of Latin origin, crammed with experience and philosophy and knowing practically everything. If the story was by Gordon Stables, R.N., moreover, they turned out to be Scotsmen, and therefore twice as conquering, hairy, noble and scornful of civilized Southern fal-lals.

If, on the other hand, the critic boy meant by 'callow' that vintage B.O.P. heroes never used beastly language, like a modern school-girl, he was correct. In the tightest corners they merely 'uttered a hasty exclamation.' More often than not, faced with fearful odds, they simply gnawed their lip, thus:

'I fear,' said Black MacTavish quietly, 'we are surrounded. Meanwhile do you, MacIntosh, hand me MacNab's knife. I fear his leg is no longer of service.'

It was the work of a moment to amputate MacNab's leg. A substitute was briskly carved from the nearest *njama*-tree by Sandy. MacNab at once leapt up and expressed himself ready to march all day. As he spoke a shower of poisoned spears rattled through the bush and laid three of the little party prostrate.

MacTavish gnawed his lip.

Callow, huh? . . .

An early volume selected at random (1887–88) and opened at random contains a passage no less tough than Mr. Wyndham-

Lewis's imaginary one. Morgana, a dark and *décolletée* matron, is
being trodden to the floor of a collapsing tumulus by a blind man,
whose leg she is attempting to hack off with a golden sickle. With
her other hand she is trying to pour out a goblet of poison. Before
she can make much progress either way the tumulus crashes on
both of them. An appropriate comment comes from one of her
adherents: 'It is time for us to become Christians.'

The same volume of the *Boy's Own Paper* contains a drawing
of a newly decapitated man with lashings of blood pouring from
his trunk, and another of a man hanging from a tree. But more
gruesome than any fictional item in this volume is a series of practical hints on taxidermy for boys, by Lieut.-Colonel Cuthell, late
13th Hussars. Here is one of the lighter passages on stuffing
birds:

The Head.—If the head is very much larger than the neck, cut the
throat lengthways to remove the head. It is immaterial whether the eyes
are taken out before the head is skinned down or after. The gouge should
go well to the back of the eye and separate the ligament which holds it
to the socket. Should the gouge go into the eye, it will let out the moisture,
which often damages the skin. Some people crush the skull slightly to
make it come out of the skin easily, but this I do not advise. Remove
the brains by taking out a piece of the skull at the back as you cut off
the neck. Pull the eyes out of their cavity and fill up their place with
wool soaked in arsenical soap. Anoint the skin of the head and the neck
well with arsenical soap, and place in the neck a piece of stick covered
with wool, the end of which put into the hole made in the skull for
extracting the brains.

Lieut.-Colonel Cuthell has another memorable paragraph
which begins: 'And now for the treatment of the head of a horned
animal . . .'

Like many boys' magazines, the *Boy's Own Paper* mellowed
with the years. It kept high standards and many of its stories, like
those of Talbot Baines Reed, were to become schoolboy classics.
It is gratifying to see it on the bookstalls still, though no longer in
its old opulent format.

Chums, another parentally approved magazine, did not appear
until 1892. The first editor was Max Pemberton, whose famous
story 'The Iron Pirate' appeared in its pages. D. H. Parry and

G. A. Henty were among the contributors. The first editorial struck an urbane, unaggressive note:

Have you, most excellent readers, too many boys' papers? And without suggesting unkindness towards my rivals, have you such good boys' papers that another may not enter into friendly rivalry with them? I think you will say that you have not.

Chums was not exclusively a magazine of fiction. It contained a profusion of articles on such topics as how gun barrels are proved, a night in a lighthouse and chats on famous schools.

A third 'respectable' boys' magazine was George Newnes's *The Captain*, edited by R. S. Warren Bell, and famous for its school stories by P. G. Wodehouse. According to C. B. Fry, who was the Athletic Editor, *The Captain* 'never persuaded advertisers that it was read by parents. Advertisers did not believe that boys are likely to buy such articles as soap and whisky. I have always thought that the disbelief of advertisers in the capacity of boys to absorb soap was the snag which eventually tripped up the career of *The Captain*.'

The class of reader at which the *Boy's Own Paper*, *Chums*, and *The Captain* aimed may be gauged, in the case of the first-mentioned, by the qualification to the take-a-cold-bath advice given by the editor—'Do not make more splash than you can help so as to give the servant trouble'; in the case of *Chums*, by the use of such phrases as *Oh quantum mutatus!* in the editorial: and in the case of *The Captain* by the preoccupation with public school cricket.

A feature of all the boys' magazines of the pre-Harmsworth era, irrespective of the class of reader at which they were directed, was the very firm handling of correspondents and the parading of a strong editorial authority. Supposed pictures of the editor always showed him to be a bearded gentleman in the sixties, with a let-me-mould-your-future look in his eyes. A reader of the *Boy's Own Paper* was very smartly slapped down for his mistaken assumption that certain articles were written by boys—'they are written by *men*.' Correspondents were kept firmly in their place and told what was good for them. A youth who wrote to the *Boy's Own Paper* expressing an interest in party politics was

THE BOY'S OWN PAPER

No. 482.—Vol. X. "   SATURDAY, APRIL 7, 1888.   Price One Penny.
[ALL RIGHTS RESERVED.]

A TALE OF THE NAVY
NINETY YEARS AGO
BY GORDON STABLES, C.M.,
M.D., R.N.,

*Author of "The Cruise of the Snowbird,"
"Wild Adventures Round the Pole," etc., etc.*

CHAPTER I.—INTRODUCING SEVERAL
OF OUR PRINCIPAL CHARACTERS.

WOULD it snow?
    That was the question uppermost in everyone's mind at Agincourt Hall on that still December morning of seventeen hundred and ninety-three.
    Would it snow?

"God save the King!"

'God Save the King!' A characteristic B.O.P. cover (1888)

G

lectured almost as severely as those youths who confessed to 'sinful habits'; the editor did not say so in so many words, but the impression gained was that a cold bath was the cure for both types of aberration.

At all times the editor was cautious not to set his readers against the established order, even in such cases as that of reader E. C. Bark, to whom he gave this not-very-satisfactory answer:

Fifteen hours a day is, we consider, much too long for a boy of fourteen to have to work; but we do not see what you can do except complete your apprenticeship. You should not have chosen a trade in which such long hours are customary.

Nor could anyone say that he went out of his way to encourage 'Cavalryman':

If you get a commission you *might* rise to be a field-marshal! But we do not think you would. Suppose you limit your notions to your becoming a sergeant?

The editor of the *Boy's Own Paper* may have been pardoned a certain asperity towards his readers, as so much of his mail seems to have consisted of carelessly packed beetles and broken eggs, hopefully submitted for identification. One feels that he got a certain amount of malicious satisfaction out of such answers as:

'BERTIE CLERK will know by this time whether the squirrel is dead or alive.'

Edwin Brett also took a stern line towards his readers and trusted them no farther than he could see them. In announcing a new competition in *Jack Harkaway's Journal for Boys* he warned that anyone submitting the work of another person would be not merely disqualified but PUBLICLY EXPOSED; and just to be on the safe side he ruled that no prizes would be sent off to winners until a month after the results of the competition were published. Brett had then been a publisher for many years and had few illusions left about readers, authors or fellow-publishers.

If editors did not trust their readers, the reverse appears to have been true. The editor of the innocent *Nuggets* had to counter allegations that his competitions were swindles, that nearly all

the prizes went to London, and so on. One reader challenged him
to a duel.

It is safe to say that the competitions run by Brett and Henderson
were mostly on a higher intellectual plane than those privately-run
contests which were advertised in small type in *The Young Briton's
Journal* (1888). (This magazine was edited by Guy Rayner, contained a serial entitled 'Guy Rayner Among the Brigands,' and
an editorial assurance that Guy Rayner did really exist—he was
'an Englishman staunch and true'.)

Here is a selection of the catchpenny contests which were to
be found in every issue:

Genuine Competition. R . . E BRIT . . N . A. Fill in five letters and
form two words. A postal order for 10s. sent to every reader who correctly
solves above puzzle. Fee 3d. only. Answer advertised. Mr. John Lewis,
2 Wait's Buildings, Staple Hill, Bristol.

Prof. Robzart offers three prizes for the most words from ROBZART.
Entrance fee 6d. First prize 6s. worth of conjuring tricks; second, three
shillings worth; third 1s. 6d. worth. List must be sent in by July 14.—
29 Fleet Street, Southsea.

Grand competition! Journ . . . Add two letters to form a common
word. 1st prize, Viaduct watch (splendid condition); 2nd, Handsome
Harry, Cheerful, Daring, Wonderful and Young Ching-Ching; 3rd,
Broad-Arrow Jack, Bravos of Alsatia, Dick Turpin and first number of
Cassell's British Battles. Entrance 6d. to W.R., 16, Trafalgar Square,
Peckham.

Genuine Competition.—Nearest to the number of times letter 'A'
occurs in the Book of Titus. First £1 1s.; second 10s.—Cummings,
53, Hurworth Terrace, Darlington.

Boys, this is genuine. Whoever guesses right or nearest number of
my watch will be owner of it. 92 . . . It is a centre-second stop-watch,
full jewelled and real silver. Guesses 6d. for one, 10d. for two. Insufficient
entries, 4d. and 8d. returned. Address C.A.H., Reading Rooms, Brixton,
London S.W.

Sheer impecuniosity must have been the reason why Rayner
accepted advertisements like these—impecuniosity which made
him invite his readers to submit stories of 'not more than six
columns and not less than three' and offer *half-a-crown* for all
printed, with 20s. for the best.

In fairness to Rayner it must be pointed out that similar—and
much bigger—advertisements were to appear a couple of years

later in a much more prosperous rival. This had an advertisement by a firm in Boston, Lincolnshire, offering £200 for counting the H's in the Book of Daniel (entry fee 2s.), £100 for counting the T's in the first eight chapters of Romans (entry 1s. 6d.), and £50 for counting the R's in the first six chapters of Genesis (entry 1s.).

And in fairness to both it must be pointed out that modern competitions run by newspapers of standing often present their readers with no less insulting a challenge to the intelligence. To be invited to complete the word JOURN . . is no worse than to be invited to solve a crossword in which JOURN forms the first five letters of a seven-letter word ending in a cul-de-sac, with an ambiguous clue which could refer either to Journey or Journal.

CHAPTER VII

CUCKOO IN THE NEST

WHILE THE SCRAMBLE went on for the pennies, and even the halfpennies, of the Victorian schoolboy, one publisher, James Henderson, was lending encouragement to a young freelance who was fated one day to buy up Henderson's firm, after crowding many of his other rivals from the map. This cuckoo in the nest was Alfred C. Harmsworth,[1] founder of the Amalgamated Press.

Harmsworth's earliest articles had been about bicycling and butterflies, but in the late 'eighties he launched in *Young Folks Paper* a characteristically ambitious project:

This interesting series of articles will contain information respecting all branches of the Civil Service, and particulars of every known trade, business, occupation or profession, with a chapter on where to emigrate.

Harmsworth's first publishing enterprise was not aimed at the juvenile market; this was *Answers to Correspondents*, quickly shortened to *Answers* (1888). It had a rocky start, but thanks to the famous competition in which readers were invited to earn £1 a week for life by estimating the total amount of gold and silver in the Bank of England on December 4, 1889, it was soon on the road to riches. Each entry in this competition had to have five supporting signatures—and there were more than 700,000 entries. Thus more than three million potential readers were introduced

---

[1] He became Lord Northcliffe in 1905.

to *Answers*. The winner of the contest, Sapper Austin, of the Ordnance Survey Department at Southampton, guessed within £2 of the correct amount.

This kind of warfare shocked the publishing traditionalists, who hitherto had kept their readers happy by giving away gold alberts and an occasional bicycle. George Newnes's *Tit-Bits* (founded 1881) could play the same game, however; one of its best contests involved the publishing of clues which led to treasure buried in different parts of the country.

In 1890 Harmsworth published *Chips* and *Comic Cuts*. They were a success from the start. Two or three years later Harmsworth was claiming that *Comic Cuts* was read by 2,500,000 persons weekly, presumably on a computation of several readers to one copy. It is possible that their success depended less on their comedy element than on such serials as 'Confessions of a Ticket-of-Leave Man,' a record of ten years' penal servitude, 'written by a gentleman convict,' and the famous 'Convict 99,' by Mr. and Mrs. Robert Connor Leighton, which started in *Answers* in 1892 and was run also in *Chips*.[1] Stories of convicts (wrongly convicted for preference) did much to strengthen the foundations of the early Harmsworth empire.

The time seemed opportune to issue more boys' papers. In quick succession appeared the *Halfpenny Wonder* (1892) and the *Halfpenny Marvel* (1893). The newsagents showed a certain amount of bloody-mindedness at being asked to sell halfpenny papers, arguing that if these were successful no one would buy penny ones, but Harmsworth promised his readers that if newsagents would not handle halfpenny papers he would appoint his own agents who would. It was not, of course, the first case of price-cutting in this field.

Harmsworth appears to have convinced himself that it was his moral duty to conduct a crusade against 'penny dreadfuls.' In *Comic Cuts* he contented himself with producing a 'fighting editor' whose job it was to throw downstairs, in addition to poets, all authors of 'penny dreadfuls' who sought to sully his pages with their unsolicited contributions. Soon afterwards the campaign

---

[1] It was reprinted in the *Boy's Herald* twenty years later.

became bitter; Harmsworth hurled into it all the reckless fervour which he was to bring to his later and more famous crusades. Number One of the *Halfpenny Marvel*, which was to carry the first stories of Sexton Blake and Nelson Lee, bore a slogan: 'No more penny dreadfuls! These healthy stories of mystery, adventure, etc., will kill them.' An editorial deplored the number of boys who, inflamed by reading 'penny dreadfuls,' were robbing their employers, buying revolvers with the proceeds and setting themselves up in the back streets as highwaymen. 'This and many other evils the "penny dreadful" is responsible for. It makes thieves of the coming generation and so helps to fill our jails. If we can rid the world of even one of these vile publications our efforts will not have been in vain.'

A later issue of the *Marvel* quoted a 'penny dreadful' with 'three spelling and six grammatical errors to every page,' and mentioned that one publisher of such works cleared £7,000 a year. 'Of course, he does not give one-fiftieth of the value we do.' There followed letters supporting Harmsworth's campaign from a police sergeant and a magistrate, quotations from court reports and a story of how a 'walking library man' had been making 24,000 per cent profit from office boys and printers' devils in Fleet Street by repeatedly re-issuing copies of 'penny dreadfuls' at half-price. Happily, he had now seen the error of his way and had undertaken in future to sell only the *Marvel*: and to sell it outright.

In a later number of the *Marvel* was quoted a letter from a reader revealing another insidious aspect of the 'penny dreadful':

In front of shop windows you may see at any time through the day a crowd of children eagerly, breathlessly following as far as they can through the glass the fortunes of some idiotic abortion of a lunatic writer's brain. Physically and morally, could there be anything more harmful to our children? No wonder they are taking as a matter of course to spectacles. Years ago we used to make fun of the Germans in this respect. In another decade or so we too shall sail our ships and fire our guns and go about our daily work spectacled.

Investing in 'Rats, the Boy Ferret' and 'Humboldt Harry, the Hurricane,'[1] I read them and have had horrid dreams ever since. There is not one good, honest paragraph in the lot; not one sentence worth a moment's

---

[1] Both of these were Aldine titles.

lingering over. . . . Were Board Schools established for the purpose of teaching children to amuse themselves with such stuff as this?

This reader who so oddly confessed to suffering from nightmares inspired by paragraphs which were not worth reading went on to say that eight out of ten boys in the streets of London had 'penny dreadfuls' in their pockets. It was, he thought, almost a case for State intervention.

Shortly afterwards the *Marvel* published prominently on its back page a tribute from the Rev. C. N. Barham, of Nottingham, expressing his pleasure that the contents of the magazine should be so 'pure and wholesome in tone.' It is conceivable that the Rev. Mr. Barham regretted writing this testimonial when he saw the front cover of the issue in which his letter appeared. The picture showed a man being tortured by Greek brigands, with the caption: 'The gaoler screwed up the horrible machine until the brigand's bones were nearly broken and he shrieked aloud for mercy, though none was shown.'

That was Harmsworth's problem: to pour contumely on 'penny dreadfuls' and their publishers, and yet to provide his readers with strong enough meat to replace the fare to which they were accustomed. It called for a nice balancing of values.

Another congratulatory letter quoted about this time in the *Marvel* was 'from a personal friend who has a son at Harrow. He informs me that at all the public schools there is a great rush for the *Halfpenny Marvel* and boys read it with evident enjoyment.'

Next came *Union Jack* (1894). It bore slogans like these across the bottom and top of almost every page: 'The *Union Jack Library* will consist of pure, healthy tales only'; 'The *Union Jack* is a market for only the very best literary and artistic wares.'

'There will be nothing of the "dreadful" type in our stories,' pledged the *Union Jack*. 'No tales of boys rifling their employers' cash boxes and making off to foreign lands, or such-like highly immoral fiction products.'

With the publication of the *Boys' Friend* (1895) Alfred Harmsworth pulled out all the stops. The first issue contained a diatribe against 'penny dreadfuls' which was intended to make their publishers curl up and die. One curious thing about this onslaught was that it contained ammunition which had already been fired in the *Quarterly Review* in 1890; and the editor of the *Quarterly Review* had been smartly reproved at the time for his intolerance and snobbishness in the pages of Harmsworth's *Chips*.

Innocent boys who got hold of 'penny dreadfuls,' said the *Boys' Friend*, little dreamed of the trickery and deceit which went into their manufacture. What could they know about 'the miserable beer-swilling wretches who write them . . . if such a word as write could be applied to their work?'

As a rule they are drunken, sodden creatures whose lives have been one long unbroken story of failure. Sometimes they are University men who in the flower of their youth gave promise of becoming noble men; but giving way to the temptations of drink they have gradually sunk lower and lower in the scale of life until at last they reach the depths of degradation and their natures have become so debased that they are fit only to write evil stories which fill the pocket of the man who prints and sells the 'penny dreadful.'

'Editor,' it seems, was a misnomer when it came to describing the person who commissioned 'penny dreadfuls'—'his capability for editing is not to be measured with his capability for drinking intoxicants.' His practice was to get hold of a lot of old and worn type which printed in 'a blurred, sight-destroying way,' and then cast around to find a set of second-hand blocks to serve as illustrations. Then he ordered a story to be written around the blocks, no matter what the pictures showed.

It is a daunting thought. Who will withhold sympathy from a hack presented with, say, six pictures showing a redskin dancing round a captive, two Frenchmen fencing, a highwayman holding up a coach, a smuggler's boat landing in a cove, a detective looking at a footprint through a magnifying glass and a bound and gagged woman, with instructions to 'keep it down to 20,000 words' and call it 'Guy Gaspereau, the Brigand Chief'?

Next the *Boys' Friend* asked: Where do they write? And supplied the answer: communal kitchens of cheap lodging-houses, the bar parlours of dirty, back-alley public-houses. The head of a beer cask was sufficient for table . . . and the man who used ink was a man of means 'compared with the usual run of this pitiful class.' Notepaper consisted of 'backs of old bills' and any dirty wrappers which happen to be handy.

Finally the *Boys' Friend* got around to asking: *What* do they write?

If you buy a copy of 'Guy Gaspereau' you will find it consists of some 16 pages vilely printed and with woodcuts which look as though they had been carved with a chopper. No paragraph is longer than four or at the most five lines.

'Guy paused.
'The villain clenched his teeth.
'The situation was terrible. No help within a league.'

There is generally a hero, bold, dashing, handsome and gifted with every possible accomplishment. There is a villain, often a hunch-back and always pitted with small-pox. There is the hero's great friend, a simple country youth who follows his chum through thick and thin and saves his life every other week.

It is curious to find Harmsworth magazines holding up the short paragraph to ridicule when it is remembered that not so many years later the *Daily Mail* offices were to contain enormous notices exhorting 'Paragraph! Paragraph! Paragraph!' and any sub-editor who allowed long-winded contributors to get away with unbroken slabs of prose was quickly on the carpet.

Alfred Harmsworth in the 'nineties was very concerned to give his readers value for money. He reminded them constantly that the 'long complete' stories they were buying meant that they were getting a shilling for a halfpenny. He even apologized for leaving the inside covers of the *Union Jack* bare of text. The paper was so thin that to print on the reverse side would have ruined the picture on the cover. Harmsworth believed in taking his readers into his confidence and telling them all about the problems of printing and block-making.

Instead of spending money on first-class glossy paper, thick cardboard covers and large type we shall give the very best value possible. . . . It would be easy to sell for 1s. 1d., but where one man will spend a shilling 5,000 will risk a halfpenny.

There was the Harmsworth theory of business in a nutshell. One can believe that the real weight of the wrath Harmsworth bore against the publishers of 'penny dreadfuls' was inspired, not by the supposed peril to the younger generation's morals or eyesight, but by such underhand and 'unprofessional' devices as using second-hand blocks. Not that such a practice was unknown in the twentieth century.

Publication of halfpenny magazines forced some of the other boys' publishers to follow suit. Brett, for instance, put out an orange-covered *Halfpenny Surprise*, containing a 'long complete' and a short serial. After a few years Harmsworth was able to raise the prices of his boys' papers to one penny, and thereby achieve a higher standard of production. There is no doubt that the type in some of his halfpenny papers was even more trying to the eyes than that of some of the maligned 'penny dreadfuls.'

A claim to be the most successful of the Harmsworth boys' thrillers launched in the 'nineties—judged by length of life—has been lodged on behalf of the *Union Jack*, which ran for almost forty years; but a strong case can be made out for the *Wonder* ('Funny But Not Vulgar') which, under the varying titles of the *Wonder*, the *Funny Wonder*, the *Wonder and Jester*, the *Jester and Wonder*, the *Jester* and the *Jolly Jester*, ran from 1892 to 1940. True, it was primarily a 'comic,' but like *Merry and Bright*, *Puck* and all the Harmsworth 'comics,' it had a powerful stiffening of adventure stories. In the case of the *Jester*, as it was best known, these ranged from the earlier tales of sleuths, iron tortoises and human bats (one performer in this category is pictured sleeping upside down with his feet in a slot) to sporting curates, convict earls and girls without a home. At one period no issue of the *Jester* was complete without a buxom heroine trapped on a target ship or pinioned in a lion's den. Serials would run on for year after year; in this department Herbert Allingham was a star performer.

The mauve-covered *Union Jack* (which incidentally bore the same title as a short-lived publication with which W. H. G. Kingston and G. A. Henty were associated some years previously) ran from 1894 to 1933, when it was merged in the new *Detective Weekly*. Number Two contained 'Sexton Blake, Detective' (of whom a great deal more in the next chapter). A certain modesty was noticeable in the announcement of future stories; 'The Phantom

Dwarf,' for instance, would be 'in the approved Rider Haggard style and written by the celebrated author Maxwell Scott. Do not imagine, however, that we would compare our series with the work of that great writer whose every new book causes its readers to go into raptures.'

The early stories were mostly open-air tales of redskins, explorers, prospectors, sailors and so on, with a few detectives thrown in. Titles like 'Fighting for the Flag' were common, heroes being drawn from the Zulu, Matabele and Ashanti wars. One story at least was written by a woman. Readers were invited to send in copies of the *Union Jack* with their comments inscribed in the margin, a prize going to the critic who wrote most neatly.

Gradually Sexton Blake stories began to grow more frequent and after about a hundred issues the magazine was devoted to the detective exclusively.

The green-jacketed *Marvel*, which ran for almost thirty years until merged with *Sport and Adventure*, published much the same kind of story in its initial stages. It had been planned as the *Miracle*, but the name was changed at the eleventh hour to avoid offending religious susceptibilities. Though it carried early adventures of such celebrated characters as Sexton Blake and Nelson Lee it did not hold on to them, and it is probably chiefly remembered for the unending tales of Jack, Sam and Pete by S. Clarke Hook (a descendant of Theodore Hook, the novelist and lampoonist).

These three adventurers, who stayed with the *Marvel* to the last number, consisted of Jack, a brave British boy with the adventurous spirit; Sam, a skilled hunter, and Pete, a negro ventriloquist, who was the real life of the party. Their stories hardly come under the heading of blood-and-thunder, containing the same strong farcical element which characterized the 'Captain, Cookey and the Engineer' stories which were simultaneously appearing in *Pluck* (1894). From Jack, Sam and Pete doubtless stemmed the numerous other stories about boy trios, in which a comic and faithful negro, Chinese or Eskimo was considered indispensable. Jack, Sam and Pete spent their time against a new, though never vastly different, background each week, returning to England occasionally when a circulation tour of the provinces seemed desirable. They had this claim to fame—they were the most balloon-minded of their contemporaries. Such titles as 'Pete's Chinese Laundry,' 'Pete's Wild West Dairy,' 'Pete's Pantomime,' 'Pete's Boarding House' give a fair clue to the later type of story. That the trio were popular is not in dispute. When the *Boys' Friend Library* was opened in 1905 to carry popular reprints from other Harmsworth publications (along with some originals), Jack, Sam and Pete were consistently prominent among the titles. As if Jack, Sam and Pete were not enough for one man, Hook launched Dan, Bob and Darkey in the war-time *Boys' Friend*.

The *Boys' Friend*, which ran for thirty-two years, was a vigorously conducted weekly under one of the 'livest' of boys' editors, Hamilton Edwards. It ran school tales ('Bob Redding's Schooldays'), romances of the Boer War, of exploration, even historical tales, and also featured from time to time all the leading performers of the Amalgamated Press—Sexton Blake, Nelson Lee and Jack, Sam and Pete. Many remember it for the Ferrers Lord stories, which ran under one title or another for years. 'Wolves of the Deep' (1900) was styled 'the story of a grim battle of life and death between two of the wealthiest men the world has ever known.' With this was linked an editorial pronouncement which, once again, sounded like a confident expression of the publisher's philosophy: 'There is no limit to the power of colossal wealth when wealth is linked with brain.'

The nature of the stories of Ferrers Lord (not to be confused with Ferrers Locke) may easily be judged from the *dramatis personae*, which included the inevitable comedy characters:

Ferrers Lord.	A British inventor. Two immense submarine boats he has constructed. A staunch patriot.
Michael Scaroff.	A Russian prince and Lord's bitterest enemy. He stole the plans of Lord's submarine ship and built a similar boat—the Tsaritza.
Rupert Thurston	Lord's companion.
Ching Lung	A Chinese prince. He is an expert conjurer and always up to some fun.
Prout and Maddock.	Two seamen of the Lord of the Deep.
Kennedy.	An Irishman in Yang's army.
Pierre Bovrille	A funny Frenchman.

Lord and his rival were made to symbolize the rivalry between Britain and Russia. 'Lion Against Bear' was the title of the second series. Everything that could and could not happen underwater happened to the rival millionaires. The fertile author was Sidney Drew.

The *Boys' Friend* hurled itself into the Great War as ferociously as it had hurled itself into the Boer War. In the second year it launched the Anti-German League. The membership form ('to be signed by every British boy') read:

I . . . living at . . . do hereby solemnly pledge that I will on no account trade with or encourage the common enemy. I will purchase no goods whatever bearing the trade mark 'Made in Germany,' and I will do my utmost to persuade my friends to register their names also.

A week or two before, tempted by the offer of a motor cycle, readers had been urged to introduce the *Boys' Friend* to as many chums as possible; now they were invited to badger their chums to join a crusade for which no prizes were offered. Soon the editor was able to report progress.

Only the other day a Balham member wished to buy a good automatic pistol. He saw one in a shop which made his heart leap with joy, but the ominous words 'Made in Bavaria' soon checked him, and he contented himself with a revolver of British make, though it was not quite what he wanted.

Other successes reported were the spurning of German pencils and rulers.

In the post-1918 years the *Boys' Friend* tended to sober down. Its final issues became quite old-fashioned in appearance. Then abruptly at the end of 1927 its readers were invited to transfer their affections to the three-year-old *Triumph*.

The *Boys' Friend* had several companion papers similar in character—the *Boys' Realm* (1902), the *Boys' Herald* (1903) and *Boys' Leader* (1903). Of these the *Boys' Realm* lasted longest. All were served by the same writers, whose names or pen-names included Sidney Drew, Maxwell Scott, Herbert Maxwell, S. Clarke Hook, T. C. Bridges, Reginald Wray, Henry Johnson, Alec G. Pearson, Henry St. John, John Tregellis, John Hunter, Murray

Graydon, Robert Leighton and Arthur S. Hardy. The school story magazines were next in the field—*Gem* and *Magnet* (Chapter XIII). Later, in 1912, came three more—the *Dreadnought*, the *Penny Pictorial* and the *Penny Wonder*. The *Penny Pictorial* offered a three-in-one bargain. A typical issue would contain a Charles Hamilton school story, a Sexton Blake story and an adventure of Jack, Sam and Pete, all much shorter than usual. The *Penny Wonder* was a curious blend of fiction for boys, girls and even housewives. It had John Flood, the River Detective, for the delectation of male readers; for women readers there were Galloping Gloria the Lady Turpin, Grace Daring the Girl Chauffeur and a third heroine whose proficiency with bow and arrow made her invaluable at firing lifelines, sending messages to prisoners in towers, and shooting down hanged men. For hearthside reading there was 'What Will Become of Her?' It was the story of 'A wife without a husband, a mother without a child, who faced the world alone.' The *Wonder* was curiously old-fashioned in that its heroines were still being lashed to windmill sails or left dangling on the clappers of church bells while more progressive journals were binding them to aeroplane propellers or suspending them from airships. Nevertheless the *Wonder* contrived to work out some novel predicaments with the aid of the old-fashioned windmill, clock tower and water-wheel. Notable was the plight of a man who, pushing his head through a grille in a clock face, had his head gripped between the hands at the lethal hour of twenty minutes to nine; a situation which was considered sufficiently dramatic to repeat in the *Boys' Friend* fifteen years later. But the most curious throwback in the *Penny Wonder* was a Gothic story entitled 'The Secret Dread, or The Mystery of Castle Hume.' Edward Lloyd would have been happy to print it in his day. Said the editorial prologue:

This story is founded upon a real life mystery and its central character had in fact his counterpart in actual existence. There are skeletons in the cupboards of our ancient noble families—skeleton secrets so awesome and so forbidding that knowledge of them needs to be kept a profound secret from every human soul but the head of the house in question. There are strange uncanny things in secret chambers, to which no light can come, that breathe and die unknown and unnamed; things that cause

a shadow in the eyes of those that know them. And of such a Secret
Dread this tale relates.

According to a later synopsis, the secret dread turned out to be
a very old friend:

It is midday at Castle Hume and a dread tempest of thunder and
lightning rages without. Guests and retainers are assembled to celebrate
the coming of age of the heir of Hume, who tonight must hear from the
old Earl's lips the dread secret of his race. On the stroke of twelve, after
the lightning has struck a goblet known as the Luck of Hume from the
hand of Lord Douglas, the heir, the old earl leads his son to the Blue
Chamber to unfold the secret to him. And as the Earl makes known to
his son the hidden secret, the solitary portrait of the wicked Earl Malpas
is split in twain and there appears through the rent—the face of a Horned
Man. Immediately flames burst into the Blue Chamber, the castle now
being on fire. Scrymgeour Hume reaches the battlements in quest of the
Lady Elaine, the destined bride of the heir of Hume, only to see the
Horned Man with the girl in his arms leap from the battlements.

A feature of the early Harmsworth boys' papers was the existence
in many stories of a heroine. The *Marvel* usually gave her a head-
and-shoulders illustration to herself. In the actual story she played
a negligible part; her duty was to rebuff the advances of the villain
and to marry the hero in the last chapter at the village church.
She was a sop towards older readers.

There was a vogue, too, for Rider Haggard queens of the 'She'
type—mysterious pale-skinned princesses ruling lost kingdoms of
negroes, or reigning over albinos in the craters of volcanoes.

These heroines were as nearly as possible sexless, even the
'She'-like queens, who wore long thick white nightdresses, sometimes with pigtails. The 'penny dreadfuls' had occasionally
offered a heroine whose bosom, in stress of motion or emotion,
had escaped from captivity, or on whose bare back a playful
pirate was proposing to brand his mark. In the early magazines
of the Brett type matrons with generously proportioned and
lightly clad torsos were no rarity, either as symbolic figures like
Britannia or Marianne, or as Boadicean-style heroines. James
Henderson's *Young Folks Budget* regaled its readers with a front-
page picture showing Queen Mab appearing before the dazzled
hero clad only in a wisp of gossamer. But the Harmsworth heroines

were careful not to flaunt their sex appeal, in which resolve they were aided in the earlier days by the prevailing fashions. Around about 1912 it became a deliberate policy to play up a 'girl chum'— possibly as a concession to the large female readership, possibly as a concession to reality. Cousin Ethel of the *Gem* was a good example (Chapter XIII). Considering the strenuous adventures which befell them, such girl chums as Eileen Dare, Nelson Lee's assistant, contrived miraculously to keep their calves concealed— even when descending fire escapes or hanging on to aerial cables. What was just as important, the crooks who tied them to railway lines were always commendably careful not to disarrange their clothing.[1] Even in the short skirt era the decencies were scrupulously observed. Grace Daring, the Girl Chauffeur who got into alarming scrapes in the *Penny Wonder*, was definitely a Good Girl: and Daisy Dare, the Girl Reporter of the *Dreadnought*, would blush innocently and retract her feet under the desk whenever a baronet paid her a formal compliment as a prelude to consulting her in some case which had baffled Scotland Yard. There is a drawing of Daisy perched at the top of a telephone pole tapping the wires, clothed entirely as Mrs. Grundy would have wished. All these girl chums as featured in the illustrations had a tendency towards flat chests and low heels. Their faces were pretty in a chocolate box sort of way, but their figures were strictly non-voluptuous—even those over whom schoolboys were occasionally allowed to go 'soppy,' until ragged out of it by their comrades.

Now and again readers would seek personal advice on the subject of feminine friendships. Wrote the editor of the *Magnet*:

A most interesting query comes from Roy Walker, of South Shields, who asks my views about boys having girl chums.

My older members know exactly the opinions I hold about boy and girl friendships. I feel they can serve a healthy and useful purpose if they are carried on with the full approval of the parents on both sides, provided no foolish thought of courtship is indulged in. A lad feels there is some-

---

[1] In a certain publishing house turning out the type of romance in which servant girls are chased by men with glaring eyes, an artist executed what he thought was an excellent cover drawing. It showed a girl lying on lamplit cobbles with her throat slit from ear to ear, and her assailant, blood-stained knife in hand, disappearing down a furtive alley. The illustration was rejected for policy reasons: the girl's dress was above her knee.

thing in the friendship of a girl chum that uplifts him, and fills him with the desire to live well, keep steady, and do great deeds. And so long as both parties to the friendship remain true to themselves, I am sure no fair-minded man or woman would wish to deny them the happiness they enjoy.

In all these papers the editorial chat was a prominent feature. The editor of the *Boys' Herald* sought to strike a more informal note at the outset than some of his predecessors when he said: 'In most cases boys regard the editor of their paper as an austere domineering old gentleman, to whom they should write, if occasion should compel them, in terms of utmost humility and deference. This is wrong.'

There was nothing frivolous in his outlook, however. He warned his readers repeatedly against those habits which could lead only to 'an early and miserable death,' and in a special note to parents urged them to introduce into their sons' lives some such daily discipline as 'an hour's woodchopping.' Otherwise the lads would assuredly behave in such a way as 'to bow down their grey-haired parents in sorrow.'

He and his fellow-editors between them advised their readers on every affliction, physical and psychological, which could beset the adolescent—blushing, pimples, short stature, pigeon-chestedness, freckles, bandy legs, protruding teeth, nervousness with girls; told them how to stop smoking, and how to remove not only blackheads but tattoo marks. As the years progressed the editors grew younger, in outlook if not in years. Rather rashly, the *Boys' Friend* during World War I published a picture of the editor—a cheerful young man. A week or two later appeared this prominent notice:

A Personal Explanation
Why Your Editor Is Not in the Forces

The photograph of your editor which recently appeared at the head of this page has lately been the cause of cynical remarks from a few of my readers who are—not unnaturally perhaps—puzzled that one so comparatively youthful is himself not in France enduring with others the inferno of the trenches. In justice to those readers I have ventured upon a personal explanation of this matter—an explanation which amply proves that no insinuation as to lack of patriotism can be laid at my door. For the information of those readers of the *Boys' Friend* who desire to know the facts of the case I would say that the explanation appears in the issue of our companion paper, *The Magnet Library*, No. 379, published last month.

There was obviously something to be said for printing a picture of an editor with a long beard.

Behind the editorial chats—which were sometimes taken over by the editor-in-chief and signed 'H.E.' (Hamilton Edwards)— could often be felt the presence of the proprietor. The frequency of stories about the invasion of Britain (see Chapter XI) was a sure sign that the newly ennobled Harmsworth did not under-estimate the importance of even the most modest of his publications.

Even when he had more ambitious projects on hand and could afford to leave his boys' papers in the hands of men who well understood both their master's whims and the whims of the public, the 'Chief' still liked to keep a paternal interest in his juvenile ventures. He did not grow ashamed of them, as other publishers had done. Indeed he strongly resented sneering references to these journals which were the foundations of his empire. Sir John Hammerton, who looked after the 'fortnightly parts' publications of the Amalgamated Press, tells in one of his books how angry Northcliffe was on one occasion when he heard that a member of the staff had jokingly referred to the 'hooligan department.' At an early stage he was so keen that no vulgar slang should creep into his boys' stories that he instituted an office censor for the purpose. Sir John Hammerton was offered the job but declined it. Hammerton's book suggests that he was not especially interested in the boys' fiction department. Could it have been in retaliation for this that one of Sexton Blake's adversaries was christened Hammerton Palmer?

In souvenir volumes published by the Amalgamated Press to celebrate important milestones in the firm's history are brief— rather too brief—references to the boys' magazines on which the Northcliffe fortunes were built. In 1912 the claim was made that 'these [boys'] journals aimed from the first at the encouragement of physical strength, of patriotism, of interest in travel and explora-tion, and of pride in our empire. It has been said that the boys' papers of the Amalgamated Press have done more to provide recruits for our Navy and Army and to keep up the esteem of the sister services than anything else.' The author of *The Romance of the Amalgamated Press* (1925) asserted: 'There is no paper with which the firm has ever been associated that, whatever its other defects, could not at any time have been placed in the hands of the most puritanical man, woman or child without raising a blush or causing the faintest thrill of distaste.' That sentence contains enough negatives to be ambiguous, but the intention is clear and most readers will endorse the truth of it.

The man who had sounded the death knell of 'penny dreadfuls' nevertheless lived to see his own publications called by the same name, though some people styled them 'bloods,' which was a shade more flattering. Long after his death the publications which he founded were still carrying paragraphs like this from the *Nelson Lee Library*:

Glad to hear, Frank Nicholls, that since your father has read some copies of the Old Paper he no longer regards them as 'penny dreadfuls.' I wish a few thousand other fathers would follow his good example.

Northcliffe to-day is remembered as the founder of the *Daily Mail*, the purchaser of *The Times*, the arch-foe of Germany, the propagandist for aviation, the eccentric tyrant of Fleet Street. In his obituaries and biographies only the most summary mention is made of his boys' papers. Just as the obituaries of Edward Lloyd had omitted to state that he was the sponsor of Sweeney Todd, so the obituaries of Northcliffe omitted to state that he was the sponsor of Sexton Blake.

CHAPTER VIII

FIFTY-FIVE YEARS
OF SEXTON BLAKE

THERE WAS ONCE a radio quiz in which a girl was asked to name a famous detective who lived in Baker Street. Her reply 'Sexton Blake' did not satisfy the B.B.C. quizmaster, though in thousands of homes it was doubtless accepted as the correct answer. Even when the quizmaster resorted to transparent prompting—'No, I mean some detective or detectives who had *homes* in Baker Street,' the girl obstinately clung to her original reply.

To offset this, there was a radio occasion in 1945 when several writers of detective stories were asked to name the most famous detective of fiction. This time Sexton Blake was not mentioned.

Sexton Blake has been called, patronizingly, the office-boy's Sherlock Holmes. Those who take detective fiction seriously claim that his successes are due less to pure deduction than to calculated coincidence, an *expertise* with fire-arms, and such specialized attainments as the power to out-stare cobras. Show Blake a sheet of writing in which the first is alternately regular and irregular, and he will be unable to tell you, from the incidence of the palsied patches, that it was written in a train travelling between Norwood and London Bridge. But nail him down in a crate and throw him off the bridge at Westminster and while you are still dusting your hands and saying 'That's that' you will feel his automatic in your back. Only an adult will accept a *tour de force* like the first. Only an adult will sneer at a *tour de force* like the second.

Miss Dorothy Sayers was probably thinking of Sexton Blake when she wrote that detective blood-and-thunders were 'the nearest approach to a national folk-lore, conceived as the centre for a cycle of loosely connected romances in the Arthurian manner.' If Sexton Blake is not a legendary hero of England ranking with King Arthur and Robin Hood it is not the fault of his chroniclers, who at a modest estimate have turned out a total of 200,000,000 words about him; or of the film makers, whose efforts are not to be decried because they have rarely been seen in the West End of London.[1] To refer to Blake as a 'legendary hero of England' is, in any case, parochial; his adventures are retailed in such diverse tongues as Dutch, Spanish and Afrikaans.

For nearly fifty-five years the interminable casebook of Sexton Blake has been profitably rummaged by syndicates of authors. It is still yielding its secrets to-day, though not quite in such profusion. There is no closed shop in the Sexton Blake industry. Anyone who feels an urge to add to the legend is free to try. Turn to 'Sexton Blake Library' in the *Fleet Street Annual* and you will read:

> The same central characters—Sexton Blake and Tinker—are invariably used, and it is therefore advisable for the writer to familiarize himself with the personalities of these.

More than one hundred authors have written Sexton Blake stories. It is the peculiar, though unavoidable, fate of most of them to be remembered not for their Blake but for the adversaries they pitted against him, or for the *femmes fatales* they introduced. Some of the names are known pseudonyms; others have that pseudonymous look about them. It is rumoured—be this as it may —that famous authors have written Sexton Blake stories under assumed names for ready cash, and that that accounts for the high level of writing and plot construction in many of the tales.

[1] Sexton Blake appeared in films as early as 1914. It is claimed that the first films to be made under the British Films Quota Act were based on Sexton Blake adventures; Langhorne Burton played the detective and Micky Brantford the part of Tinker. More recent Blake films featured David Farrar.

In latter years—since it became policy to play up authors' names—those who have created outstanding opponents for Blake, or who are linked with major developments in his story, include Robert Murray, George Hamilton Teed, Gwyn Evans, Anthony Skene, Edwy Searles Brooks, Lewis Jackson, John Hunter, Anthony Parsons, Donald Stuart, Rex Hardinge and Gilbert Chester. One who must not be omitted from the Blake roll of honour is the indefatigable artist Eric R. Parker, who was also the designer of the Sexton Blake bust, now something of a rarity. The bust went to console competitors who failed to win Austin Sevens, and was also widely distributed at cinemas which showed Sexton Blake films.

Sexton Blake can be traced back, without much difficulty, to the year 1893, but only a rash researcher would claim that this was positively his first appearance. Sherlock Holmes, on whom Blake is commonly supposed to have been based, made his début in 1887 in *A Study in Scarlet*, attaining much wider popularity four years later in *The Adventures of Sherlock Holmes*. But it is noteworthy that the Sexton Blake who appeared in the sixth number of Alfred Harmsworth's *Halfpenny Marvel*, published in 1893, in a story called 'The Missing Millionaire,' had almost none of the characteristics of Holmes. The illustrations showed a well-built, not particularly distinguished Victorian gentleman with a high-crowned bowler, carrying a heavy walking-stick. Nor did he work in Baker Street but in New Inn Chambers (the next story put him in offices in Wych Street, off the Strand). He was operating at that time in partnership with a French investigator, Jules Gervaise. In those days it was a privilege to be linked with a French detective, so well had Messrs. Gaboriau and Leroux done their work.

The author's name was given as Hal Meredeth—almost certainly a pen name. Whether Mr. Meredeth himself invented the name Sexton Blake is open to doubt; a survivor of those days states that the original intention was to call the detective Frank Blake, but the demand went up for a more unusual first name, with a dash of the sinister. Somebody hit on Sexton—and the name stuck.

Blake was of the 'new order of detectives,' which could have meant the Conan Doyle stories, the French school or the American school. In the 'nineties detectives were spawning in both hemispheres, as the next chapter will show.

Number Seven of the *Marvel* also contained a Sexton Blake story. He and Gervaise seemed to be doing fairly well, for they had a clerks' office 'with three doors.'

Even at this stage there was a woman in Blake's life. Not for the last time the detective was to feel tenderly towards a young woman who was destined to be kidnapped and not restored till the last chapter. The style of Mr. Meredeth's Blake is worth quoting:

'I never believed until now,' reflected Sexton Blake, 'that I should ever seriously fall in love and especially at first sight: but I must confess that if I could succeed in winning the affections of Lillie Ray I should account myself the luckiest of earthly mortals. Bah! I'll not trouble the office any more to-day. . . .'

It was not long before Blake and the arch-crook of this particular episode were fighting hand-to-hand in the basket of a balloon drifting over the Channel. Neither man could break his adversary's grip.

He [Blake] then determined on taking a desperate course, for the present position of matters had become maddening. He pulled the trigger of his revolver and sent a bullet crashing through the silk of the balloon! The gas came hissing from the rents and the two men descended with a rapidity which robbed both of them of their senses!

What exactly happened after this Blake could never tell. When he had at last opened his eyes it was to find himself in the comfortably furnished cabin of a steamer. . . .

The heroine, once rescued, came into a good deal of money. Blake was distressed at this development:

For a little it seemed to Blake that her accession to such vast wealth placed another barrier between them; but she has given him more than half a promise that she will some day reward his devotion to her in the way he most desires.

In spite of which Blake was destined to remain a bachelor. Or was he? Mr. Reginald Cox, writing in *The Saturday Book* (sixth year), mentions a crony who claims to have heard of a companion

Sexton Blake in mid-career.—The Union Jack, 1915

paper of *Union Jack* in which there are disconcerting references to a Mrs. Blake. Researchers have taken up the scent but it is no easy task to traverse 200,000,000 words; meanwhile the report should be treated with reserve. Whatever the truth, it must have been borne in upon Blake's sponsors at an early stage that while it was not unreasonable for him to cheat death at least once a week, it would invite accusations of profligacy if he fell in love with a different woman every week.

To return to the *Halfpenny Marvel*. Blake made only spasmodic appearances in this journal, which like all Harmsworth's new publications was exceeding the Editor's 'most sanguine expectations.' Some of the stories were attributed to Harry Blyth—perhaps an alias of Hal Meredeth. Blake took turns with stories about gold prospecting and the Matabele wars. Then in Number 25 came the announcement that 'Sexton Blake has been secured by the *Union Jack*,' due to make its début in April 1894. It was this pink-jacketed *Union Jack*, then also a halfpenny paper, which was to make Sexton Blake famous. Not that it held any exclusive title to him, for he has appeared in *Boys' Friend, Boys' Herald, Penny Pictorial, The Jester*, and of course the *Sexton Blake Library*, which started as a separate institution during the First World War. To those who to-day pay sevenpence for their Sexton Blake it will come as a shock to find that the first novels were half the price of a 'penny dreadful.'

A redskin story—'The Silver Arrow'—was selected to open *Union Jack*. Then in Number Two came a Sexton Blake story with a cover picture showing an exhumation in a churchyard. The editorial preamble said:

> Some time ago we arranged with Mr. Sexton Blake, the celebrated detective, to furnish us with particulars of the most remarkable and sensational cases he has been concerned in. From some of the materials he has placed at our disposal we have framed the following exciting and authentic narrative, feeling sure that its strange details will excite world-wide interest.

Heroes and villains in these early stories were pretty easy to identify. No detective (or reader) would be likely to waste time checking up on the credentials of Ernest Truelove, or Harry

Armitage; or of Ninian Joyce, 'the sweetest maiden that Heaven ever blessed with a dainty form and a beauteous grace.'

It was early made clear that Blake was not interested in money. To a naval officer who consulted him, he said:

'I would rather work for nothing for a naval man like yourself, one of the best protectors of our precious flag, the pride of England, than I would take bank-notes from those who are careless of the honour of old Britain.'

The naval officer was relieved to hear that, and even more relieved to hear:

'With Heaven's help, my word shall be kept. The promises of Sexton Blake are written in adamant.'

To the villain, when finally unmasked, Blake said:

'Your cunningly erected edifice of fraud has now collapsed and you stand a good chance of being involved fatally in its ruins.'

In *Union Jack* Blake's adventures still alternated with stories of the Matabele and Ashanti wars, and in a readers' poll he took third place to 'Fighting For the Flag' and 'The Silver Arrow.' His popularity easily survived a brief spell during which the editor of *Union Jack* printed abridged versions of works by Dickens, Scott and Fenimore Cooper.

Not that the *Marvel* was now neglected. In No. 33, still in collaboration with Jules Gervaise, Blake laid down his working principles in near-Johnsonian prose to a client:

'We do not interfere in disputes between man and wife, nor do we pursue defaulting clerks, but if there is wrong to be righted, an evil to be redressed, or a rescue of the weak and suffering from the powerful, our hearty assistance can be readily obtained. We do nothing for hire here; we would cheerfully undertake to perform without fee or reward. But when our clients are wealthy we are not so unjust to ourselves as to make a gratuitous offer of our services.'

Hereabouts the Editor of the *Marvel*, claiming that 'thousands of correspondents' had written demanding more Blake stories, invited criticisms of the stories published to date. Puzzlingly, soon afterwards appeared a Hal Meredeth story of Jules Gervaise in which Blake received only a passing mention.

What Blake needed, obviously, was a build-up. At some early stage he became hawk-like, aquiline and acquired the habit of putting on his dressing-gown in order to think. Probably it was sheer pressure of public opinion which forced him into Baker Street. In any case, offices provided an unsuitable background for a detective. Clearly he needed someone to look after him, someone old enough and respectable enough to be called a housekeeper and not a 'housekeeper.' Hence Mrs. Martha Bardell, with her genius for mispronunciation and malapropism. It was a happy stroke to furnish him with a bright boy assistant instead of a dull fellow modelled on the lines of Watson. Blake badly needed someone to prevent him being pompous. At the same time it was probably considered that an errand-boy reader could more easily project himself into the narrative by imagining himself to be Blake's assistant. So arrived Tinker, that young man of doubtful years (old enough to pilot an aeroplane) and doubtful antecedents, irrepressible, resourceful, susceptible to female charm, addicted to suits 'which would have made Solomon want to retire from the glory business,' and possessing a fathomless admiration for the 'Guv'nor.' On one of the occasions when Tinker was 'wanted for murder' (a misunderstanding, of course) the police posters with which Britain was placarded showed him to be an intelligent, eupeptic-looking youth, with curly hair.

Mr. Cox claims in the *Saturday Book* that Tinker had three predecessors. The first, a Chinese boy called We-wee, was dropped for reasons which may readily be conjectured; the second was a waif called Griff; and the third was one Wallace Lorrimer. Tinker did not arrive until 1904. He is supposed to have been living on the fringe of the underworld, though later evidence has it that he was also a regular soldier (in which case he must have bought himself out very rapidly). Blake educated his assistant rather sketchily. He himself had been brought up at two distinct public schools and had subsequently studied at both Oxford and Cambridge, so that he may well have decided that a man can have too much education.

Tinker was the only survivor of the great purge of 1904 when Blake—heavily overworked—dismissed all the other members of his staff and retired to the country under the name of Henry Park. 'Tinker always would remain. They were part and parcel of each other's lives.' Tinker at this time was refusing bribes of £5 to disclose the detective's private address to importunate clients. Then came the day when Henry Park was falsely accused of theft, and Blake had the stimulating experience of being engaged to track himself down. (He rather liked that kind of operation. Once he wagered £500 with the police that he would disappear in London and that they would not find him. He joined the police who were hunting him.) The unusual case of Henry Park convinced Blake that he would never be able to give up the game of detection. 'I shall remain in harness till the end,' he said.

There was another addition to the household—the bloodhound Pedro (or was he a bulldog?). He was sent to Blake with £100 by a well-wisher called Mr. Nemo. And then came the Grey Panther, which sometimes turned out to be a motor-car and sometimes a monoplane (designed by Blake himself). This was confusing, but latterly the name Grey Panther was reserved exclusively for Blake's bullet-proof Rolls.

Thus equipped and befriended, Blake was able to settle down to his ordained task of combating the Brotherhood of Silence; the Brotherhood of the Yellow Beetle; the Criminals' Confederation (featuring Mr. Reece); George Marsden Plummer, the Scotland Yard renegade, and his beautiful accomplice Vali Mata Vali; Huxton Rymer and his equally beautiful female accomplices Mary Trent and Yvonne; Leon Kestrel, the Master Mummer, whose real features no one knew; Waldo the Wonder Man; Mr. Mist, the Invisible Man; Dr. Satira; Carlac; Professor Kew; Paul Cynos; the Baron von Kravitch, 'luxury-loving aristocrat by night and picker-up of cigarette ends by day'; the reincarnated Prince Menes; Zenith the Albino, afflicted with a colourless skin but far from colourless personality, whose possession of infra-red binoculars put all London's wealth at his peril; a variety of numerical groups like the Black Trinity, the Double Four and the Council of Eleven; a string of coloured geometrical gangs like the Red Circle and the Green Triangle; an endless succession of megalomaniac banditti calling themselves the Slasher, the Phantom, the

Vulture or the Spider; and a lesser but equally interminable rout
made up of German spies, Soviet trade spies, anarchists, apaches,
mad scientists, hooded terrors, fraudulent Atlantic flyers, crooked
lawyers, rascally rajahs, American racketeers and human bats.

Not all Blake's adversaries sought to destroy him, or he to
destroy them. Mr. Mist, who caused some dislocation in the
nation's business by stealing the Mace from the House of Com-
mons and spot-lighting a Budget scandal in which the Chancellor's
wife was being blackmailed, sent the detective the friendliest of
notes (beginning *Morituri te salutant*) when he decided to go out
of business. Waldo the Wonder Man cherished no hard feelings.
Blake could show magnanimity too—even in the case of Leon
Kestrel who went round impersonating the detective, thus fogging
the issue to a bewildering degree. And it was hard to be cross with
Miss Death, the lady with six months to live, who broke the law
in order to speed up her measures for the underdog.

Other adversaries were definitely out to 'get' Blake. One of the
more ruthless arranged to have him fired to the Moon by rocket,
but Blake, with nine hours to go, cut himself out with his pocket
hacksaw. There was a scientist who sought to rob him of some of
his surplus energy. This 'man who stole life' sat the detective in
a glass chair and threw over the master switch. Blake seemed a
likely customer, in contrast to the previous occupant of the chair
('That girl was tired. I was only able to take a little life from her').
But Blake was able to escape with his life force unimpaired.

To every famous detective, if he stays long enough in the
business, comes the day when he pits his wits against his double,
arrests the chief of Scotland Yard, finds himself in jail (Blake was
lashed to the triangle and all but flogged at Bleakmoor), sees his
lodgings blown up (dynamitards visited Baker Street in 1912),
reads about his death and attends his own funeral. When Blake
was reported dead in 1927 an illustration showed page-boys and
top-hatted City gentlemen all with stunned expressions gathered
round a newsboy, united in their common loss. And the detective's
Fleet Street collaborator, Splash Page, was so overcome he could
hardly bring himself to turn out the required two columns on
'Sexton Blake As I Knew Him.'

The call for Blake's services came from every corner of the globe, from rajahs and Red Indian chiefs, from the Lord Chancellor, the Bank of England (repeatedly) and even from a local authority worried at the number of men who were disappearing and leaving their wives chargeable to the rates. One of Blake's major assignments was that in which he was granted plenary powers over everyone in the country for twenty-four hours; one of his minor assignments was in intervening to save a Highland laird from an addiction to the bottle. (This story, entitled 'Drink!' bore one of the few monosyllabic titles in the long list.) At one stage Blake had a taste of the fate which was to overcome his professional rival, Nelson Lee. A serial in the *Boys' Friend* described how, in order to break up some fell conspiracy, he joined the staff of a public school; Tinker, of course, became a schoolboy. It is worth noting that Sexton Blake and Nelson Lee, though rivals, were perfectly good friends. A story by Maxwell Scott, 'The Winged Terror,' in the *Boys' Herald* of 1910 had Blake stepping in to warn Lee of an impending attempt on his life by an ex-convict. Together the two detectives, aided by Tinker and Nipper, tracked down their man in a highly mechanized campaign which cost the nation the Tower Bridge and London Bridge. When, at one stage, Lee drove the car in which he and Blake were travelling into the hedge, to avert a calamity, Blake said, 'It was a smart idea of yours, old boy . . . an inspiration of genius.' To which Lee modestly said, 'It was a choice of evils.'

The era of short skirts and shingles produced a succession of beautiful and unscrupulous heiresses who sought to compromise Blake's reputation as a bachelor *sans reproche*. One night, returning to Baker Street, he found in his bedroom a young woman dressed in a kimono and not much else who coolly asked him to go outside while she slipped a dress on. Mrs. Bardell denied having admitted the hussy. It turned out that she had entered disguised as Tinker, carrying nothing but a change of clothes and £100,000 in jewels. The girl was Olga Nasmyth, alias the Girl of Destiny, who was taking time off from her implacable pursuit of her family's foes to vamp the detective. When the scent of her hair was in his nostrils and her lips were very close Blake pulled himself together and 'put her from him gently.' Piqued, the girl blew smoke in his eyes and under cover of this ground a glass phial under her shapely heel. When the detective came to Olga had vanished. It was good riddance.

Then there was the affair with Roxane. For a man of Blake's well-tamed instincts it was quite a sultry little episode. He found himself on some pretext or other aboard the lady's luxury yacht (she was his client at the time). Roxane was a reigning beauty and her picture was constantly in the shiny weeklies. On this occasion she made it clear that her patience was exhausted:

'I'm not going into details again,' she said slowly, 'but I am forced to ask you once more if you will join me. . . . It is true that I have reached the limit of endurance. I want some—happiness in life. Am I ugly? Am I repulsive? Am I lacking in intelligence? Other men have not found me so.'
'Nor have I,' said Blake in strained tones. 'You are none of those things. It is necessary for me to tell you that you are very lovely and very, very desirable.'
'Then why won't you . . .?'
He shook his head.
'No. If I admit any of the softness of what you suggest into my life it means my career would suffer. I have always put it first and must continue to do so. I am sorry, but I can't.'

Roxane had no glass phial, but she had something just as good— a gas pistol. She fired it, not at Blake, but at herself; a white cloud suffused her lovely head. Blake caught her as she slumped, 'the warmth of her body intimately close through the wisp of silk that covered her.'

Blake was in pretty bad shape. He implored her to tell him with what gas the pistol had been loaded, so that he could search in the yacht's laboratory for an antidote (it was that kind of yacht). Nor did he stop there, but promised recklessly that he would do anything she wished. 'It was a bursting of the forces of control such as Sexton Blake had never experienced. . . .'

In due course Roxane came to and before he realized what was happening 'she was drawing his head lower and lower until his mouth was upon her half-open lips. How long they stood thus neither could have said.' It was always something that they were standing.

Suddenly Roxane smiled and announced that the whole thing was a hoax. She had filled the gas pistol with harmless scent. 'I tested you,' she said.

It was just as well, in order to take Blake's mind off the treachery of women, that at this stage the infamous Felix Dupont, entering without knocking, announced that he had witnessed the whole episode, that he had photographed it and proposed having the picture of the detective 'embracing with such fervour . . . this clouded bit of nudity' published in a disreputable journal.

This was Blake's bad day. He whose name was a 'synonym for austerity' would be disgraced and forced out of his profession. London, Paris and New York would ring with the news of his downfall . . .

Happily this fate did not come to pass. But it was a narrow escape, and perhaps a salutary warning. Already he had been lucky in the case of June Severance, a charmer whom he had gone out of his way to assist. His enemies might have made a good deal out of the fact that he had set her up in the antique business.

During the ten years preceding World War I Blake had a long and curious association with Kaiser Wilhelm. His adventure entitled 'The Conscript, A Tale of the German Army' (1908) ended with Blake thrown into a Prussian prison. He had failed in his object of extracting a British recruit who had been forced into the German Army. To his surprise Wilhelm came to visit him in his cell. The Emperor was displeased:

'On former occasions you have come to my country to do me service. This time your hand has been against me, and you have broken my laws.'

However, in recognition of the esteem in which he held the detective, the Emperor magnanimously decided to grant him a free pardon and a passage home; this dispensation also covered Tinker and Pedro (each languishing in their separate cells), and even the young Briton whom Blake had sought to rescue.

'Again I thank Your Majesty,' exclaimed the detective. 'Never will I forget your great kindness.'

His voice 'choked with emotion,' and in his gratitude he kissed the hand of the Kaiser. The last sentence described the party of

I

four leaving for England, 'thanks to the mercy and generosity of the Emperor.'

Blake did not allow his gratitude to the Kaiser to outweigh his patriotism. When, shortly afterwards, the British Prime Minister asked him to investigate some ugly reports connected with the German Naval manœuvres, Blake warned:

'I have had the pleasure of meeting the Kaiser—having worked both for him and against him—and I can assure you that even his wildest speeches have truth in them—a good foundation of truth.'

'The only man in Britain for the task,' was the Prime Minister's comment when Blake left the room, and mentally made a note to put him down for a peerage. Blake refused this almost on the same day that he declined the Kaiser's offer to appoint him head of the German Secret Service. At that time it really looked as if he had succeeded in persuading the Kaiser that his doctrine of 'might is right' was folly. But it was hard to reconcile the Kaiser's 'reform' with an intercepted document in which Wilhelm rashly committed to paper a plan whereby Bulgaria was to receive her 'independence,' the Emperor Franz Josef was to annex Bosnia, the Kaiser was to march on Paris and Britain was to come cap in hand to the peace table.

Five years later—in 1913—Blake again undertook a mission for the Kaiser. A telegram delivered at Baker Street read: 'Come here at once. Wilhelm.' He wired back to Potsdam: 'Regret too busy to accept honour. Sexton Blake.' But eventually he went to Berlin. He had already been followed by German Secret Police in London, somewhat to his surprise. ('I wonder what the deuce the man wanted to follow me for. If the man had been a Russian I could have understood it, but—'.) The Kaiser ordered him to recover a document stolen from the German War Office. It was to be returned with seals unbroken and the contents could not be divulged even to Blake. To assist him, the Kaiser gave the detective a ring which he had only to show to receive every official co-operation. Blake and Tinker recovered the document, which was 'a most complete and detailed plan for the invasion of England,' and returned it to the Kaiser, after sending a photographed copy to Whitehall, with the detective's compliments. The Kaiser did not seem put out at this. He recognized in Blake not only a clever sleuth but a great patriot, and realized that a patriot could have done nothing else. Indeed he presented Blake with a ring in recognition of his services (in exchange for the original *laissez passer* ring). Everyone parted on good terms. It was a puzzling episode.

The 1930 Blake

One by one Blake cleaned up the big cities of Britain— 'Sexton Blake in Nottingham,' 'A Manchester Mystery, Sexton Blake in Cottonopolis,' and so on. It is impossible to escape the conclusion that his provincial tours were prompted by the circulation department. (About this time, incidentally, a Sexton Blake play 'Hush Money' was touring the provinces.) Then came a series of crimes which involved the assumption of the most improbable disguises—'Sexton Blake, Bath-chairman,' 'Sexton Blake, Ice Cream Man,' 'Sexton Blake, French Gardener,' 'Sexton Blake, Tax Collector,' 'Sexton Blake, Trainer,' 'Sexton Blake, Santa Claus,' and so on.

Next, one by one, Blake tackled the rackets which were disfiguring Britain—slum landlordism, the sale of children, the worn-out horse traffic, food profiteering and hire purchase abuses. This perhaps was Blake's finest hour (if one excepts his war service).

There were the occasional political cases too. Once, to Tinker's pained surprise, Blake insisted on going out of his way to record his vote at an election. It is not disclosed how he voted, but from his admission that he happened to own property in the constituency it is possible to make a guess. His attitude on the question of votes for women was clear-cut. At one stage Mrs. Bardell joined the

Women's League of Freedom and said, in reply to a query about some insignia she was wearing:

'That lurid thing, sir, as you 'ave called it, is a mark of honourable extinction and in no wise deserving of the finger of scorn. I would not part with it for orders or jewelled garters or for the Company of the Bath nor for any other boasted insignitaries of 'igh degree. It is a toking of the fact that I have joined the Women's League of Freedom. Sir, I am proud to state that I 'ave become an 'umble decipher of the great Mrs. Spankhard. . . .'

Exasperated, Blake spoke sharply to Mrs. Bardell and threatened to pack her off bag and baggage at a week's notice. This was probably the only time he really lost his temper with his loquacious housekeeper.

Another time Blake was called in to tackle the case of the Labour M.P.

Honest Tom Mills, the Labour Member, was respected by everyone throughout the land. A hardy son of toil, he had raised himself unaided to the high position he now held.

Unfortunately, Honest Tom's son was suspected of selling the plans of the new Australasian defence scheme. Blake recovered these just in time to avert the collapse of the Government. Thanks to Mr. Orwell (see Introduction), one is left harbouring a possibly base suspicion that Blake would not have exerted himself quite so hard if it had been a Labour Government in jeopardy.

About 1910 it was revealed in 'Sexton Blake, Territorial' that the detective, like Tinker, had once been a regular soldier, a circumstance which might have accounted for his political orthodoxy. For the purpose of this story Tinker also had to join the Territorials. Those who expected him to chafe at Army discipline were disappointed. He was sorry he had ever laughed at 'Saturday soldiers,' and found that the service did him a power of good. It was noticeable that Blake and Tinker never missed an opportunity to put in a good word for the 'Terriers.'

Despite his regular training, when World War I came along Blake was in a reserved occupation. True, he did a certain amount of snooping about the Low Countries in disguise (with pot-shots at the odd Uhlan), but mostly he was too busy at home recovering kidnapped Ministers or preventing the gassing of Greater London. Usually he was briefed by Sir John ——, but sometimes it was Sir James ——. Once Sir James —— offered him a C.B. even before he had begun his investigations, but the detective brushed this aside pretty snappily.

Blake was relieved, it may be supposed, when the nightly dumping of spies on these islands ceased, and he was able once more to choose his own cases. But all too often extravagant crime persisted in occurring around him when he was trying to avoid it, or in circumstances which made it impossible to disregard it. There was the 'Case of the Silent Jury,' for instance. The detective was a spectator at the Old Bailey. Ordinarily he did not care to watch his man being sentenced, but it was important to take precautions; the judge might turn out to be Leon Kestrel in disguise, or the court attendant might have omitted to test the witnesses' drinking water for arsenic. On this occasion Blake had stayed to hear the judge's summing up—a masterpiece of lucidity. Then the jury retired. Their verdict was a foregone conclusion. But the jury failed to emerge after a reasonable time. They refused to answer a knock at the door. When the door was broken down there they were—all mysteriously dead. The judge, a fellow club-member of Blake, was worried by a remark of the detective, and said:

'Good heavens, Mr. Blake, you surely are not insinuating that this is the result of foul play?'

The judge put Blake on the case at once. It was a very sticky one. The next shock was when the murderer whose fate the jury had been discussing was delivered to Blake dead in a crate. It was not long before Blake found himself being prepared for a crate too. If he had not filled the villain's hypodermic with water the *Sexton Blake Library* would have closed there and then.

The murderer? It was one of those cases in which the least-likely person is the guilty one. Yes, the judge. 'We do not credit the Old Bailey Judges with the passions and emotions of ordinary men,' explained Blake. They found in the diary of this unhinged justice the entry:

'Presiding at the Royal Courts of Justice, and listening to the incredibly fatuous cases of criminal stupidity has become a weariness unto the flesh. Now that my retirement is due I shall put into execution a crime unique in the annals of the Old Bailey or indeed of criminology. . . .'

To this end the judge had inserted a capsule containing a deadly, volatile, odourless gas in the keyhole of the jury-room door. Turning of the key had crushed it and the dust cover on the key-hole had prevented the gas blowing back into the court room.

In the later issues of *Union Jack* leading Blake authors were persuaded to pit their wits against each other. The first test of strength was a series in which six authors had to write separate stories all building up to a common climax: the discovery of Sexton Blake unconscious from a blow on the head on a tram top at Wood End depot. There was a good deal more to it than that, however. Slumped on a seat beside Blake was to be a stoutish, clean-shaven, elderly man, dead of heart failure. Other stipulations were:

At his (the dead man's) feet lying on the floor is a rolled-up banner, such as is used for processions. The wording on the banner is: 'We Demand Justice For Our Fellow Sufferers.'

On the seat beside him, tied up roughly in brown paper, is a brass fireman's helmet with a dent in it. The helmet is tarnished. The window of the tram on the man's left is broken. Only a few fragments of glass——not enough to fill the hole—are inside the tram.

The man's name proves to be Albert Mowbray Pound, and his age is about 45. He is wearing an ordinary grey lounge suit, but there is no sign of hat or cap. The contents of his pockets are:

Coat

One pawnticket for a mandoline.
One pawnticket for a carpet.
A pipe and pouch of tobacco (shag).
A packet of postcards of London views, banded with a paper band, and obviously just bought at a shop. There are only eleven cards in the packet, one presumably having been extracted.
A map of the London underground system.
A map of the London tram system.
A break-back mousetrap, wrapped in paper.

Waistcoat

An old silver watch.
Two pencils; one H.B., one blue.

A packet of book matches.

An electric torch in the shape of a fountain pen.

A wallet containing a 10s. note.

TROUSERS

4s. 9d. in coins.

A knuckle-duster.

These articles may or may not be relevant to the events which lead up to his presence on the tram. The conductor of the tram says he looked on the upper deck when he arrived in the depot before signing off for the night, but did not see either the man or Blake.

Readers were invited to vote on the respective merits of the six tales which ensued, with a prize of a pedigree bloodhound to the one who correctly put the tales in their order of popularity. (The nervous were informed that this prize could be commuted to £10 in cash.)

In the final issues of *Union Jack*, just before it became *Detective Weekly*, appeared a Blake serial—'The Next Move'—instalments of which were written by four authors in turn—Robert Murray, Anthony Skene, G. H. Teed and Gwyn Evans; the editor was the 'referee.' Thus Robert Murray would end an instalment with Roxane locked in an air-tight safe of which only she knew the combination, and leave it to Anthony Skene to extract her. Skene would leave Blake drowning in an underground catacomb (and Roxane still in the safe), and hand over to G. H. Teed. Finally Robert Murray brought the whole thing to a plausible end. Readers were invited to give their opinions of this experiment. Some may have found literary exercises of the kind disillusioning; for there have always been a minority who believed Blake to be a real person and who from time to time have plucked up the courage to write to him, congratulating him or even seeking his aid.

The *Detective Weekly* (1933) proved to be modelled on the more spacious lines of the *Thriller*, which had emerged from the same stable with loud trumpetings in 1929, and which had carried in its first number a full-length story of J. G. Reeder by Edgar Wallace. Some of the Sexton Blake 'regulars' had also been writing for the *Thriller*: it had carried, too, 'Saint' stories by Leslie Charteris and tales by Sidney Horler. It was time to give Blake a fresh boost, to sustain him against the strenuous competition of the 'thirties.

The nature of the Blake build-up in the first number of *Detective Weekly* was not calculated to disillusion the credulous who believed in a real-life Sexton Blake. Readers would discover, it was stated, that 'Sexton Blake is not merely a name or a puppet figure of fiction. From our stories, phase by phase, will emerge the real and rounded portrait of a living man—and one who has already won and held the attention of a world-wide audience. Sexton Blake is not a detective; he is *the* detective.

The *Detective Weekly* was launching Blake on a new lease of life, so the build-up contained a wealth of imaginative detail. Blake, it was claimed, had 'added much to the foundations of criminology laid down by such pioneers as Lombroso and Charles Goring, M.D.' The reader was blithely referred to a list of his monographs in Appendix B of that great German crime classic *Der Verbrecherkreig*, by Ludwig Schroeder. Blake's titles were said to include:

Some information on the use of methylene blue as an anti-toxin.
Single-print classification.
Finger-print forgery by the chromicized gelatine method.
Speculations on ballistic stigmata in fire-arms.

It may be noted in passing that Blake was up against gelatinous forgery, not merely of finger-prints, at a very early stage. In one of his first cases he accidentally put his hand on an unconscious man's face, and the 'face' came away in his hand.

The *Detective Weekly* went on to remind readers that Blake was an honoured figure at international police congresses at Vienna, Paris and London, and referred to his early training in the world of medicine (his father was Berkeley Blake, of Harley Street). It seemed a little hard, after this, that the first issue of *Detective Weekly* should have sought to drag a skeleton from the Blake cupboard—the only one there, as far as is known. However, the author, Lewis Jackson, had Blake's 'full permission.'

So for the first time followers of Blake learned that the detective had a brother Nigel, a waster, whose conduct had brought 'the grey hairs of his old father in sorrow to the grave.' Blake had met Nigel in the Cameroons, where he was drinking himself to death in a fever swamp, with occasional time off to beat his wife; and

Nigel had ordered him away at the revolver point, calling him a 'snivelling parson.' Blake left, and tried to think no more about the distressing episode.

Twenty years later in his study in Baker Street the detective was looking through his earliest collection of finger-prints. In his youthful enthusiasm he had finger-printed his family and even himself, heading the list with 'Sexton Blake, His Mark.' The adjacent print was Nigel's. Gazing horror-stricken at this, Blake recognized it as the same print left by a mysterious forger currently enjoying an unusually prosperous season in London. Blake, in fact, already had all his resources marshalled on the case, and aiding him was Nigel's son, whom the waster had deserted along with his wife. Once again Blake was faced with a diabolical problem. It was the Roxane dilemma afresh:

He could picture the stories, the publicity and scandal of it. 'A brother of the world-famous private detective.' How one or two at the Yard would relish it; and what a titbit for some of his 'friends' in the criminal fraternity!

Luckily it proved possible to hush up the criminal's capture, and Nigel was shut away in a fortress-like house in Buckinghamshire; but not before brother Sexton had had a show-down with him, exclaiming in a voice 'acid with bitterness': 'Nigel Blake— forger and crook! What would our mother have said to that!'

That was probably the only reference to Sexton Blake's mother.

No sooner was Nigel locked away than Leon Kestrel, who never knew when to let well alone, began to go about made up as the wastrel brother. His object was the theft of Blake's Magnetic Picklock, which in conjunction with Blake's Manual of Crime was calculated to make him a considerable menace to society.

The *Detective Weekly* inaugurated a 'round table' at which readers were invited to criticize the fare provided. There were some readers who wanted to see Blake married off; there were even some who wanted him killed off. Both proposals provoked an angry reaction from the faithful. When the second world war came along there was an agitation for Blake to tackle the Hun, but there was an even stronger agitation to keep him fighting criminals out of uniform. When he did tackle the occasional

Gestapo plot 'it was only after all the skill and resources of Scotland Yard, aided by the British Secret Service, had failed.'

In the closing days of *Detective Weekly* there was a serial by Edward Holmes—'A Case For Sexton Blake'—which ran in conjunction with a Tuesday night serial on the radio—a piece of pre-Dunkirk escapism featuring a man in an iron mask. Then, in the issue of May 25, 1940, came the half-expected announcement that *Detective Weekly* was closing down on account of paper shortage—but that the *Sexton Blake Library* would go on.

No disciple of Blake would claim that the master has remained unchanged since he began to operate from Baker Street. He was not long in discarding a style of speech which was better suited to one of the more virtuous characters in the Red Barn. He ceased to say 'Hist!' and once he even used the expression 'vamoose.' But generally Blake left the slang to Tinker, and Tinker's slang was a baffling mixture of 1900 *Comic Cuts*, post-1920 Wodehouse and 1930 Hollywood. Even to-day he uses expressions like 'deucedly,' 'with knobs on,' and 'sufferin' cats.' Then, in the next breath, he says of a lady visitor, 'Nice bit of homework!' Blake finds it necessary to snub him from time to time:

'Can I come in now, Guv'nor, or am I de tropp?'
'You are usually de trop,' rejoined the detective, 'but you can come in anyway. And, incidentally, the "p" in "trop" is silent as in "phthisis." '

Or the reader is allowed a superior, and rather unfair, smile at Tinker:

'Besides, Rampadula Shah happens to be a Jain.'
'A Jane?' Tinker fairly gasped.

The remarkable speech of Mrs. Bardell has already been quoted. Her exclamations are 'Hevvings!' and even 'Lawks-a-mussy!' She refers to America as 'Merikee. Rarely is she at a loss for an unsuitable word, but on one occasion at least she was reduced to inarticulateness. That was when Blake, who was no snob, invited her along to the Hotel Magnificent's ornate Regency dining-room—'the smaller private one'—to join with the Yard and Home Office chiefs in celebrating the downfall of the Criminals' Confederation. Alas, the profusion of glasses was Mrs. Bardell's undoing, and 'her remarks, never very intelligible, became more wildly incomprehensible towards the end of the proceedings.'

Blake, of course, has always moved with exquisite *savoir faire* in the highest circles. His *aficionados* were suitably gratified when the detective, sitting down to a meal, would exclaim 'Ah, Bollinger, and '12 at that!' To those who could not tell Bollinger from Condy's it was good to know that their hero could keep his end up in a fashionable restaurant, especially when dining with such dignitaries as Sir Felix Felton of the Home Office (who as a grubby small boy was Blake's fag at school).

Devotees of Sexton Blake in his vintage years will want to know how he is faring to-day. The titles of his more recent adventures give a fair clue—'The Man from Arnhem,' 'The Case of the Missing G.I. Bride,' 'The Mystery of the Three Demobbed Men,' 'The Case of the Conscript Miner,' 'The Affair of the Fraternizing Soldier,' 'The Yank Who Came Back.' Among routine knifings and kidnappings 'The Mystery of the Three Demobbed Men' stands out for novelty of plot. Tinker, accustomed to peculiar behaviour by his master, is astonished to see him not only accepting a bribe from a lawyer but demanding that the original offer of £1,000 be doubled. Blake observes his misgivings:

'I owe you an explanation, Tinker. You've been very helpful to me. You see, before I went to see Mr. Gradstone I took a small dose of a certain Eastern drug. We didn't know the effect of it and we wanted to find out. It appears that a measured dose of this drug lulls the moral sense. In other words, it makes the victim blind to common honesty and capable of any theft or unscrupulous piece of work.'

He sat up, his nostrils quivering impatiently.

'Tinker,' he said, 'on the shelf in the bathroom you will find a small box containing a white powder. Bring it to me and bring me half a glass of water as well. Quickly!'

There's a nasty situation for you. One false step, and Blake will become a criminal, with Tinker as his hunter. But Tinker is equal to the occasion. He darts to the bathroom and destroys the remainder of the drug. Blake is exceedingly angry, but after a tremendous struggle with himself he shakes off the effects of the powder. He then gets down to the task of exposing the activities of a demobbed soldier from the Middle East who is incorporating the drug in the old-fashioned headache-powders manufactured by a respectable firm in the North. The result is a wave of minor crime in Lancashire. Women of unimpeachable integrity, after taking a headache powder, start to steal each other's clothes pegs off the line, or to lift packets of sugar at the grocer's without paying. The drug happily causes only minor peccadilloes, but the statistics of petty crime have the police chiefs worried. No more insidious threat to the nation's well-being has ever been removed by Sexton Blake.

In 'The Case of the Night Lorry Driver' Blake finds himself drawn into the sort of case which, but for his strong sense of public duty, he would doubtless have preferred to decline, if only out of respect for Tinker's tender years. The crime he is invited to investigate begins to look ominously like something out of the *News of the World*. This conversation occurs between two characters:

'Tell me, Dr. Gribley, what inclines you to the idea that the woman had been criminally assaulted?'
'She was young and rather attractive and in my opinion slightly hyper-thyroidal.'
'What does that mean in Basic English?'
'I would say,' said the pathologist, smiling, 'that she was not under-sexed.'
'Theories, eh?' said Harker with a grin. 'Anything else?'

Blake (who did not grin) had his own theory. Tinker held no very firm views; he was a little out of his depth, one hopes. And Blake was using words like 'empirically' and 'militating,' which put a strain on Tinker's vocabulary; possibly more than one long-standing reader read with raised eyebrows:

Blake had investigated a large number of what the police called 'sex crimes' in his time and had studied the reactions of a large number of sadists.

But while Blake is wiser in the ways of human wickedness, some may wonder whether he is quite his old resourceful self. In 'A Date With Danger' he is driving in his bullet-proof Grey Panther on the heels of a car-load of crooks. Unluckily he is cut

off by the closing of level-crossing gates. He waits two minutes—
two minutes, mark you—and then hails the signal-box.

'Can't you open up for us, signalman?' he called. 'I'm a detective in
pursuit of crooks. They're getting away.'
'Sorry, sir, but there's no openin' of gates once they're closed. The
train's due, and orders is orders.'
Blake went back to his assistant.
'We've had it, old chap,' he announced.

That flat acceptance of defeat is rather shocking. Was this the
man who, forty years earlier, had allowed Tinker to drive a
Packard through police barricades on a wild dash to London?
Why didn't he say, 'I'm Sexton Blake' instead of 'I'm a detective'?
In the old days, of course, every signalman would have recognized
not only Sexton Blake but the Grey Panther, and cheerfully risked
dismissal or the wreck of the Irish Mail to speed his passage.

It looks, too, as if Blake has come to lean more and more on
gadgetry. Looking into his consulting-room is a periscopic mirror:

The apparatus which, prior to its present installation, had seen dramatic
service in one of the Kaiser's U-boats, had been dubbed 'The Secret Eye'
by the detective's assistant Tinker.
The detective himself was not proud of it, and was sufficiently self-
conscious about it to admit no reference to its existence 'outside the
family.' Its justification was that it had proved, over the years, a valuable
adjunct to business. On many occasions the unsuspected observation
of a client waiting to see him disclosed clues of genuine help and value,
psychological and otherwise. He could tell, for instance, sometimes when
agitation or anxiety was real or assumed.

There is also an infra-red contraption of which the working
principles are not too clear:

It was a device which the detective had played with for years and
which was only just beginning to emerge from the category of a scientific
toy. Because the special lenses of the stereoscope converted an infra-red
ray into normal white light it was possible to illuminate a room which
remained, apparently, in darkness.

Finally, how has Blake been bearing up all these years under the
strain of celibacy? Read the last page of 'The Mystery of the
Bankrupt Estate.' The case is solved, but it has cost the life of a

charming and eminently nubile young woman. This is the scene at the close:

Sexton Blake and Tinker sat again with the Assistant Commissioner of the C.I.D. round a table piled high with flowers and the debris of an excellent dinner such as only the famous Valois appears able to serve in these parlous days. But upon this occasion they were in a private room.

Tinker, rather tastelessly, and possibly under the influence of the Bollinger, referred to the dead girl as a 'smasher.' Blake overlooked this. Then the Assistant Commissioner, who should have known better, also made some unfortunate reference to her. Possibly he called her 'a nice bit of homework.'

'She's dead,' Blake said quickly, rising to his feet. 'I've given you the woman you wanted, Sir Edward. Let Anne Mallory rest.'

There was a moment of surprised silence. Then the Assistant Commissioner rose with him.

'By all means, Blake,' he said, 'if that's how you prefer it.'

'I do, sir.'

'Strewth!' gasped Tinker under his breath. 'By gosh, I believe I was right. I believe the old war-horse really had got a pash on her. Oh my stars!'

CHAPTER IX

MORE DETECTIVES

SEXTON BLAKE lived to lead the field of popular detectives, but he was only one of a huge and struggling bunch of runners when he made his first appearance.

The setting up of private detectives was a major literary industry in the 'nineties. By the end of the year the Aldine Company alone could boast more than 250 detective titles. Earnest attempts were made to spin a web of romance round the private investigator, however squalid his role might be in real life. Said an Aldine advertisement in the 'nineties:

These thrilling SHADOW REVELATIONS of the deep and cunning meshes of concealment woven by astute and criminal men and women often in high positions and spotless before the world and the deadly dangers besetting the daring professional MAN HUNTER are vividly depicted in these absorbing narratives.

Among the earlier detectives who achieved a transitory fame in Aldine publications and elsewhere were Joe Phoenix, Brandt Adams, Caleb Drage, Gilbert Scott and Harry Hunter. Some of the more peculiar titles were *The Demon Detective, The Jew Detective, New York Nell, the Girl-Boy Detective, Fritz, the Bound Boy Detective, Old Stonewall the Shadower, Lynx-Eye the Pacific Detective* and *Old Electricity, the Lightning Detective*. Female sleuths included Daisy Bell, Sarah Brown and Kate Scott, the Decoy Detective. Then there was a whole range of specialist

detectives, such as The Post Office Detective, The Revenue
Detective, The Naval Detective, The Hansom Cab Detective,
The Science Detective, The Actress Detective and even The
Mountaineer Detective. There were also brother detectives,
brother-and-sister detectives, father-and-son detectives, father-
and-daughter detectives, uncle-and-nephew detectives, husband-
and-wife detectives—there may well have been man-and-mother-
in-law detectives; and, of course, there was no scarcity of dog
detectives.

Some of these detectives were native-born; others were
imported from America. During the 'eighties the famous Pinkerton
Agency had put out a series of supposed selections from the
firm's casebook, with the Pinkerton eye—'We Never Sleep'—on
the cover. These had encouraged other publishers to issue 'casebooks' linked to reality only by a couple of hairs. Many of these
were reprinted in Britain and enjoyed ephemeral life.

Since the competition was acute, it followed that the mortality
rate was high. A sleuth would be hailed as 'none other than the
celebrated' so-and-so (though he might never have achieved
print before), would flourish for an instalment or two and then
vanish into limbo. Others, more modestly introduced, would
crop up at long and irregular intervals in unexpected places. A good
detective might outlast a poor magazine, but equally a poor
magazine could ruin a promising detective. It was not necessarily
a tribute to a detective's brilliance that he survived; it was just as
likely to be due to the publisher's financial staying power or to
the size and brilliance of the coloured plates he could afford to
give away. No one will ever know how many stories written
around a given detective were rejected and then successfully re-
submitted to another publisher with another detective's name
substituted; nor how many stories, once accepted by an editor,
had the hero's name changed to that of another detective to meet
some emergency of publishing.

The origin of Nelson Lee, the detective who turned schoolmaster, is as uncertain as that of Sexton Blake. There was a real-
life Nelson Lee who figured in the 1850's as some sort of theatrical
impresario, but there is no evidence to show that he mingled

detection with his other accomplishments. The fictional Nelson Lee, again, was a Harmsworth detective, and his earliest appearances appear to have been in the *Halfpenny Marvel* and *Pluck*. His creator was Maxwell Scott (Dr. John Staniforth), who planned his stories so meticulously that he knew exactly what would happen in chapter 30 before he had written a word of chapter 1.

Lee's first exploit in the *Marvel*—'A Dead Man's Secret' (1894)—was the solving of a blow-pipe murder mystery on the West of England Mail. Nipper, his future assistant, figured in this first story, arriving at Gray's Inn Road to claim half a sovereign for information. He was very much the guttersnipe.

Readers of *Pluck* who missed this story in the *Marvel* must have been puzzled by their first introduction to Nelson Lee. This mettlesome weekly, started in 1894, was described as 'Stories of Pluck—being the daring deeds of plucky sailors, plucky soldiers, plucky firemen, plucky explorers, plucky detectives, plucky railwaymen, plucky boys and plucky girls and all sorts and conditions of British heroes.' An editorial in the first number said that *Pluck* would contain true stories, but no one was to imagine that truth would be dull. The first number carried stories of General Gordon and of Nelson's powder-monkey; succeeding numbers featured Lobengula, Livingstone and Lord Roberts. In the fifth issue was a story of 'Roland Dare, the greatest fireman America ever had.' As a name like Roland Dare plainly invited suspicion the editor disarmingly admitted that it was a false name but said that the hero's identity was 'so thinly veiled that it will be readily recognized by most readers.' In Number Eight came another announcement which may or may not have caused misgivings:

Long ago and with irresistible acclaim the world gave Gideon Barr, the famous detective, one of the highest places among the men who have immortalized themselves by strenuous deeds of courage. It was he who accomplished one of the most brilliant achievements in recent social history by so coolly dealing with an already lighted bomb that he saved the best part of a large city from destruction.

His noble bearing in the fearful mining disaster in Wales will hold the memory for ever; and who can forget that Gideon Barr single-handed was the valiant one who subdued and banished that infamous confederacy of highly trained and murderous criminals known as 'The Black Vultures'?

This time the editor did not state that Gideon Barr was a disguised name. It is doubtful whether any of his readers were sufficiently interested in establishing Barr's bona fides to search for Bayland's Inn off Holborn and there hunt out a lithe, blue-eyed detective whose flaxen hair had a 'golden glow.'

Succeeding issues of *Pluck* were still sprinkled with the adventures of such incontestable characters as the Duke of Wellington. An examination of these early numbers suggests that while fact may have been stranger than fiction, fiction may have sold better than fact. Was it proved that 'real life' was as dubious a recommendation for an adventure story as 'home made' for a window-full of cakes?

But what of Nelson Lee? In Number 23 came this announcement in bold type on the back page:

Some of our readers may remember reading the newspaper account of the wreck of the steamship Sandown, which took place on the 19th of last December. It was rendered more than usually interesting by the fact that the ill-fated steamer was bringing an enormous amount of bullion (or bars of gold) from Capetown to England, and that after the wreck no less than twenty of these bars (valued at as many thousand pounds) have been stolen. The Steamship Insurance Company, with whom the vessel was insured, placed the matter in the hands of Mr. Nelson Lee, of Gray's Inn Road; and the celebrated detective after nearly three months sojourn in foreign climes has now returned to England, flushed with success. Newspapers and magazines have vied with each other in publishing more or less fanciful accounts of his latest and most brilliant triumph; but thanks to our arrangements with Mr. Maxwell Scott the true and complete account will appear in the pages of *Pluck*. It will be published in the next issue under the title of 'A False Scent, or the Adventures of Nelson Lee in Search of Sunken Gold.'

So, out of this half-world of fact and fiction, emerged Nelson Lee, hero of Lhasa and Limehouse, confidant of Lloyd George and Kitchener, the man who in later life saved from nameless and numberless disgraces the venerable public school of St. Frank's.

Lee was introduced in his headquarters in Gray's Inn Road 'pacing his room with the rapid stride and muttered growls of a caged and hungry lion.' He was offered 10 per cent of the value of the Sandown's missing bullion, if he recovered it.

'That is £2,000,' said Nelson Lee, musingly. 'You will pay me £2,000 if I succeed, but what will you pay me if I fail?'

A foolish speech, as he realised at once when his client reminded him with a smile:

'There is no such word as "fail" in the dictionary of Nelson Lee.'

It was easy money, as it turned out, involving nothing more arduous than an underwater fight with long-handled axes.

Later evidence showed Lee to be aquiline, with sunken yet clear eyes—'he could even be called good-looking.' He was a dressing-gown detective, liked comfort and Turkey carpets. His chief vice was a continuous knitting of the brows. There is evidence in the *Boys' Realm* of 1902 that Lee was working in uneasy alliance with another of those French detectives, Jean Moreau. But Moreau, though brilliant, was treacherous, and Lee did well to shake him off.

Lee's adventures appeared in many of the Amalgamated Press journals. It was not until 1915 that he achieved the distinction of being chronicled in a library all his own. There was as yet no serious paper shortage, and readers were invited to compete for a 3½ h.p. Rudge-Multi by getting the names of as many boys as possible to read the *Nelson Lee Library*. Five thousand lads at once rose to the bait. The motor cycle eventually went to Master Willie Jones, of 102, Wellsby Street, Grimsby, who submitted 8,634 names and addresses. It was probably the hardest earned motor cycle in history.

Gray's Inn Road was the scene of thinly disguised criminal activity in those days. One afternoon the detective, still served by Nipper ('pert as a magpie, keen as a weasel, and clever as a cartload of monkeys'), was looking idly out of the window. To Nipper he said:

'Do you see that man there? European clothes, but with the slant eyes of a Chinaman. Probably his pigtail is coiled up in his bowler hat.'
'You mean the lame one, sir—the one with the club foot?' Nipper, the young assistant, answered brightly.
'The man who appears to have a club foot,' Nelson Lee corrected. 'If you watch him closely you will see that the bend of the knee is not

natural, that his leg would be the same length as the other if he cared to stretch it out and——'

'But what's the idea of that?' Nipper demanded.

Nelson Lee shrugged his shoulders and the expression on his face suggested that he was bored to death.

'Opium smuggling,' he answered briefly. 'I have often thought that there was a depot of that kind round King's Cross and now I am sure of it.'

Nipper wanted his master to take action, but the detective said it was an affair for the police. He was bored with routine small-time stuff. With an ill grace he consented to rescue an American millionaire's kidnapped son, receiving for his pains a cheque for £10,000. Nipper suggested that this was 'almost enough to take us away for the week-end,' but he received curt instructions to distribute it among the detective's ten favourite charities. Lee did not care for the way the millionaire had made his money and declined to be corrupted by it.

There is no doubt that Lee was one of the choosiest detectives when it came to taking up a case. When the Great War came the State had first call on his services; he was kept busy stamping out the 'serpent of secret service that writhed its insidious coils through every town, city and hamlet in the British Isles.' With the 'fervent thanks of his grateful country ringing in his ears' he could afford to take a very off-hand attitude towards the War Office. When a Staff major rang him up late at night and asked him to come at once, he exclaimed,

'Bally Government offices! Deuced cheek I call it. Think everybody's got to dance attendance on them. Jolly well wish I hadn't said I'd come.'

And it was only a trumpery little matter of preventing the Goswell Road district being asphyxiated by barge loads of German 'fertilizer.'

It seems probable that Nelson Lee was overworking at the time. As Nipper pointed out when the phone rang:

'My word, sir, Mr. Lloyd George hasn't given you much rest since he appointed you Inspector of Government Factories.'

When Lee, in response to the phone call, went across to see the Premier he was received instead by Sir Reevely Chart, Lloyd

George having been suddenly called away. This was a disappointment for Lee, to whom Kitchener was always at home, but then Lloyd George was a busy man, too. Sir Reevely Chart got down to business:

'Look at this Table of Output. Over 2,000 hands are employed yet the number of rifles, shells and small ammunition is a bare half of what it should be.
'This is grave indeed,' said Lee. 'I am at a loss to account for it.'
'They were running at full speed when you were down there?'
'Day and night, double shifts. No lathe or machine idle.'

Here an unworthy thought occurred to Sir Reevely Chart. He asked:

'Do the men drink?'
'No. There may be a slacker here and there, but the bulk of them are splendid fellows—good, honest, hard-working Yorkshiremen.'

The villain in the piece turned out to be General ('*und tousand teufels*') von Schoffen, who was out to weaken output before giving the signal for a mass insurrection of Germans from prisoner of war camps.

Much timely and versatile assistance was given to Nelson Lee by Eileen Dare, the girl detective. She was of special use when he wanted to plant a parlourmaid in some house of mystery. Nipper, knowing that there were limitations even to his powers of disguise, seems to have borne no ill-feelings—rather the reverse. When Eileen Dare was around he paid more attention to his appearance, and slicked back his hair. He always called her 'Miss Dare,' as did Nelson Lee. It is improbable that the girl detective shared the bachelor quarters in Gray's Inn Road, but she was always readily available. The partnership lasted many fruitful years.

Nelson Lee's first visit to St. Frank's was with the object of hiding from a gang who were pursuing him too hotly. But if he hoped to find calm in the groves of Academe he was mistaken. His professional rival Ferrers Locke was continually being called to Greyfriars or St. Jim's to investigate a stabbing or kidnapping, planting his juvenile assistant in the Remove or the Shell as required. It must have been to the mutual advantage of Nelson Lee and

Dr. Stafford, the Head of St. Frank's, when the detective agreed
to join the staff; doubtless the Head was astounded to see what
new, unsuspected and perverse machinations the detective was to
uncover. Lee had the good sense to keep things as quiet as possible,
including the outbreak of Communism (see Chapter XIII). He knew
as well as the headmaster how grave would be the effect on the
reputation of St. Frank's if the papers got hold of 1 per cent of
what was happening. Nipper enjoyed the move to St. Frank's.
He had never had any formal education, and held his own among
the Sir Monties and Hon. Douglases. Only occasionally was he
'framed'; then he speedily cleared himself.

Now and then Nelson Lee and Nipper slipped back to Gray's
Inn Road to keep the old practice going, but these reversals were
not popular with the imperious readers of the *Nelson Lee Library*.
The editor had to admit that separate stories of Lee and Nipper,
divorced from St. Frank's, were 'about as popular as fog at a football match.' 'You want the detective element, but you want it
intermixed with a school yarn. All right, you shall have it.' And
have it they did, right to the end, when the *Nelson Lee Library*
was merged with the *Gem* (1933).

The Aldine detective, Dixon Brett, was a highly organized
performer when Blake and Lee were still comparative tyros; the
archives show that he had routed many an anarchist by the middle
'nineties. This scientific sleuth owned one of the first Mercedes
race cars. He was usually to be found cigar-smoking at the wheel,
wearing 'immaculate evening dress' under a fur-lined overcoat.
The 'Night Hawk,' his car, was a redoubtable performer too,
and did not seem to suffer from the heartless way in which the
detective set her in motion. ('The sleuth put in the clutch, slipped
it in gear and let the clutch back again with a jerk. A second later
the great car leapt forward . . .'). Beside Brett in the 'Night
Hawk' was usually to be found his Number One assistant, Pat
Malone; his Number Two assistant, Bill Slook, was more often
left to look after the chambers in Lincoln's Inn. Slook was a
curiosity—'a freak even,' in that he was 32 years old but looked
like sixteen. His youthful appearance was the more remarkable
when it is remembered that Brett plucked him from a life of

" I am serious, Lee, and your flippancy is not in keeping with the present circumstances ! " snapped the Night Owl. " I have come here for the Don Santos Treasure, and I shall take it away with me ! "

degradation in an opium den. There were obvious advantages in 'combining the face and form of a boy with the age and ripe experience of a fully-grown man.' But for all his ripe and specialist experience Slook seems to have caused the detective a good deal of worry. In case after case he was rescued only at the eleventh hour from sudden death, or would turn up at Gray's Inn Road 'foaming and chattering like an ape' from a musk-maddened tarantula's bite. Malone was nearly as bad; he narrowly escaped torture by liquid air one day and by heat ray the next.

When not tearing about the country in his Mercedes, Dixon Brett was sitting in his loose dressing-gown in a deep chair, smoking an 'evil-smelling briar' or 'igniting a choice weed.' For a man with so many enemies it seemed odd that he should have had a speaking-tube extending down from his sitting-room to the front entrance; and for a man of his acumen it seemed even more odd that he should have been unsuspicious of a sweet scent in the room, and, having detected it, that he should have dismissed his giddiness with 'Shall have to put in a bit more exercise. Nerves getting a bit slack.' For Dixon Brett knew as well as the reader that Fan Chu Fang, the Wizard Mandarin, was abroad in London.

Fan Chu Fang, 'a veritable archangel of evil,' was one of the few fictional villains to raid Buckingham Palace successfully. The Chinese Government used regularly to deny that the Mandarin was an agent of theirs, but Dixon Brett knew better.

Fan Chu Fang was one of many Brett characters who seemed to have unpleasant optical trouble.

'At last he unveiled his green and evil orbs, and with something very like a shudder of disgust Dixon Brett observed that with the uplifting of the heavily folded eyelids a filmy grey substance was likewise drawn upward over the pupils, something like the moving membrane—the *membrana nictitans*—seen in the eyes of a bird.'

Soon after the Mandarin left a young man called, 'an obvious neurotic, slender, fragile, eager.' He had wide-open blue eyes with broad pupils 'in which could be seen plainly the characteristic "hippus"—the incessant change of size which marks the unstable nervous equilibrium.'

The eyes of Brett himself 'glowed a cat-like green' when he was excited. A hand-to-hand struggle between him and an albino would have been good value.

As a scientific sleuth Brett had an up-to-date laboratory. Some of his triumphs to-day would seem like the pottering of a small boy with a chemistry set, but he performed one feat at least which would still take some rivalling. It was necessary to identify some small seeds which looked like being an important clue. Brett laid them on soil which he steeped with a secret fertilizer, and then turned on the Röntgen rays (maintained by him for detecting forged banknotes).

In about ten minutes the shoots had reached the height of nearly an inch, and were then observed to grow much slower. Brett tipped the remains of the fertilizer from the phial into the jar.

The effect was almost magical; slowly but surely the shoots stretched upwards until the tops were at least eight inches from the earth. They then began to swell till they formed a dry-looking bud which a moment later burst, bringing forth a magnificent flower of a deep red colour.

'Great Scott! A poppy!' gasped Malone.

He was right. There was no mistaking the nature of the beautiful flower.

'Quick, Pat!' rasped Brett. 'Switch off the current of the rays and pull back the curtains.'

Why Brett got so excited at the end, or why he was operating behind drawn curtains, is not clear, unless it was that he did not want to be caught monkeying with the forces of Nature.

But if Brett was a scientist he had not neglected his modern studies. When Dr. Yoshimaro, to whom he took the poppy for identification, greeted him with 'Welcome, O Friend of ten thousand virtues!' Brett took a deep breath and countered with 'Greeting, O faithful son of ten million illustrious ancestors! The sight of thy radiant countenance, beside which the sun at noon is even as a dishonourable farthing candle, has healed me of all things. O Yoshimaro, the wise, beside whom the Sacred Owl of Wisdom is a babbling and absurd idiot!'

Nobody could complain that the characters in a Dixon Brett story died by natural causes. Leon Markheim collapsed suddenly, not from that overworked arrow poison but from sipping what he thought was a bottle of cognac and which turned out to be a flask of liquid air. 'His throat had been frozen solid the second the terrible liquid touched it, every blood-vessel in his neck being instantly congested.' Another victim was literally scared stiff by seeing an evil figure beckoning to him from what he had supposed was a mirror; another fell to the whispering death, a sibilant, all-pervading voice which urged him to get up and hang himself (one of many anti-social uses to which the innocent microphone has been put).

It was about 1900 that a powerful new rival strode on to the scene: Nick Carter. Perhaps it would be better to say that he was dumped on the scene. 'Remainders' of the Nick Carter Publishing House in New York were put on the British market at a low price, and enjoyed a considerable success. The house of Harms-worth, who had done their best to undercut their rivals a few years before, tried to enlist the wholesalers against this threat, but failed. Nick Carter established a beachhead, and began to fan out. But his weakness was in his supply lines. When the remainders were exhausted Nick Carter had to withdraw and await his next chance, hoping that his legend would survive.

Not that his reputation depended only on remainders. He made many appearances under the aegis of one publisher or another. And he was a much-translated detective. The Germans, for instance, saw in him a challenge to the dubious sensational fiction from which their market suffered. He had a keen following in France and Belgium. So many incarnations had Nick Carter, in so many places, that it is uncommonly difficult to chart his career, or to determine his real origins. The authoress of a book on pen names lists Nick Carter as a writer's pseudonym. She says: 'Discounted by the moral mentors of the youth of yesterday was "Nick Carter," or Francis Dougherty, whose tales of adventure seemed too spicy in tone, lacking literary merits.'

The Nick Carter who was introduced to the public of Great Britain in 1911 in the *New Nick Carter Weekly* was undoubtedly an American citizen. The magazine was priced five cents and bore a New York address. Amalgamated Press promptly took the opportunity of pointing out that Sexton Blake was a BRITISH detective, and issues of *Union Jack* bore the notice 'This is NOT

an American reprint.' Number One of the *New Nick Carter Weekly*
showed the detective examining a safe on which a robber had been
considerate enough to leave, not just a fingerprint, but an entire
handprint, or as entire a handprint as he could leave with only
three fingers. It seemed as adequate a clue (or clew) as any detective
had a right to expect.

There was a powerful piece of promotion for the benefit of
those, if any, who had never heard of Nick Carter:

The name of Nick Carter has spread to every land where the English
tongue is spoken, and his exploits have won tremendous popularity in
the picture palaces everywhere.[1] He is undoubtedly the cleverest detective
and criminal investigator the world has ever known. Nick Carter, with
the aid of his two assistants, Chickering Carter, generally termed Chick,
and Patsy has unravelled more astounding mysteries and been the central
character of more thrilling adventures and hairbreadth escapes than any
other man. He ranges his wonderful powers on the side of law, order
and justice against the criminals of five continents.

Notice that Nick Carter is credited with two assistants. (Chick,
just to make things difficult, sometimes made up as Nick.) There
were many others, though not all stayed the exacting course.
When it was suggested to the Grand Duke Ivan that Carter was
just the man to mop up the nihilists ('The nihilists! The nihilists!
That cry which is the most awful that can be heard in Russia!') The
Grand Duke asked:

'Does he know anything about Russia? Does he speak the language?'
'My dear Cousin, Nick Carter knows every country and speaks all
languages like a native.'
'Then let us send for him.'
'By the way, there is more than one of him.'
'What do you mean by that?'
'He has two or three assistants, I really don't know how many, and
they usually work together in big cases. We'd better have them all,
hadn't we?'

Really only a Grand Duke or a Maharajah could afford to take
all Nick Carter's assistants on the payroll. It was not only that
Carter had assistants, but his assistants had wives who sometimes

---

[1] Exploits of *Nick Carter, Master Detective*, were being screened in Britain as
recently as 1940.

joined, or were called into, the chase. On the rare occasions when
they were home in New York they all lived together *en famille*.
Patsy Garvan and his wife had a private sitting-room, but they
dined with the detective, who sat at the head of the table. It was by
no means unusual to find Nick smoking a cigar in the library
with Adelina (Patsy's wife) curled up opposite him with her
embroidery. This was a striking break with the masculine traditions
of Baker Street. Adelina, 'beloved by every member of the household,' would sometimes 'take liberties with the detective that
others would not think of doing.' All this meant was that she
would sometimes rally him when he was unduly silent or secretive.

There was a girl called Ida Jones who would cross oceans at
the detective's request; there was the 'youngest assistant,' whose
name was Jack Wise; and there was an Indian called Jack Rabbit;
the household also included a 'faithful servitor' called Joseph and
a housekeeper, Mrs. Peters.

On the top floor of the house was the strong room, a high
windowless (yet ventilated) room which came in useful from time
to time. Nick thought nothing of locking up a couple of women
crooks inside the strong room and holding them, without fear of
habeas corpus, until he had decided what to do with them.

Nick Carter flattered himself that he was pretty good at disguises. He would cheerfully run the clippers over his hair, stain
his teeth, and torture his ears with gold wire. And when he became
a hunchback—his strong line—he was not content with a hump
which came away when he removed his coat (as some operators
apparently were): the hump lay 'deeper than the coat or the
flowered waistcoat that covered it. It was deeper than the shirt
beneath the heavy, coarse woollen undershirt he wore, in fact, so
that if occasion should arise to remove his coat, as was likely to
happen, the hump was still there.' Even when he took the last
garment from his back you had difficulty in spotting that the
hump was a dummy. When not in use the hump was kept in a
cupboard and must have baffled Mrs. Peters when she came round
tidying up.

Yet when Nick Carter joined the nihilists in order to bore from
within (having sent his assistants to Moscow by different routes,

and ordered Ida Jones across from New York), in spite of his skill
at disguise and facility at languages he was unable to convince
the evil Vlasda that he was the peasant Beppo who lived 'about
ten versts from Tver.' She ordered him suddenly in French to sit
down, but Nick did not fall for that one. Nor did he bat an eyelid—
this illiterate peasant—when told to report to the arch-crook with
an open document which said that he was Nick Carter, a traitor.
Soon he was in a rough-house, punching his assailants 'in American
fashion' under the back of the skull, and at the same time exclaiming,
'That's English, if you understand it, you villains.' Had he fought
a less clean fight he would not have landed in Siberia, chained to
a murderer and a thief.

Carter was at his best when pitted against beautiful, unscrupulous
women. Deliberately he courted a battle of wits with a female
Svengali in Paris. He wanted her to believe that she had him in a
state of hypnosis, whereas he would still (he hoped) be in possession
of his wits. It was tough going. Under the lady's gaze he felt a
tightening of his throat, 'a feeling like that of a rubber band around
his brows.' He allowed himself to be lured to an easy chair where
the lady stroked his forehead, covered though it was with beads
of sweat.

'Nicholas Carter,' she said, with odd formality. Then sharply, 'Answer
me.'

Nick did not answer, but continued to play 'possum.'

'I am about to waken you now. You will believe that you have slept.
You will believe that you held me tightly in your arms; that your head
has been pillowed upon my breast; that you have told me of your love
for me; and that I have confessed my love for you. You will implicitly
believe all this when you awaken.'

Nick declined to 'awaken' fully, and his adversary put him to
sleep again. Just about then the master villain came in and suggested
that it would save a lot of trouble if the detective in his hypnotized
state were sent out on to the boulevards with instructions to jump
in the Seine. For private reasons the lady was unwilling to do this.
The plot hereabouts became very complicated, but at no time did
Nick yield the initiative.

After enduring many a trying experience like this Nick Carter was entitled to hold strong views on his pet subject:

'Throughout my experience I have been repeatedly annoyed by the escape of criminals whom I have arrested only after great and continuous effort. With the aid of my two assistants I track down a criminal and get him or her in durance vile and then some official turns his back and permits that criminal to escape. No man likes to do his work over a second time, no matter how much he may be paid for doing it. But this present case out-Herods Herod. . . .'

It is disconcerting, after studying 'this wonderful American' against his cosmopolitan background, to find that in 1915 he apparently took up permanent headquarters in, of all places, Manchester. (*Further Exploits of Nick Carter, Detective:* C. A. Pearson, Ltd.) He was down to one assistant, Chick Wilson, who was familiarly, if unoriginally, known as the Nipper, but still enjoyed the power to arrest or to say to police officers, 'You will arrest——'

Another English publisher—George Newnes—put out stories of Nick Carter against a sometimes ambiguous background, which could have been either Britain or America. Perhaps that was all part of the secret of the popularity of the Nick Carter stories.

In 1933 Nick Carter made a notable come-back in the *Nick Carter Magazine*, published in New York. The stories were stated to be 'by Nick Carter,' although the narrative was in the third person. Nick Carter the author did not hesitate to praise the initiative and acumen of Nick Carter the detective.

Carter was by now very busy and very rich; too busy to observe the normal courtesies, and perhaps too rich to care. He lived in a house on Fifth Avenue with a Filipino valet 'whose name was changed every time Nick Carter felt like it.' Adelina was no longer there to practise her gentle raillery. She would have found the new Nick Carter very hard and self-sufficient, and would almost certainly have been snubbed if she had tried to jolly him along. Chickering Carter was still alive and serving the sleuth faithfully.

Nick was now tackling big gangster organizations and kidnappers. Experience had taught him to practise an even higher degree of personal preparedness. Here he is at breakfast:

Holding his glass of orange juice in one hand, Nick started deftly shucking the envelopes off his mail with the other. It was an unwritten law with the master detective never to use two hands for anything if he could possibly manage with one. This was because there were so many times in Nick Carter's life when he couldn't use one hand because it had a gun in it.

One out-of-the-way case was the recovery of a stolen yacht loaded with a drug which had been hailed as the new anaesthetic, but which, belatedly, had been found to drive patients crazy and to give them the characteristics of apes. Carter searched for the yacht from his own aeroplane, which was fitted with a large magnifying glass in the floor. Being Nick Carter, he was allowed to mount offensive weapons on his aircraft and to carry bombs, even while flying over New York.

He also routed a master crook who had hit on the happy idea of priming his unwilling helpers with the details of cracking a chosen crib and then clamping on their heads an electric helmet which paralysed cerebrum and cerebellum, leaving the *medulla oblongata* still functioning. In this mechanical state the victim would proceed to execute uncritically the last instructions registered by the *medulla*.

With the *Nick Carter Magazine* was launched a Nick Carter Club, members of which were given a badge resembling a police shield. This accorded the wearer no special powers, but he was expected to help uphold the law on all occasions, to give evidence in the face of intimidation and to resist all demands for protection money. The hope expressed by the sponsors was that there were 'hundreds of thousands of citizens who will no longer remain passively standing by while crooks drench our streets with their bloody killings and flaunt their crimes before us.'

Certainly Nick Carter set an example of incorruptibility. To a father who offered him two million dollars to save his son from the consequences of his folly, he merely said, 'Your son is going to burn.'

He had become a very hard man indeed.

Among later detectives who dared to be different was Falcon Swift, who flourished in the pages of the pink-jacketed *Boys'*

Magazine[1] (1922). He was a sporting detective; not the first of that genre, for Aldine had run a *Dr. Grip, the Sport Detective*, nearly a generation before. But Swift was the only detective to play in international soccer wearing a monocle.

This sleuth with the 'keen aristocratic face' was a Cambridge triple blue who was equally proficient at boxing, soccer, sculling, and fencing. He had his headquarters in what was described as a 'cosy' sanctum hung with boxing gloves, rapiers and many trophies of the chase. Here sat his assistant Chick Conway—'the London street urchin whom he had literally taken out of the gutter.' Chick spent all his time reading the *Sporting Chronicle* and trying to match up his master for a prize fight. The *châtelaine* of this establishment was Biddy Malone, who cooked the meals when she was not lying clubbed or drugged in the kitchen.

One of Falcon Swift's early adversaries in the ring was a bruiser, who was also a member of an international gang of crooks. Swift found himself facing this rugged character in the ring on one of those days when everything had gone wrong. Chick Conway had vanished in suspicious circumstances, and just before the contest was due to begin it was revealed that the box office had been robbed of the £10,000 takings. A lesser man than Falcon Swift might have been put off his form. But he prepared to do battle.

The men shook hands. What a contrast! Swift with a skin of satin whiteness looked a picture of the English fighting man, with long arms and slightly sloping shoulders. And the Smasher. A man who might have been carved out of old mahogany, his body tanned to a red-brown hue, his mighty neck and shoulders suggesting some great forest oak.

A dirty blow in the stomach nearly knocked out Swift in the first round. He played for time, trying to recover his wind. Then during one of the intervals, while he was breathing heavily, a note was pushed through the ropes.

'I am sending this to the house by pigeon post. Biddy will bring it to you. Come at once, Boss, Mellish has trapped me. I am locked in an underground cell with the tide coming in through the grating. By eleven o'clock I shall be flooded and drowned. The Owls are robbing the box-office. Come as soon as possible to the Blue Lamp Laundry. Wharfside Alley, Rotherhithe. It's SOS, Boss.'

---

[1] Later absorbed in the *Champion*.

It was ten o'clock when Swift received this note. Chick Conway was due to die in an hour's time. If he left the ring now, on whatever pretext, Swift would be mobbed by 'a thousand angry men.' What could he do? What could anyone do, lacking the vegetable resources of a Popeye? Hastily he scribbled a note to Scotland Yard. Then the gong went.

Swift boxed listlessly. But just as the Smasher was moving in for the kill he suddenly became 'a thing of fire and tempest,' and in no time at all the Smasher was dead meat. Exactly five minutes later Swift was climbing into his Hispano-Suiza—in full evening dress—for another spell of slogging, this time in the alleys of Rotherhithe.

With remorseless regularity Falcon Swift's adversaries in sport turned out to be master crooks. Playing football one day he charged the crack opposing player—a man with bright red hair—and dexterously pulled out two of his hairs in the process. The hairs were not red right down to the roots: they were dyed. The player was an escaped convict.

Soon afterwards Swift was given a temporary commission in the Black Dragoons (Conway being taken on as batman) with instructions to locate a traitor in the regiment. It was all too easy. When the toast of 'The King' was given in mess only one man— the major—did not drink. As glasses were dashed to the floor (it was that kind of regiment) the major's glass left a red puddle, and Swift was the only one to spot it. It fell to Swift to fight the major with foils, though why he had to fight on a roof top with a sheer drop behind him is not clear. Swift was for ever being drawn into these unequal combats.

It was a character called Claude Montana—who sounded like a dance band leader but who was the arch-crook of five continents—who gave Swift his most worrying week-end. Montana was fond of a 'dare,' and he sent Swift the following document:

'As perhaps you and I are the greatest rivals for fame—each in his own method of interpreting the British Laws—I am challenging you to a little combat of wits before putting up the shutters on what I can proudly boast to be the most successful career in the history of crime. I have decided to take possession of the English Cup at Stamford Bridge

L

Ground to-morrow, Saturday, April 9th, at 3 p.m. precisely. There
promises to be a record crowd present, and after all have paid admission
I will call round and collect the gate money. I am retiring from active
life and I feel that I cannot write success on the last page and close the
book until I cross swords with you in this last adventure. One word of
warning—be careful that this little affair of mine is not your last as well.
I am hoping to bring off a big coup.'

In the succeeding operations Chick Conway got himself kidnapped again. It is doubtful whether that mirror ring he wore in
order to see behind him was really much use. But bruised as he
was, he was able to unscrew the perforated sphere, twice the size
of a cricket ball, which he habitually kept underneath his jacket
(and which his captors unaccountably overlooked) and release a
miniature pigeon with another message to his master.

Montana kept his promise. He did succeed in seizing the English
Cup and the 'gate' at the time appointed. It was all done from the
air, with smoke bombs and lassoos, and a confederate here and
there on the ground. But Swift's plane was hard on his heels and
after a brief chase Montana was shot down.

Swift's adversaries frequently turned out to be exhibitionists.
There was one who caused a warning charade to be projected on
to the vacant wall of a building. It showed the master crook about
to drop the glove which was the signal for shooting a row of
gagged and bound victims. But the criminal who best combined a
sense of the dramatic with a sense of humour was the one who had
Chick Conway suspended upside down in such a way that when
Falcon Swift came to his rescue the opening of the door would
lower his assistant into a cauldron of acid. There was an attractive
simplicity about this scheme; it required less technical preparation
than an alternative device in which the opening of a door closed
the circuit which fired a gun aimed at the victim's head.

All the detectives noted so far were content with a modest
pied-a-terre in which to live and consult their clients. Not so
Martin Track, the detective of *The Dreadnought* (1912). Here was
an operator who attached high importance alike to his personal
comfort, his personal dignity and his personal safety. He lived in
a barbaric palace which looked like a lamaserie, built on a high
pinnacle over the North Sea. Round the base of the hill ran a high

wall a mile in circumference, guarded by armed men, and without visible entrance. Baffled visitors seeking an audience would find themselves suddenly and disconcertingly confronted by a Chinese dwarf dressed in a monk's robe, who would blindfold them and lead them in by an underground passage. Others would be netted from the wall and whisked over the parapet. Still others would be picked up eagle fashion, by padded claws operated from underneath Track's box-kite aeroplane homing to its eyrie, and dropped down a chute on to something soft, there to await the master's pleasure.

Once inside, the clients were usually so overawed by the owner's bizarre taste in furnishing that they would forget to be indignant about the manner of their delivery. The main reception room was resplendent with ottomans, rich silks, tapestries, wild beasts' skins and stained glass windows. Priceless objects of art lay all around; any rash visitor who, fancying himself unobserved, picked up one of these to examine it was liable to find himself surrounded by a device resembling a giant glass cake-cover dropped from the ceiling. Through this the gipsy features of Martin Track would be seen registering disapproval. The chamber was frequented by Grip the Chinese dwarf, two Japanese servants, a parrot, a raven and a white dove—sometimes all together. There was another audience chamber where Track occasionally chose to receive his clients. It was a cavern cut in the living rock, and patrolled by lions and tigers, who ambled up to sniff the suppliant. Track sat on a stone throne, with a black eagle perched above his head. He wore neither the beard nor the leopard skin which such a situation seemed to call for, merely a lounge suit of undistinguished cut.

In spite of the elaborate defences with which he surrounded himself, Track spent a good deal of time repelling attempts to assassinate him by syndicates of criminals. Once his castle was bombarded with six-inch shells by a pirate cruiser; another time there was an attempt to dynamite his castle rock. Spies who succeeded in crossing the wall were liable to fall into the 'pit of treachery,' already littered with the bones of the too-inquisitive. Others were set to work night and day in an underground chamber, in an 'enforced repentance.' Even though they fully repented they were never allowed to emerge; they were lost to the world as irrevocably as Mrs. Lovett's pieman in Bell Yard.

Martin Track was a real literary curiosity—a Gothic detective who employed the latest inventions of science. There is no record of him ever playing in a Cup Final.

CHAPTER X

PURE INVENTION

IN THE LATE Victorian years was born a fashion for tales of invention—pure invention, invention for invention's sake.

All too soon was Science to become the bride of Mars. But in those closing years of the nineteenth century warfare and invention were still two separate conceptions. Warfare meant donning a frogged uniform and riding down Zulus or Fuzzy-wuzzies, or exchanging leisurely cannon balls with the Russians at Sebastopol; invention meant nothing more sinister than labouring with two chums in a secret workshop to devise a more gratifying means of locomotion in the air, on land or under the sea—in other words building an aeronef,[1] a steam man or a submarine.

Electricity was still a miraculous and exciting novelty, all the more fascinating because it was imperfectly understood. Machines, whether aerial, terrestrial or submarine, were frequently driven by a baffling mixture of pure electricity, hydraulics, steam or liquid air. Writers of early 'scientifiction' did not go to any great pains to brush up their subject, or to make their inventions plausible. The more cautious authors kept to ballooning. It was hard to make any technical *gaffes* in a story of lighter-than-air craft; and if it was essential to cover vast distances rapidly it could always be done by harpooning a whale and hanging on.

---

[1] Jules Vernese for power-operated flying machines. Verne's output of scientific romances began in the eighteen-sixties and continued into the twentieth century; those of H. G. Wells were published between 1895 and 1905.

The heavier-than-air machine which did service for the best part of a decade, in scores of aerial romances, was shaped like a short, fat airship, with a railed observation platform on top. Above the platform an array of propellers revolved horizontally. These served to raise or lower the vessel, and to scare off pterodactyls. At the front and rear of the craft were vertical airscrews, often two or three to a shaft, and any protuberance in the design was also fitted with an airscrew for good measure. Occasionally the craft had rudimentary wings, usually shaped like those of a bat.

Now and again, however, an inventor turned out something really original. In an early *Marvel* story—'The Witches' Clutch,' by Owen Meredith—was described a flying contraption (if anything 700 feet long can be called a contraption) based on a principle which seems to have been overlooked by the de Havillands and the Messerschmitts. The artist who illustrated the story baulked at drawing the machine. Let the inventor explain:

I have simply adopted the old theory of Professor Lanis, which was based on the fact that if a vessel is exhausted of its air it becomes lighter than the air and will float in it. He suggested that a metalline vessel might be made so large that when emptied of its air it would not only be able to raise itself but to carry passengers along with it. This is a fact admitted on all sides, but hitherto no metal has been found which could be beaten out sufficiently thin to float in the atmosphere and at the same time be able to resist the external pressure.

The secret of making such a metal is mine. I can manufacture steel which when rolled out into sheets as thick as tissue paper will defy the assaults of any bullet you can fire at it. With this wonderful steel I have constructed an immense tube some 700 feet long and nearly 150 feet in diameter. This, exhausted of its air, will raise a prodigious weight any height. Internally it is divided into chambers which, by a contrivance of my own, can be filled or deprived of air at will. Thus I can regulate the speed of ascent or descent, or if I wish we can remain motionless suspended in space. . . .

Along each side of the tube large collapsible wings are attached. They are reversible in action, and guide as well as propel. So closely do they fold up that when in this position they are not easily discernible. Rigidly suspended beneath by hollow columns through which my machinery works is a commodious car built in the shape of a ship. Here is luxurious accommodation for hundreds of passengers and here are placed my electrical engines which control the great wings and the air-exhausting pumps. I have invented storage batteries which will re-charge themselves automatically. The nature of the fluid I use is again my secret.

That this invention was packed with menace towards others besides the passengers was admitted by the designer:

Consider how soon I could make the greatest city on earth a seething mass of ruins if I assailed it from my airship with a sufficient quantity of the proper explosive, and I be out of harm's way all the time! In less than half an hour I could sweep the combined armies of the old world off the face of the earth. Therefore I say my discovery will make war impossible.

He was, alas, only one of a long line of fictional visionaries who were confident they had found the secret of making war impossible. So obsessed was this designer, nevertheless, with the danger of his invention falling into the wrong hands (thus making war possible) that he had it built by Red Indian slave labour in a remote township, suitably called Eureka, of the American West.

Another bizarre flying machine was that which figured in a story, 'King of the Air,' by 'Professor Gray,' also in the early *Marvel*. Its body was shaped like a launch. Rising from its decks were two pairs of bats' wings, and extending horizontally fore and aft from the body were shafts bearing multiple propellers. The test flight was conducted rather optimistically from the top of a tower, instead of from the ground, but there was a reason for this. Here is the inventor's explanation:

'The reason why the outside appears so much greater than the inside is that all round are air-tight chambers in sections. These are filled with gas, and the gas can never escape. Notwithstanding this, I say the tendency of the machine is to gradually approach the earth, though very slowly. Were no one in it, but only the dynamo and batteries which work the wings, it would keep almost level in the air. Get in, and I will show you that theory put into practice.'

Somewhat dubiously, the hero consented, and with difficulty found room among the rifles, pistols, ammunition, provisions, condensers, chemicals and electric stoves which the 'Bat' contained. In no time at all they were shooting buffalo from the air and rescuing a young woman from mutilation by a tribe of gorillas.

The most successful and industrious of the inventors for

invention's sake was Frank Reade, whose adventures were retailed under the Aldine banner, in the *Invention, Travel and Adventure Library*. There were, in point of fact, two Frank Reades—father and son—but nothing is gained by distinguishing between their exploits. According to the first story in this Aldine series:

Frank Reade was noted the world over as a wonderful and distinguished inventor of marvellous machines in the line of steam and electricity. But he had grown old and unable to knock about the world as he had once been wont to do. So it happened that his son Frank Reade, junior, a handsome and talented young man, succeeded his father as a great inventor, even excelling him in the variety and complexity of invention. The son speedily outstripped his sire.

The great machine shops in Readestown were enlarged by young Frank, and new flying machines, electric wonders and so forth were brought into being. But the elder Frank would maintain that inasmuch as electricity at the time was an undeveloped factor, his invention of the Steam Man was really the most wonderful of all.

For all his fecundity of invention Frank Reade, junior, persisted in designing machines in the form of men and horses; as far as he was concerned the locomotive might never have been invented. His justification was that his Steam Man was a magnificent sight, far more impressive than any puffing billy of the age. The coloured cover showed what looked like an outsize suit of armour, surmounted not by a casque but by a top hat, from which flames were issuing. In his hands the Steam Man held the shafts of a small chariot, which was walled with bullet-proof mesh, and contained apertures for rifles. The young inventor, looking just a shade anxious, held the reins and appeared to be calling on his robot rickshawman for a spurt. In the wake rode a band of hostile cowboys.

For the benefit of new readers, every story contained a summary of how the Steam Man operated:

Steam was the motive power. The hollow legs and arms of the man made the reservoir or boiler. In the broad chest was the furnace. Fully 200 pounds of coal could be here placed, keeping up the fire sufficient to generate steam for a long time.

The reins operated the throttle and whistle respectively. In the chariot at the rear was a store of ammunition and a box of surprises.[1]

Hardly had the Steam Man emerged from the shops than the call for his services came from the West. Reade, junior, with his faithful retinue, Barney O'Shea and Pomp the negro, jumped aboard, and 'the Steam Man plunged at once into the unexplored wilds of the mighty West . . . for hours he kept on with long strides.'

His normal speed seems to have been in the thirties or forties. He could negotiate rivers, always supposing that the water did not come up to his furnace-chest.

The Comanches Indians had thought themselves inured against the shocks of the White Man. But the Steam Man panicked them. It bore down on their encampment, trampling the tardy under its metal feet and scything the horses' legs with the Boadicean knives attached to the chariot's hubs.

When beating up an Indian camp or a Western township it was important to keep the Steam Man going all the time. If he was faced with a physical barrier he was finished. Running out of fuel was not the problem it might have appeared. Usually 'a coal mine chanced to be near and the bunkers were refilled.' Eventually, after a running fight with desperadoes on a railway train, and the rout of cowboys who sought to halt its progress with lassoes, not to mention the rescue of its inventor from the stake, the Steam Man plunged over a cliff and was destroyed.

Frank Reade, junior, did not mind. He now had the opportunity to build a Steam Horse. It was a fine-looking beast, with steam gushing from its nostrils and powerful pistons in its flanks. The chariot was rather better armed and armoured, and could tackle anything up to cannon. There was no need to feel nervous at night, out in the Comanches country, with the Steam Horse for company:

[1] *The Aldine Garfield Boys' Journal* (named after America's canal-boy-to-White-House President) contained, *c.* 1894, a description of a steam man made by a Mr. George Moore in Canada. The designer had been obliged to clothe his invention in medieval armour instead of the contemporary frock coat. Inside the chest was a boiler filled with water, and steam was expelled from a cigar between the model's teeth. The steam man was five feet six inches in height, developed half a horsepower and was credited with a speed of between five and eight miles an hour.

The eyes of the horse lit up by the fierce glow of the magnesium coils threw a brilliant light far out upon the level plain. Frank pulled the whistle cord, and the Steam Horse sent forth his shrill note of defiance.

After surviving peril from quicksands and theft by the Red Indians, the Steam Horse blew up, inexplicably, in a fire. But another was ready in time for the next instalment, an improved model with rubber joints and capable of running on sea-coal, wood or even turf; which did not mean that it could be turned out to graze. Then came the great day when the Steam Horse and a new Steam Man set off across the prairie together. The Man, as was only to be expected, lagged a little, so the Horse had to be throttled down. The two were capable of very effective combination against the Indians; at one point they bore down upon a bunch of braves with a trip wire extended between man and horse. When it was desired to frighten the Indians by night, chemical fire in a variety of colours was discharged from the hollow uprights of the chariot. The box of surprises now included an electric stockade which could be laid out at night. Redskins who touched the wire could not let go and were plucked off when a suitable opportunity arose.

The next development was obviously a Steam Team. This equipage, which could easily exceed fifty miles an hour, needed a certain amount of skill to handle. When cornering it was necessary to slow down one horse and speed up the other (it was never explained, incidentally, how the other steam monsters were steered). The Steam Team could also be reversed.

In time Frank Reade, junior, grew really ambitious and invented such hybrids as the Electric Air Canoe, which could hover under its 'suspensory rotascopes' and train a dynamite gun on any object desired; and the Electric Submarine Boat in which the three adventurers travelled under the ice to the North Pole. But it is by the adventures of the more modest steam men and horses that Frank Reade is best remembered.

There is a bit of a mystery about Frank Reade's rival inventor, Jack Wright, who also had a town named after him on the eastern seaboard of America. It is entirely possible that Wright, who figured in the Aldine *Cheerful Library* (1894), was Frank Reade under another name, though why Aldine should have wished to change his name is not apparent.

Almost parenthetically, the reader was told in the first story of a project on which Wright was working in his spare time—a project which made Edison and Faraday look like amateurs of Science:

Behind Wrightstown there was a vast mass of iron in the ground, a mile long, a mile wide and several miles thick, around the top of which miles of wire had been wound by the young inventor. He had formed an induction circuit in which he was going to have the most powerful of electric currents, and as telephones are made by running wire round the top of a magnetic bar, when this one was charged with electricity the boy expected to hear the explosions which are supposed to be going on continually upon the sun by this big telephone.

While he was able to squander vast quantities of raw materials merely in order to listen in to the rumblings of solar indigestion, Wright was conscious of his duty towards the town of Wrightstown. It was quite a place:

In the central building the boy constructed various kinds of submarine and other kinds of boats; in the right wing he devised the most singular-looking vessels for navigating the air, while the left wing was utilized for building overland contrivances, run, as most of his inventions were, by electricity, steam, compressed air, gas, vacuum and wing force.

It was Jack's concern to provide his township with bigger stores and better factories. Perhaps that is why his inclination was towards building under-water craft rather than flying machines. It was a bad day if one of his submarine catamarans or electric turtles (with jaws which could snap off a ship's rudder) did not come back with the gold of half a dozen sunken galleons.

He also penetrated the West from time to time in extravagantly conceived vehicles. One of these was the 'Magnetic Motor,' which had a cowcatcher, a pneumatic gun, a searchlight and a steel-meshed cabin for the protection of the occupants. Carried externally was an imposing array of spare 'horse-shoe' magnets, arrayed in neat patterns. These were to be operated, in some unexplained way, 'to increase the speed of the locomotive if it became necessary.'

In this vehicle the intrepid inventor made a Thermopylae stand against hordes of Apaches. By pulling a lever he could make the vehicle impart electric shocks to any Indians who were rash enough to touch it. But the Indians seized him nevertheless, tied him to a golden stake and set fire to the faggots. He was rescued just as the warriors were commenting on how bravely he burned, and they probably did not grudge him the load of gold he shipped away, to defray expenses. After that Wright went back to submarine navigation, where the worst that could happen was being sucked half-way into the sac of a giant octopus.

It is fortunate that neither Reade nor Wright entertained dreams of world conquest. They were restless experimenters, and never seemed satisfied with one invention for long. Mere accumulation of wealth was no object. Otherwise they might have been tempted to equip Readestown or Wrightstown on Willow Run lines in order to mass-produce steam men or herds of iron horses, with results which defy contemplation.

Over-soon, this halcyon age of pure invention was to end. The Northcliffe boys' magazines began to see in the fertility of inventors all manner of threats to the security of Britain.

CHAPTER XI

BRITAIN INVADED

No one who was born just before the turn of the century and who was nurtured (as who wasn't?) on the boys' papers of the Amalgamated Press is likely to forget the remorseless spate of serials which described the descent of foreign hordes upon these shores and their subsequent bloody repulse (at the cost of a sacked St. Paul's and a shattered Clock Tower at Westminster).

So fierce became the Northcliffe propaganda against Germany (chiefly in the *Daily Mail*) that in 1910 an American newspaper was prompted to exclaim:

> It will be a marvel if relations with Germany are not strained until war becomes inevitable as a direct result of the war-scare campaign inaugurated and carried on with the most reckless and maddening ingenuity by the Northcliffe syndicate of newspapers.

The 'maddening ingenuity' might well have been a reference to the campaign as conducted in the *Boys' Friend*, *Boys' Herald*, the *Marvel* and other Northcliffe boys' papers. Unable to convince adult citizens of their danger from invasion, Northcliffe did his best to convince their sons.

His early broadsides were fired, not primarily against Germany, but against the French and the Russians. In 1900 the *Boys' Friend*, already heavily weighted with a profusion of drawings showing Boers riding down fleeing natives, shooting up flags of truce and bombarding the Red Cross, carried a series of pictures of warships at death grips. One which was headed 'What Will Happen in the Next Great Naval War' bore the caption: 'Here is seen the sinking of a French man o' war battered by the guns of the British Navy. There can be no question that our Navy is more than equal to any two of the great European powers. Long may it be so!' Another in the same issue was captioned: 'This sketch shows a French warship trying to enter the Thames being blown up by a submarine mine.' A third bore the legend: 'The Russian Fleet being driven back into the Baltic by a flying squadron of British warships. This is what would happen if war between Russia and Britain broke out.' To bring the peril right home there was also a drawing, supposedly based on an incident in the news, showing a Frenchman beating an Armenian beggar for daring to address him in English. It bore the title: 'How The French Love Us.'

This policy appears not to have received wholehearted acclamation, for shortly afterwards an editorial note revealed that a reader had pleaded for fewer war pictures to be printed:

He [the protesting reader] will already see that the *Boys' Friend* has once more returned to its old serene style of being purely a boys' paper.

It was all very well making a burst of patriotism when the war first commenced, but to maintain it would be to my mind unnecessary and calculated to annoy my readers. So my friend will find that war will not occupy a very prominent position in the only boys' paper in the future.

Hence those of my readers who have objected to war pictures will now find their objection no longer exists.

The note was a little premature, for in the issue in which it appeared there were more than a dozen pictures of war-like incidents. Soon afterwards the editor, who seems to have repented of his decision, returned to the urgent theme:

Will my readers believe that there are at the present time but a few hundred trained soldiers in this country to resist any attack an antagonistic foreign nation might choose to make on our little island home?

An issue or two later the *Boys' Friend* carried a full-page drawing on its cover showing a shell exploding smack in the middle of Big Ben, with stampeding horse omnibuses in the foreground.

The heading and caption ran: 'Bombardment of London—The French at Our Doors: Indeed then would come our great hour of woe when French shot and shell fell in horrible rain along the fair streets of the Empire's City. One shell, for instance, would strike the Clock Tower of the Houses of Parliament, flinging it down in a hail of destruction.'

Inside Hamilton Edwards described how easily Britain could be invaded from the Continent. He wrote:

'The Invasion of England'—it is no wild dream of the imaginative novelist, this threat of an invasion of our beloved shore. It is stolidly discussed in French and Russian—ay, and in German—newspapers.

The Frenchman and the educated Russian talk of such a thing as coolly as we talk of sending out a punitive expedition to the Soudan or up to the hills of North-West India.

The *Boys' Friend* returned to the theme week after week, month after month, year after year. So did the companion papers. The *Boys' Herald* had a series in 1903 describing how a Captain Strange fought a one-man war against the French in the English Channel. (In the *Boys' Realm* a Captain Handyman performed a similar office.) Strange's vessel was equipped with a giant grab, and almost every week he would steam triumphantly into harbour trailing a bantam-weight submarine which he had discovered exploring the British minefields. From it would be decanted a handful of 'shaken Froggies' who would be handed over to the grateful authorities. Captain Strange also frustrated various treacherous attacks on Gibraltar by the French. He was the first to realize the deadly peril contained in the announcement that 'M. Santon Dumas,' the aerial inventor, had put his knowledge and his wonderful flying machine at the disposal of the French Government. In no time at all M. Dumas's craft was sinking the British Fleet at the rate of one bomb, one battleship.

In 1905 a *Boys' Friend* serial, 'Rule Britannia' (containing a Lion and a Bear in the heading design), described a British punitive expedition to St. Petersburg rendered necessary by the outrageous act of the Russian Fleet in firing at defenceless fishing vessels on the Dogger Bank. This story was stated to be on the lines of 'your editor's story "Britain in Arms".' A story with this title,

republished in the *Boys' Friend Library* in 1909 and sub-titled
'The Death or Glory Boys,' started with massed French and
Russian invasion fleets steaming on the United Kingdom (the
German Ambassador in Paris had been privy to this plan). For
once Britain was in a state of preparedness; on the word of command
a fully trained Army Corps of 34,000 was ready to take the field
—more than enough to handle an Armada bearing 150,000 troops.
Spirited cavalry charges in the Light Brigade manner routed the
vanguard of the 'Frogs' who landed at Newhaven. A Russian
assault on Edinburgh was contemptuously repulsed, and from that
point the Russians were ignored.

It was decided to teach the French a lesson, however, so a
British Expeditionary Force under Lord Roberts set out to invade
France. And here comes a revelation which the 'inventors' of the
Mulberry Harbour might care to hear about:

As they steamed in towards shore the soldiers were astonished to find
that a landing stage had been erected for them, and everything was ready
for the ships to run alongside and the British troops to land.

The move of Lord Roberts had been well calculated. A detachment
of Royal Engineers had constructed a floating wharf made to fit this
particular point in the shore. This wharf had been towed across the
Channel and fixed while the British Fleet was bombarding Havre.

In a few hours everything was complete and 60,000 British troops,
50,000 cavalry and 300 guns were landed on the French shore.

Britain had commenced to take her revenge.

Against cavalry on a scale never dreamed of even at Camberley
no defences could stand. Very soon the French had concluded
peace, promised to pay an indemnity of £100,000,000 and agreed
to limit their army to not more than a million men. 'This,' said
the author, 'indirectly worked for the benefit of the French people
who were relieved from the horrible conscription which every
year sucks the life-blood of the best of the younger generation of
Frenchmen.'

Meanwhile, with almost monotonous frequency Sexton Blake in
Union Jack was uncovering plans of the German High Command
to invade Britain by sailing up the Thames, or by arriving 'the
unexpected way, from the north; or to bring Britain to her senses,
and her knees, by first overrunning the Continent. These docu-

ments he would send with his compliments to the Cabinet or the
War Office, but the only action ever taken was to offer Blake a
peerage; nobody thought of getting down to the job of reorganizing
Britain's defences.

The warning was sounded even in the stories of Greyfriars and
St. Jim's, of Rookwood and St. Frank's. Some Territorials taking
cover near St. Jim's were mistaken for Germans. One of the
schoolboys said: 'It can't be the Germans. We all know they are
coming some day, but they have not finished their fleet yet.'

In 1908 the *Boys' Herald*, introducing a new serial of aerial warfare, printed a symposium of views by famous military leaders and
statesmen on 'Will there one day be a world at war?' Wrote the
editor:

It is no secret that the Britisher is hated abroad. In many countries
a Britisher is not safe from insult or assault. In parts of Germany, to give
one example, our countrymen are openly reviled and sneered at. Why?
Because of our huge possessions and colonies, because of our prosperity
as a nation, because of our enterprise and grit. Foreign nations are
jealous of our progress. They fear that one day we will make a bid to
be the conquerors of the world, that one day Britishers will rise up from
their homes in every part of the world and make a concerted blow at
every other nation.

Foreign spies in Great Britain and our possessions abroad have for
years been gathering information with regard to our fortifications and
defences, the weak points on our coast line and a thousand other items
invaluable to a Power intending one day to strike a blow at us.

Spies have again and again been caught in our forts and dockyards.
Regular reports are despatched by spies in Great Britain as to our progress in submarines, airships, guns and other implements of warfare.
Foreign army observers are as familiar with the maps of rivers and railways and roads and canals of Great Britain as with those of their respective
countries.

And while all this was going on, said the editor, the number of
men in our Army was steadily decreasing.

Simultaneously the *Boys' Friend* was playing up an invasion
story called 'The Peril to Come.'

As 1914 neared the invasion stories came thick and fast. John
Tregellis was the name under which many of them appeared. In
1912 this author had 'The Flying Armada' running in the *Boys'*

M

Friend, and 'Britain Invaded,' followed by 'Britain at Bay,' in the *Marvel*. In the *Dreadnought* was 'The War in the Clouds,' not to mention a serial called 'Doom,' which told of a great cataclysm overtaking the earth.

'Britain Invaded' and 'Britain at Bay' which formed a continuous story, ran as end-of-the-book serials, in very short instalments. The impression given, perhaps wrongly, was that here was something which the editor was printing only because he had to. Pride of place went to Arthur S. Hardy's boxing stories and the interminable adventures of Jack, Sam and Pete.

This particular invasion—for which the excuse was a dispute over the East African frontier and the German seizure of a British arms ship—started with the sudden cutting of the North Sea cables and the simultaneous dawn landing of five Army Corps—totalling 200,000 men—at Hull, Boston, Cromer, Lowestoft and Frinton. In the battle from the word 'go' were the cadets of Greyfriars (not *the* Greyfriars) who rapidly became an élite corps. The Kaiser, whose yacht was on the scene at an early stage, was not to be killed. That instruction came from 'higher up.' He was to be taken alive.

Britain's gallant armies, under General Sir Sholto Nugent and Lord Ripley, could not hold back the invaders from the northern half of London. Uhlans and Prussian Grenadiers marched through the City. Von Kranz ran up the German flag over the Mansion House, which he made his headquarters, and accepted the keys of the Bank of England. The Lord Mayor elected to remain in office rather than leave his beloved capital, or what was left of it. St. Paul's, once again, had become a casualty. The dome was crushed in at one side, like an egg assaulted by a spoon. Big Ben was cleft down to the clock face, and London Bridge was broken down. On the occupied side of the river the Londoners were bearing up 'wonderfully well on the whole . . . as patient as heroes.' In parts of the West End life went on much as usual, though there were no cabs as the War Office had commandeered all horses at an early stage. Food was not plentiful, but the rich were able to buy commodities which they were decent enough to share with the poor. Rioting by the still far-from-docile population was frequent, and was bloodily put down, men, women and children being shot in batches. Barricades were thrown up in Covent Garden and defended to the last woman and boy. Von Krantz began to get desperate. Perhaps he had heard that the Colonies were sending ship-loads of arms to the defenders. His worries were not lessened by the destruction of a second wave of German troops in the North Sea. Two cadets of Greyfriars had accomplished this feat by spilling petrol over the ocean, sailing powder hulls into it and then tossing in a match when the German vessels came near enough. Setting the sea on fire had been thought of long before World War Two.

Helping to maintain the morale of Londoners in the southern half of the city was the *Daily Mail*. In the northern sector it came out under German censorship, but in the south it was free to report, with suitable comments, each German ultimatum. Typical headlines were:

THE KAISER'S DEMANDS
BRITAIN TO PAY INDEMNITY OF £100,000,000
CESSION OF NATAL, TRANSVAAL AND RHODESIA
EGYPT AND CAPE COLONY TO BE GERMAN PROTECTORATES
HALF THE NAVY TO BE SURRENDERED TO GERMANY
A GUARANTEE NOT TO BUILD MORE THAN TWO SHIPS PER YEAR
    IN FUTURE WITHOUT THE GERMANS' CONSENT
DISARMAMENT AND SUBMISSION TO GERMAN RULE

This was greeted by the loyal populace with cries of 'No surrender!' 'God Save the King!' and the hoisting of every Union Jack in town.

The 'smartest of the afternoon journals'—oddly enough, the Northcliffe *Evening News*—commented:

The great fact remains and the blame with it lies not with our military or naval leaders but with those above them.
WE ARE NOT READY!
We have been taken unprepared; the greatest military nation of the age has caught us napping. Thanks to this belief in our security we have been sleeping, dreaming of universal peace. This is our awakening.

The Northcliffe boys' papers were not alone in their forecasting of war with Germany. In the Aldine *Boys' Own Library*, which started about 1907, appeared a highly imaginative story (No. 44) entitled 'The Aerial War, A Tale of What Might Be,' heralding a clash between a scientifically armed Germany and a Great Britain left in the lurch. Doubtless it was digested, like all the others, by German Intelligence, and filed away in the Wilhelmstrasse with a black mark against the author, John G. Rowe.

The story began with a welter of Nihilist plotting in Ireland, where a secret aerial battleship, 'Hope of Russia,' was almost ready to set off on a lethal mission, as a result of which 'the name of the Czar would be spoken no longer by the sons of men.' Somehow the Nihilists faded out of the story, and the scene was switched to an aerial dockyard in the South of England where two aeronefs were almost completed. The plans of these had been stolen some time previously by the Germans.

Then the bombshell came.

Long threatened had been the war which had just been declared with our old medieval foe, Germany. Our relations with that country had been strained to breaking-point for months on account of the high-handed treatment of English interests and British-owned property in Germany, by the German Government, and the inflexible attitude adopted by the latter.

Hostilities opened with the arrival of five 'aeroplanic battleships' described as 'huge-winged monsters unlike any bird that ever flew with their wide spread and complex arrangement of aeroplanes [wings] sailing up from the south-east at a speed that was annihilating distance.' Halting over our aerial dockyards, the Germans chivalrously, if rashly, offered to fight duels with our new vessels ship for ship.

The challenge was accepted, and scores of gunners of the Royal Artillery were rushed on board the British aeronefs, which rose to do battle with a great buzzing of 'typhonoids.' There followed an aerial slogging match, rather in the style of a naval battle, but with a greater variety of weapons, including 'dynamite torpedoes' and 'liquid bombs.'

When one of our aeronefs went down crippled, the Germans unexpectedly forebore to fire on her.

It was the one redeeming point about their behaviour, which otherwise looked almost like treachery, though everything is fair in war.

Despite the loss of this vessel, the British won the engagement and captured three enemy craft. 'So ended the first aerial battle between two great Powers on earth.' But while the country began to maffick over this 'second Trafalgar' came the news that the German battleships which had escaped had bombed and wrecked Woolwich Arsenal on the way home. Also one of the vessels had made a determined effort to kidnap the King at Windsor, hovering above the window of the Royal bedroom and landing boarders. In the nick of time the Royal Family had been smuggled out and removed to unknown destinations. (The Monarch was not always so lucky as to escape kidnapping, as will be seen.)

Public Enemy No. 1 was now Aeroduce Swaffenbach (the rank was the equivalent of Admiral). Operating their new fog-dispeller (a wireless wave of great intensity) Aeroduce Blundell and Vice-Aeroduce Thorpe cruised the skies over London looking for him. They found him only after he had flattened St. Paul's and Westminster Abbey. During a temporary truce, called for by the British, Swaffenbach explained that he had destroyed the cathedrals not out of malice but only as an object lesson. He expressed surprise at his moderation. 'The whole of the metropolis was at our mercy, but we have contented ourselves with destroying those two buildings. We spared the Houses of Parliament as they were sitting.'

There was a lot more thrilling action, including a battle staged over the Thames (to avoid damage to property!), a German raid on Tilbury and Shoeburyness, and a big naval battle off Margate, where the German Fleet was easily routed by the doughty British blue-jackets. But this success was not enough. The enemy's aerial strength had to be destroyed at its source. So was carried out the first British air raid on Berlin, where nine aeroplanic battleships were on the stocks. It was so successful that not only were the aerial dockyards burned out but the German Government, in panic, capitulated and undertook to defray the expense of rebuilding St. Paul's and Westminster Abbey.

A little later a conference of all the chief powers met at Geneva and signed a treaty by which they mutually agreed to preserve the peace of the world and to submit every international dispute to arbitration by the other neutral powers and abide by the decision arrived at if this were agreed by two-thirds of the arbitrators.

Lord Blundell (as he became) was to be regarded as a benefactor of the human race, since 'by his great victory he probably made war impossible between civilized nations and opened the way for universal peace.'

He was a long way before his time, was Mr. Rowe. Technically, he was inclined to be on the defensive, to judge by frequent footnotes quoting scientific justification for his aeronautical detail. In one chapter he tells how the windows of an aeronef iced over, in spite of which the navigators could tell where they were by the ice patterns on the glass. Says the footnote:

Grand, the founder of the Copenhagen Academy of Science, vouches for a case where frost traced upon windows of a coach an accurate outline of the surrounding scenes. No satisfactory theory has yet been advanced to account for this curious phenomenon; but it is well known that lightning has also the singular power of tracing the outline of distant objects on the surface of the bodies through which it passes.

The long-prophesied war with Germany duly arrived, and proved to be a very different proposition from what had been forecast. Four years after it was over, the Amalgamated Press *Champion* (1922) ran a serial describing Germany's 'War of Revenge.'

The author, Leslie Beresford, seems to have under-estimated Germany's powers of recovery, for he placed World War Two in 1962. He declared in his preamble that in the 'next war' navies and armies would have a small part to play beside the chemists and the scientists.

Powerful wireless will control the most terrible weapons of death, flattening out cities and wiping out whole communities without a single man moving more than to press a button.

The 'war of revenge' was not an undeclared war. Posters had mysteriously appeared all over Britain reading:

In retaliation for the humiliating Peace Treaty of 1919 which the German Government was forced to sign the hour has come when German honour must be avenged. Ignored by the signatories of the Washington Conference of forty years ago and therefore not pledged to peace, the Imperial Government considers itself fully justified in announcing that on and from the morning of Tuesday, April 13, 1962, a State of War will exist between Germany and Great Britain, unless the conditions imposed by the Imperial German Government and handed to the British Ambassador at Berlin a week ago—namely on April 1, 1962—have been accepted by Great Britain.

(sgd.) Johern von Kreutz.

Von Kreutz was described as 'the sabre-rattling Imperial Chancellor' who had come into power when the Republic was replaced by a new Emperor Wilhelm.

The British newspapers and public laughed at this threat and at the accompanying demand for a £10,000,000,000 indemnity. After all, Germany had an inadequate army, no navy whatever and an air fleet inferior to ours. But those who held the British nation's secrets knew that Germany had elaborate plans for bombarding England by radio-controlled aerial torpedoes from the Frisian Islands (and if that wasn't V2, what was it?).

The cover of the *Champion* containing instalment number two of this story showed a crowd in Ludgate Circus staring at a vast information board which read:

LATEST NEWS

Liverpool and Manchester were bombarded for two hours after daylight this morning.

Bombardment of Birmingham reported just begun.

London meanwhile was taking it in a big way. The news was grave enough to bring the King—King Albert—back from the North.

After the bombardment the Germans invaded. Their chief secret weapon was the walking machine, a robot-like tower on mechanical legs, armed with machine guns and poison gas, which patrolled English cities spreading havoc. There were also 'flaming balls'— 'a new form of spherical explosive,' and such chromatic novelties as a green ray and a red gas.

It must not be supposed that the Germans had a monopoly of inventions. The British leaders, with the fortifying names of General Duff-Cavan and General Sir Francis Drake, were able to counter with some very effective triphibians. The winning weapon proved to be a ray before which all metal vanished—navies dissolved at sea, aeroplanes disintegrated in the sky, spilling their human freight, and guns, tanks and even the trouser buttons of the infantry disappeared into nothingness.

It was a novel illustration of the old principle of catching your adversary with his trousers down.

CHAPTER XII

PLANETS AND LOST CITIES

Aᴄᴛᴇʀ ᴛʜᴇ atom bomb had been dropped on Hiroshima and
a dubious world had been invited to hail the birth of the
Atomic Age, someone rang up the editor of a 'scientifiction'
magazine in New York and suggested that Fact had at last caught
up with Fiction. Somewhat austerely, the editor replied that for a
considerable time past his contributors had been writing about the
state of affairs which would exist after the world had been destroyed.

Authors of scientific romances in the British blood-and-thunder
market were never in quite the same hurry to polish off the world.
One or two of them destroyed civilization, but usually gave it a
second chance—perhaps with the moss-grown ruins of the London
Underground as an example of what their forefathers could do
when they applied their energies to peaceful progress. Blowing up
the world or throwing it off its orbit into outer darkness were
considered bad form.

Possibly it was the *Champion*'s futuristic vision of a German
war of revenge (see last chapter) which inspired the Allied Newspapers' *Boys' Magazine* to go a step farther. In 1923 this lively
newcomer with the pink jacket described the war which destroyed
civilization in 1934. The story was Michael Poole's 'Emperor of
the World.' It had a memorable title picture showing the Emperor,
clothed in the skin of a wild beast, presiding at a savage Olympiad
amid the ruins of a great city, in the skyline of which stood the
reproachful outline of one half of the Tower Bridge.

The nations which initiated this death struggle were not individually specified, but were cloaked under names like the Quadruple Alliance. No details were given of the fighting, but the weapons were chemical. It was 'sufficient that man had created something more powerful than himself and against which he could devise no protection.' Professor Marckstein, the mad scientist who had done more than a little to precipitate the war, locked himself and a chosen few in an underground laboratory, and drugged everybody, including himself, with a serum which would keep them quiet for 200 years, or long enough to let the gases disperse. He was careful to ensure that he himself would be the first to wake. And he kept a few ray pistols handy, just in case.

By August 1934 the earth was 'much as it was at the morning of time.' By the year 2134, when the party came out of suspended animation, it had progressed little. The few descendants of those who had survived the world war in caves and remote places were wandering round in skins, carrying clubs. It was not difficult for anybody with the evil genius of a Marckstein equipped with a ray pistol to make himself emperor of the world. The youths of the party, however, did not care for the professor's leadership and fled to America, which again was in the possession of Red Indians. One of the tribal ancestors had left a message foretelling some such invasion as this and urging a policy of Isolation:

They will come again by sea and by air, but never again shall America join with Europe, though they speak fair words and utter many promises. There is but one thing to do when Europe comes to America again.

That one thing was to slay the invaders, who were promptly tied to the stake in the old-fashioned manner.

Hereabouts the story seems to have come rather precipitately to an end. In the space of a couple of hundred words or so the heroes toured the world, rallied the vestigial tribes everywhere, saw the spread of knowledge, the rebirth of radio and aircraft, the formation of Parliaments and the welding together of the peoples of the world, ruled by the Council of Three (the three youthful adventurers).

It was in the *Boys' Magazine* of about the same time that there appeared an exciting serial, 'The Raiding Planet,' describing the war between the Earth and the planet Thor in 1987. Wrote the author, Brian Cameron:

The years between 1923 and 1987 were remarkable by virtue of the colossal forward march made by the world's scientists. There had been extraordinary discoveries; extraordinary inventions were incorporated in the common life of the people.

The tides were harnessed and made to furnish power for the huge mills which thundered day and night along the coast. The sun's rays were captured by day and the electricity manufactured by their heat lighted whole countries at night. A means of transmitting power by wireless had been invented and the huge aeroplanes which plied the world's trade routes were propelled by small electric motors fed from tall steel towers set near the generating stations. The danger of fire in the air was thus practically eliminated and the only disaster which ever befell this method of locomotion occurred when the world's electrical workers came out on strike suddenly and cut off the current. Every machine flying at the time was immediately forced to descend.

Commercial shipping was a thing of the past and the only vessels to be seen upon the seas were the pleasure yachts of men of wealth or else vessels of the gigantic navies of the greater powers.

Among the novelties in the armaments line were the Wilkinson double-explosion gun, which fired a shell for eighty miles, at which point a second explosion in the shell propelled another projectile for sixty or seventy miles; and Flamvior's Gaz de Mort, one canister of which could destroy Paris.

In 1987 astronomers began to get excited about the new planet Thor, 'named after the great push Britain made in the European war of 60 years ago'—i.e. 1927. One professor announced that it was heading towards the earth at 40,000 miles an hour.

'That means,' said the professor, 'that unless something occurs to divert Thor from the course it is taking the event which is popularly known as the end of the world will be an accomplished fact in three weeks from now.'

The earth seemed to know what was coming to it. Quakes were frequent and mysterious fissures appeared everywhere. An epidemic of Fear ran round the world. In Trafalgar Square a speaker attracted an enormous crowd by proclaiming: 'Woe to the people of London, for death is upon them!' Another prophet tried the same game in

Paris, but the crowd, showing more spirit—or more fright—
hanged him on the spot.

When Thor had grown very big indeed in the sky the last
bastion of Britain collapsed: the Stock Exchange closed. Looting
began in the big cities. Downing Street crumbled under earth
stresses, and the Houses of Parliament were choked by hundreds
of refugees from the tidal wave which had engulfed Southwark.
Suddenly Thor stopped and began to circle the earth like a moon.
This looked like a respite, until Thor began to send out raiding
battleships, packed with thousands of men. The invasion was on.
Soon the air was full of Thorians in chain mail, each descending
individually with the aid of a small propeller behind his shoulders.

London by now was badly bruised. Whitehall and the Houses
of Parliament were in ruins. A 'caterpillar machine' had reared
itself in the air and fallen smack on the Marble Arch, where the
Cabinet were suspected of hiding. An eighty-foot tidal wave caused
by a burst dam swept down Bayswater Road. Towers of Terror,
each bowling along on a huge ball, were stretching out giant grabs
to pick up cars and shake out their occupants. Ray guns were
being erected by the invaders right across the Midlands. And a
Thorian plan was afoot to create a vast magnetic field to embrace
every division of the British Army, causing all items of metal
equipment to stick together—an even more embarrassing weapon
than depriving the enemy of his trouser buttons. Meanwhile,
lashed by Thorian foremen, slave gangs of Englishmen were
digging a gigantic circular pit for some unguessable purpose in
Huntingdonshire.

The rest of the world was being savaged too. Berlin and Vienna
had been destroyed, though Paris—as usual—had got off with an
occupation. England—as usual—was the one hope of the world.
And the one hope of England was the 'atom-destroyer,' a powerful
disintegrator which operated on the ray principle. It could bisect
an aerial battleship or a skyscraper considerably more quickly than
an oxy-acetylene flame could bisect a safe. The Thorians were
unable to counter it or to capture it.

Why had the Thorians invaded, anyway? The answer was that
theirs was a dying planet, and it was a question of finding new

living room or perishing. From the outer void Earth had seemed as good as anywhere. But unrealized by the Thorians the moving of their planet from its orbit had solved their problem for them. The axis had been altered and the poles had begun to melt. This meant—as any reader of 'scientifiction' knows—the unfreezing of brontosauri and mastodons and sabre-toothed tigers which had been locked for centuries in their remote caverns of ice. These were a bit of a nuisance for a while, but you can't have a new world without new (or rather, very old) problems.

The Thorians evacuated Earth in space-ships fired from the great pit of Huntingdonshire. They made a final vengeful effort to destroy Earth by moving up closer to fry everybody, but this attempt was frustrated by Earth's schoolboy delegates on Thor. At the end it seemed probable that the few Thorians remaining on Thor would settle down and make the most of the revived world left to them.

This was only the start of inter-planetary skull-duggery. A later story in *Boys' Magazine*—'Buccaneers of the Sky'—chronicled the departure of a fleet of spaceships, commanded by Lord Harkness, to the Moon in order to foil a plot by the emissaries of Venus. Having discovered the secret of moving heavenly bodies, the people of Venus, who had long wanted a moon of their own, had decided to divert our moon from its orbit and to set it spinning round Venus. That a 'have-not' planet should seek to help itself to bits of the Universe like this occasioned great indignation on Earth.

That attempt by Venus to steal the Moon was only one illustration of a failing which characterized the inhabitants of other planets: they were not sporting. Time after time, in stories of planetary adventure, this deficiency was stressed. The dwellers on alien stars might be, and usually were, ahead of us technically; they might have robots working for them as slaves; they might have attained the twin goals of perpetual motion and perpetual life; but they had no more sense of fair play than Neanderthal Man.

In 'The Raiding Planet,' for example, the two lads who were kidnapped from Earth and transported to Thor found themselves set down in a mighty arena to entertain the Emperor of Thor and his assembled subjects. Resigned to face bull, bear or lion, they were shocked to find that their adversary was a fighting machine:

It was a thing of steel which moved on a whirling ball at its base, in the manner of the Thorian tower. Above this ball was a square box-like structure, at each corner of which was a moveable arm holding a revolving knife. On the top of this was a smaller box of the same shape as the lower one, and in this was the brain of the machine. The thing was about the same height as a Thorian and as it moved across the sanded floor of the arena it gave a horrible impression of intelligence and grimness of purpose.

The robot was able to judge its distance from its opponents by electrically nerved feelers (presumably a form of radar) and to frame its approaches accordingly. Very soon it had its human adversaries at a disadvantage.

The Thorians were cheering wildly, anxious to see their mechanical idol—so synonymous with progress—slash its victims with its revolving knives and spill their blood about the arena. Their wish would have been gratified had not the boys' guardian professor arrived unexpectedly and yanked the machine's head off, to the crowd's fury.

Not only were the men of other worlds unsporting, they were humourless and void of all ordinary human emotions except the lust for power and the lust for revenge. They were too highly mechanized—that was the plain truth of it. Oddly enough there never seemed to be any women or children; the populace were apparently bred in laboratories. As fighters they lacked initiative and could be swatted in hundreds by any British schoolboy (especially as the lowered force of gravity on an alien planet gave schoolboys ten times their normal agility). In their civil wars— one group were always trying to become a Master Race— experience showed that whichever side could first call in the aid of a British schoolboy would win. One planet even sent a space-ship to fetch an Earth scientist to ascertain the cause of a mysterious plague among the people of the planet. The scientist rapidly diagnosed the complaint and prescribed lime juice.

Not that the inhabitants of other planets were necessarily human or even approximately human. In a *Union Jack* story entitled 'In Trackless Space' (1902) the Moon was found to be occupied by giant spiders fitted, for no very adequate reason, with electromagnets. A trip to Venus revealed only giant centipedes and scorpions. There was gold in vast quantities on the Moon, but the hero declined to allow it to be exploited for the admirable reason that there was enough gold causing trouble on Earth already.

The method of propulsion of a space-ship was left vague in those days.[1] Someone would just discover the secret of overcoming the force of gravity, just as someone else would trip across the secret of invisibility, and that was that. An anti-gravitational device would be incorporated in the sky-ship. You turned it one way to start and the other way to stop. As you were liable to be travelling at more than a million miles an hour you had to be careful how you handled it. The crook who had stowed away on board usually chose the difficult moment of deceleration to emerge from his hiding-place with a flame pistol.

There had to be a reason for inter-planetary travel. Mere lust for scientific knowledge was not enough. Sometimes (as has been seen) it was necessary to prevent the theft of the Moon or the wanton destruction of, say, the Pole Star. Sometimes it was necessary to check up on what another planet was doing in the Milky Way, or to forestall an attempt at colonizing useful nebulae. In the more advanced stories it was a case of protecting trade routes through Space. Or it might be necessary to do battle with a Space Emperor.

Those who today devour stories of inter-planetary adventure in American-style magazines like *Astounding Science Fiction* may find the details more plausibly worked out, but the basic plots are not necessarily more ingenious or audacious. The space-ship Llanvabon in one of these stories was introduced when she was decelerating at full force because she was 'a bare half light year from the Crab Nebula' (itself six light-years long) and a matter of 4,000 light-years from the Earth. Experts on board the atom-powered, radar-equipped Llanvabon had been photographing the Nebula on the journey 'by the light which had left it from 40 centuries since to a bare six months ago.' The space-ship's speed had been stepped up

---

[1] In the first recorded story of an interplanetary voyage—Bishop Godwin's *Man in the Moone* (1638)—the hero was carried to the Moon in twelve days by birds called 'gansas,' harnessed to an intricate framework.

to seven times the speed of light by an over-drive. She was equipped with blasters

. . . those beams of ravening destruction which take care of recalcitrant meteorites in a spaceship's course when the deflectors can't handle them. They are not designed as weapons, but they can serve as pretty good ones. They can go into action at 5,000 miles, and draw on the entire power output of a whole ship. With automatic aim and a traverse of five degrees, a ship like the Llanvabon can come very close to blasting a hole through a small-sized asteroid which gets in its way. But not on overdrive, of course.

That 'of course' points the difference between the super-confident science fiction of today and that of forty or fifty years ago, with its defensive footnotes. Another extract from a latter-day story in *Astounding Science Fiction* will show how the language and the mood have changed:

He was looking into a long, severely utilitarian room, lit only by flickering glows reflecting from the grouped scanner videos and the moving centre strip of the Ro-Eye Relay.
Standing back a few feet from the disks and frames and the fluxing panels was a lean man in Tech overalls, a knob micro adjuster in his hand. He was curiously rigid.
Lodner clawed at his belt, failed to find his disciplinary stun gun, turned to Horovic, who was entering behind him, and yanked the cruel stud-nosed electronic clubber from the chief guard's waist clip.
The Tech man said, 'Sir, I've done nothing.'
Lodner threw the gun on him. The Tech man tried to dodge. But the bolts sledged the quick-turning shoulder and head. The Tech man was slapped over. He lay huddled on the floor.
Lodner tossed the stun gun on a flange between the stills and the fluxing panels. 'I'll teach you to stand and gawk at me, you swine,' said Lodner coldly. . . .

While British authors always sought to teach Thorians and Plutons to play a straight bat, some American authors have used the universe as just another place in which to play cowboys and Indians. Mr. S. J. Perelman quotes this science-story description in his *Crazy Like a Fox* of the main street in Jungletown, a stop-over town full of clip joints somewhere in the Cosmos:

Here were husky prospectors in stained zipper-suits, furtive, unshaven space-bums begging, cool-eyed interplanetary gamblers, gaunt engineers

'*The thing curled itself round the space ship and its weight nearly pulled the machine to the ground. . . .*'—The Hotspur

in high boots with flare pistols at their belts, bronzed space-sailors up from Jovopolis for a carousal in the wildest new frontier-town in the System.

The hero of this particular story, 'Captain Future, Wizard of Science,' had a bodyguard which Mr. Perelman considers one of the most paralysing in modern fiction. It consisted of a white-faced, green-eyed, rubbery android, or synthetic man, and a giant metal robot with a pair of photo-electric eyes who carried a transparent box in which was housed a living brain, with two glittering lens-eyes.

Against this, an extravaganza in a recent British thriller, in which a hovering space-ship is encircled and dragged to the ground by a giant earth-worm is a trifle of the imagination. Or is it?

Closely akin to the inhabitants of other planets in that they lacked the sporting instinct and a sense of humour, and were too easily exploited by Master Races, were the inhabitants of Atlantis. This fabled land—first hinted at by Plato—was rarely discovered in the same place twice. Sometimes it appeared mysteriously as an island right in the middle of the shipping lanes; sometimes it rose and sank at the whim of the Lord of Atlantis; sometimes it was to be found snarled up in the Sargasso Sea; and once at least it was found flourishing in a gigantic air-lock at the bottom of the Atlantic. Ferrers Lord discovered a rival to Atlantis in Mysteria (*Boys' Friend*, 1905). This was a rising-and-sinking island which surrounded itself usually with a mysterious rosy glow but was capable of changing hue—in fact, it seemed to have most of the properties of a mighty Wurlitzer. It was an over-lush and over-odorous isle, full of armoured crabs and black owls as big as rocs. Ferrers Lord did well to blow it to smithereens.

As unpredictable in location as Atlantis was the City of El Dorado, which shifted between the Peru of the Incas and the Upper Amazon. The natives of El Dorado were rarely friendly, which is not surprising in view of the numerous attempts made by syndicates of crooks (and even honest men) to rob them of their basic raw material. Those inveterate discoverers of lost civilizations, the boys of St. Frank's, once chanced upon El Dorado (in Brazil) when it was being administered by the master crook, Professor

Zingrave. Their flying machine disabled, the boys found themselves marooned on an island of molten gold, from which they were eventually rescued in a giant chariot drawn by triceratops. The flying machine became airworthy again, and it only remained to beat off an attack by claw-winged pterodactyls before returning to England, home and school. Short of a love interest, it is hard to think what other ingredients could have been introduced into that memorable story.

But others may remember the lost England discovered by the boys of St. Frank's in the Antarctic. Warmed by a hot stream flowing below an unexplored part of the ice cap, this Kingdom of Wonder was inhabited by settlers of English descent, who had strayed there three centuries before. They wore olde Englishe smocks, their architecture was neo-Elizabethan and they talked prithee English. As so often happened, the explorers arrived just in time to take part in a civil war; in this case between the subjects of King Arthur and King Jasper, whose territories were separated by a mighty wall beside which the Great Wall of China was a trench in the ground.

That elusive temperate land beyond the Antarctic icecap had been cropping up for years. It had figured in Sidney Drew's serial 'Wings of Gold' in the first *Boys' Herald*, a story which began with the shooting of a mysterious bird-lizard in far southern latitudes and followed, week by week, with the shooting of pterodactyls (these always came first), labyrinthodons, plesiosauri, giant crustaceans, mastodons, dog-apes, and ape-men; with fitting accompaniments in the way of volcanic eruptions, meteor showers and sub-aqueous explosions.

In the case of a serial by Reginald Wray in the *Boys' Friend* (1915) the lost world with its full range of prehistoric monsters was located under the Yorkshire moors—a vast world complete with sea and sky buried beneath the earth's crust.

A lost civilization story—whether set in the Antarctic, the Himalayas, the Amazon or the high lands of Africa—was always a good excuse for trotting out the prehistoric zoo.[1] The reader

[1] Conan Doyle's *The Lost World*, which possibly inspired some of these stories, was published in 1912.

soon grew to know the warning signs. If it wasn't a strayed bird-lizard or a sea-serpent, it was an obscene smell rising from the primal mists in a valley where no man had trodden before. It was unnecessary for the explorer-hero to say, 'We are on the edge of the oldest things.' An author who worked affectionately through the Book of Evolution was John Hunter. Not content to leave his saurians in their lost valleys he must needs bring them to Britain. In 'The Menace of the Monsters' in an early issue of the *Boys' Magazine* he described the return of a vessel known as No. 913, 'homeward bound from a place that lay beyond the dark curtain of one of the world's unknown places, her open hatches emitting a sickening odour of musk and foulness, a slow steam of hot and monstrous living creatures.' Behind glass shot with wire two serpents lay, thicker than the body of a bull and 120 feet in length.

They stood, the two boys and the Big Game Hunter, in a hallway of the world that was before man trod the heated earth, in the presence of the things that waded in the stinking marshes of the forming world, that sunned themselves on the steaming mudflats, that fought and tore and ravened across this cooling universe aeons and aeons ago.

How the big game hunter proposed to off-load this old-fashioned cargo was not made clear. The point is of no consequence because the ship was wrecked and the animals made their way ashore. It was the invasion pattern all over again, with prehistoric monsters instead of German armies. Pterodactyls clawed down aircraft, stegosauri derailed the Royal Scot and invaded packed football grounds. A giant ape clung to one side of Tower Bridge and plucked a taxi from the opposite bascule. A dryptosaurus measured its length on Brighton pier, crushing it into the water. One motoring party found themselves driving into the jaws of a pelagosaurus, which had cunningly opened its mouth where a bridge had once been.

But the monsters did not have everything their own way. The wastage was considerable. One was torpedoed by a naval craft, another was bisected by the *Bremen*. Some killed each other, and some were slain by the most formidable foe of all—the English climate. What the monsters really missed was the good white mist they had been accustomed to. Nature played into their hands and sent a London fog. So the monsters, having concluded a triumphant provincial tour (with special attention to Newcastle), concentrated on long-suffering London. St. Paul's for once was spared, but before the last creature had been accounted for Nelson had been lashed from his monument. There was some satisfaction in the fact that the Admiralty Arch resisted all efforts by a dryptosaurus to overthrow it. It is one of the few London landmarks which have not been gutted by fire wrecked by gunfire or sapped by earthquake.

CHAPTER XIII

MAGNET AND GEM

EARLY IN THE Second World War a seventy-year-old author sat skimming critically through the current issue of the new literary magazine *Horizon*. He saw that it contained a picture which did not resemble a picture, a poem which did not resemble a poem and a story which did not resemble a story. From this he deduced with some accuracy that it must be 'a very high-browed paper indeed.'

But he was not really interested in the poems, the pictures and the stories. He kept turning back to an article on boys' school stories by a writer called George Orwell. The article came as a surprise to him: he was not to know then that it was only one of a series in which Orwell sought to assess the social significance of sundry neglected art forms, including the comic postcards of Donald McGill and the hard-boiled novels of James Hadley Chase.

The author found Mr. Orwell's article on boys' fiction to be 'entertaining' but misconceived. After all, the author himself, whose name was Charles Hamilton, alias Frank Richards, alias Martin Clifford, alias Owen Conquest, alias Winston Cardew, alias Hilda Richards, alias nearly a dozen other names, claimed to be something of an authority on school stories. He had been writing them for about thirty years at the rate of a million and a half words a year, and had been receiving £2,500 a year for his pains. To his publishers he was a prodigy; to his readers—under at least two of his pen-names—he was already a legend.

It was with particular exasperation that Charles Hamilton now read a statement by George Orwell that, since the school stories which had filled the *Magnet* and *Gem* for a generation could not all have been the work of one man, that was why they were written in a style easily imitated. The vast majority of the *Magnet* and *Gem* stories were in fact the work of one man, and that man was Charles Hamilton. Numberless authors had striven to imitate his style but—in his own view and equally in the view of his more discriminating admirers—they had failed. It was not enough for an imitator merely to borrow the familiar standardizations and stylizations. Only Hamilton could bring credibility to the academies of Greyfriars and St. Jim's. (A researcher has revealed that at least one deputy did not know in which county to put Greyfriars, a lapse which horrified the faithful.)

It was galling, too, to see Mr. Orwell arguing that the Greyfriars and St. Jim's stories were derived from the school stories of Desmond Coke and Gunby Hadath, authors to whom Charles Hamilton owed nothing; and that the slang was inspired by Kipling's *Stalky and Co.*

There was only one thing for Charles Hamilton to do: he would have to write a rebuttal of this onslaught and *Horizon* would have to publish it. Which *Horizon* did.

The reader will be aware (if he read the Introduction) that George Orwell charged boys' papers with encouraging snobbishness and cheap patriotism. He averred also that the stories ignored the harsh realities of life, funked any mention of sex[1] and habitually poked fun at foreigners. 'The mental world of the *Gem* and *Magnet*,' he summed up, was something like this:

The year is 1910—or 1940, but it is all the same. You are at Greyfriars, a rosy-cheeked boy of fourteen in posh tailor-made clothes, sitting down

---

[1] Mr. Noel Coward has registered a similar complaint. In his autobiography *Present Indicative* he claims to have derived great enjoyment in youth from reading *Magnet* and *Gem*, but adds: 'They were awfully manly decent fellows, Harry Wharton & Co., and no suggestion of sex, even in its lighter forms, ever sullied their conversation. Considering their ages, their healthy-mindedness was almost frightening.' Re-reading one of the later *Magnets* (*c.* 1937) he was conscious of a 'tender emotion.' 'There they all were, Harry Wharton, Frank Nugent and Billy Bunter, still "Ha-Ha-Ha-ing" and "He-He-He-ing" and still, after twenty-four years, hovering merrily on the verge of puberty.'

to tea in your study on the Remove passage after an exciting game of football which was won by an odd goal in the last half minute. There is a cosy fire in the study and outside the wind is whistling. The ivy clusters thickly round the old grey stones. The King is on his throne and the pound is worth a pound. Over in Europe the comic foreigners are jabbering and gesticulating, but the grim grey battleships of the British Fleet are steaming up the Channel and at the outposts of Empire the monocled Englishmen are holding the niggers at bay. Lord Mauleverer has just got another fiver and we are settling down to a tremendous tea of sausages, sardines, crumpets, potted meat, jam and doughnuts. After tea we shall sit round the study fire having a good laugh at Billy Bunter and discussing the team for next week's match against Rookwood. Everything is safe, solid and unquestionable. Everything will be the same for ever and ever. That approximately is the atmosphere.

Any *Horizon* readers who themselves read *Magnet* and *Gem* in their youth—and they were probably more numerous than might be expected—doubtless took a personal, if restrained, pleasure in Hamilton's spirited defence of himself and of his schoolboy creations.

What (asked Hamilton) was life like in 1910—the period which Orwell appeared to hold in peculiar horror?

I can tell him that the world went very well then. It had not been improved by the Great War, the General Strike, the outburst of sex-chatter, by make-up or lipstick, by the present discontents or by Mr. Orwell's thoughts upon the present discontents.

Young readers ought not to be allowed to worry over the instability of life, he said; a sense of security was good for them and made for happiness and peace of mind.

Mr. Orwell had been disappointed that sex was never mentioned in *Magnet* and *Gem*. These journals, pointed out Hamilton, were intended for readers up to the age of sixteen. 'If Mr. Orwell supposes that the average Sixth Form boy cuddles a parlour maid as often as he handles a cricket bat, Mr. Orwell is in error.'

On the charge of snobbishness, Mr. Hamilton had no need to apologize.

It is an actual fact that in this country at least noblemen generally are better fellows than commoners. My own acquaintance with titled Nobs is strictly limited; but it is my experience, and I believe everybody's that—excepting the peasant-on-the-land class, which is the salt of the earth—the higher you go up in the social scale the better you find the manners and the more fixed the principles. The fact that old families almost invariably die out is proof of this; they cannot and will not do the things necessary for survival.

In any case he claimed that a working-class boy at Greyfriars or St. Jim's was represented in a popular light.

Mr. Orwell would have told him that he is a shabby little blighter, his father an ill-used serf, his world a dirty, muddled rotten sort of show. I don't think it would be fair play to take his 2d. for telling him that!

Accused of habitually representing foreigners as funny, Hamilton merely pointed out that foreigners *were* funny. They lacked our sense of humour.

There was one criticism which Hamilton did not answer in *Horizon*, perhaps because he was not happy about his audience. That was that in all the millions of words about Greyfriars, St. Jim's and Rookwood there was never any mention of God, not even in the form of 'My God!' Some time later he disclosed in an article in *The Saturday Book* that this, too, was deliberate policy. He remembered with displeasure the way the Almighty was dragged into *Boy's Own Paper* stories by Kingston and Ballantyne, and resolved not to commit any similar error of taste.

Whatever he may have thought of the charge of 'drugging the minds of the younger proletariat into dull acquiescence in a system of which Mr. Orwell does not approve,' Hamilton returned to his labours. But a bigger blow was to fall. It was Dunkirk year; and in that early summer both *Magnet* and *Gem* and a score more boys' papers were discontinued. The toil of thirty years was over.

Now let's see how the *Magnet* and the *Gem* began. They were not, of course, the first popular boys' magazines to exploit school stories. The fathers of the boys who bought the first *Gem* could well remember reading the rather less inhibited adventures of Jack Harkaway at Pomona House School (see Chapter V).

In the first years of the new century school stories grew markedly more popular; the writers avoided the excesses of Jack Harkaway even as they avoided the anguish of *Eric, or Little by Little*. Hamilton, then free-lancing prolifically, proved to have a special

flair for school fiction, though others were turning it out too.[1]
It was in *Pluck* that he first wrote about St. Jim's. The earliest
boys there were Jack Blake, Herries and Digby of the School
House and Figgins & Co. of the New House. Later arrived the
monocled Arthur Augustus d'Arcy ('Bai jove, deah boy!'), second
son of Lord Eastwood, whose passion in life was the study of
trouserings. He is said to have been based on an unusually
elegant sub-editor (a profession not usually remarkable for
immaculacy).

In 1907 Hamilton was invited to turn out a series of fortnightly
school stories for a new magazine to be called the *Gem*. He was
also invited to find himself a suitable nom-de-plume, and eventually
settled on Martin Clifford.

But Martin Clifford did not open the *Gem*. The cover of the
first number showed a bulldog bloodily at grips with a python—an
incident in an adventure story called 'Scuttled.' Clifford did not make
his début until No. 3 with 'Tom Merry's Schooldays.' The school
was Clavering College. Newly arrived Tom was considerably
embarrassed by the attentions of his nurse, Miss Priscilla Fawcett.
He found himself in a study with Harry Manners, Lowther and
Gore. But all was not well at Clavering. One day there was much
speculation because a stout gentleman with a fur-lined coat called
to see the Head. All too soon 'the grip of the moneylender fell on
Clavering, and the fine old buildings came down to make room
for a newly discovered coal seam.' Tom Merry was consoled by
the news that he would be transferred to St. Jim's.

Behind this outrage on a venerable seat of learning (who said
that harsh reality never impinged on a school story?) the astute
reader of the day may have deduced an editorial merger. Henceforth the St. Jim's stories from *Pluck* were to be amalgamated
with the Tom Merry yarns in the *Gem*. In succeeding stories
Merry, Manners and Lowther all made their several ways to St.

[1] Writing in *Lilliput* (August 1947) Walter Tyrer, self-confessed author of
20,000,000 words of popular fiction, said: 'For years I wrote about mysterious
public schools with neither discipline nor lavatories, where everything happened
in the same queer place called the Quad and my characters never emerged from
an odd form called the Shell.'
Few will wish to upbraid Mr. Tyrer for his reticence about lavatories.

Jim's, there to be known for the next thirty years as The Terrible
Three of the Shell.

The change of schools was a bit hard on Tom Merry, who had
been well ragged already on joining Clavering. This was the scene
when he arrived at St. Jim's:

Jack Blake of St. Jim's fell into the arms of Herries, while Digby
collapsed into the embrace of Arthur Augustus d'Arcy.

The chums of Study No. 6 in School House seemed completely overcome.

'What is it?' murmured Blake in tones of exaggerated faintness.
'What can it be? I wonder if it has a name?'

'It is something new,' said Digby. 'I have never seen anything like
it before off a Christmas tree. Fancy meeting that!'

'It is weally too extwaordinary,' said d'Arcy. He pushed Digby into
a sitting position on the step and solemnly adjusted his eyeglass, and
through it took a survey of the wrathful Tom Merry. 'It is alive. I
can see its features move. What a stwange object!'

This elaborate display was conducted in full presence of Tom
Merry's nurse, who was chaperoning her charge. Not surprisingly
she began to wonder whether St. Jim's was all it was cracked up
to be. However, Merry was strong enough to stand up for himself
and soon earned more suitable recognition. His stock rose after
he had helped Ferrers Locke, the detective (of Baker Street), to
investigate some nefarious activity in the vicinity of St. Jim's.
Said the detective afterwards:

'You've been a lot of help to me in this case. I am deeply obliged to
you and I shan't forget it. I do not know what you will be when you
leave school, my boy. But if you want a start in life as a detective there'd
be a place for you as assistant to Ferrers Locke. You can bear that in
mind. Good-bye.'

Thus Tom Merry might easily have become a Tinker or a
Nipper, but he seems to have preferred to be the leader of the
Terrible Three. Ferrers Locke (a relative of Dr. Locke of Grey-
friars) grew tired of waiting and acquired the services of Jack
Drake, who was to masquerade when occasion demanded as the
duffer James Duck; a cynical example of playing ducks and drakes.

The *Gem* was by now prospering. It became a weekly, which
meant twice as much work for Hamilton. Then the restless schemers

of Amalgamated Press, quick to distinguish a steady demand from a passing craze, had the idea of launching a companion paper to the *Gem*. They looked speculatively at Hamilton. He was wasting a good deal of his time on music and art. Obviously he ought to be properly harnessed. They pressed him to do the same for the *Magnet* as he was doing for *Gem*. Hamilton, with only slight misgivings, agreed. He ceased composing songs. After all this demand might not last long, and he was well able to satisfy it. Actually, the demand lasted for a generation.

For the *Magnet* Hamilton, under his best-known pseudonym Frank Richards, invented a new school, Greyfriars. Here he launched his most famous character Billy Bunter—'a really first-rate character,' as even Mr. Orwell has testified; a character who was to become a household word not only in Britain but in the more improbable parts of Empire.

The first story in the *Magnet* was entitled 'The Making of Harry Wharton.' It started with Colonel Wharton draining a glass of port at Wharton Lodge, and saying, with an air of decision, 'Send Harry Wharton to me.' His nephew entered with a bad grace. He was wilful and headstrong, completely wild and given to insulting his tutor. There was but one solution: Greyfriars.

On the train Wharton met Frank Nugent and fought with him, unsuccessfully. Wharton at this stage did not know how to scrap and that was fatal. Nugent, the bloodshed over, offered a gift of toffee, which was spurned. Soon Wharton found himself in the same study in the Remove as Nugent, Bunter and the bully Bulstrode. The job now was to learn how to master Bulstrode. His stock rose when he saved Nugent from drowning; so that was one firm ally. . . .

The two juniors—friends now and for life henceforth—shook hands upon the compact. And so Harry Wharton faced his difficulties again to fight his battles out with a true chum by his side to help him win.

Gradually he triumphed—rescuing a lad from drowning or a maid from burning—until he became the established leader of the Famous Five (Harry Wharton, Bob Cherry, Frank Nugent, Johnny Bull and Hurree Jamset Ram Singh).

William George Bunter, of Bunter Court, the Fat Owl of the

Scene from an earlier Greyfriars—'Tom Torment, or The Lads of Laughington School'

Remove, leading keyholer and tuck fancier of Greyfriars, was meanwhile being groomed for stardom. It has been said that he was derived from four persons—one a fat sub-editor (the staff of Amalgamated Press again), another an acquaintance who was always blinking over his spectacles, another a person who was always expecting but never receiving a postal order, and an un-named Victorian statesman of more than ordinary fatuousness. The owner of 'the tightest trousers in Greyfriars' (for some reason they were striped horizontally and vertically, instead of just vertically) was the perfect butt. He had few praiseworthy qualites, other than the power to incite mirth. He would borrow money with no intention of paying it back, he would pirate another man's tuck without a qualm. Therefore no one felt markedly sorry when dogs ran away with his sausages, when he sank his teeth into decoy pies filled with pepper, when pins punctured his hide or when he slipped or was thrown into stream, fountain, barrel or horse trough. Withal he was never really unpopular—a fat boy never can be. His machinations were so barefaced and his *bon-*

homie so suspect that it was a fellow's own fault if he was taken in
by them. His eager 'I say, you fellows—' generally earned an
exasperated 'Kick him, somebody.' Doomed to be the object of
everybody else's japes, Bunter devised retaliatory ones and was
the victim of those too.

Bunter never walked anywhere; he rolled. He did not possess
hands, but paws. He did not speak, he bleated. Where other boys
laughed 'Ha! Ha! Ha!' Bunter laughed 'He! He! He!' Under the
simplest cross-examination he was a total loss. Here he is accused
of playing pranks with a pin:

'No, sir! Nothing of the kind,' stuttered the confused fat Owl. 'I never
had a pin, sir. Besides, fellows are allowed to have pins, sir. I—I—I—
was going to pin a page into my Latin grammar, sir. Not that I had a
pin, sir!' added Bunter cautiously. 'You can ask Skinner, sir. He knows
—he gave it to me.'

From a modest début, Bunter grew steadily in popularity until
in due course the cover of the *Magnet* carried as a sub-title 'Billy
Bunter's Own Paper.' His fame was enough to warrant the creation
in a girls' paper of one Bessie Bunter; but that is another story.

Soon after Wharton got his measure of the bully Bulstrode,
Bob Cherry arrived. He was described as a 'finely built, nimble
lad with shoulders set well back and head well poised. His hair
was thick and curly and he wore his cap stuck on the back of it.
His face would not have been called handsome but it was so pleasant
and cheerful that it did you good to look at it.' And then arrived
a survivor from another school tragically but unavoidably closed
down—the Nawob of Bhanipur, Hurree Jamset Ram Singh. After
Bunter he is one of the best-remembered characters of Greyfriars.

His complexion, of the deepest, richest olive showed him to be a
native of some Oriental clime, and though clad in the ordinary Eton
garb of the schoolboy there was a grace and suppleness about his figure
that betrayed the Hindoo. Slim and graceful as he was, however, there
was strength in the slight form, and although the lips and the dark eyes
were smiling there was resolution about the chin and a keen observer
would have seen that the Indian was no mean antagonist if put upon
his defence.

Singh's greeting from Bulstrode was slightly less than cordial:

'My only pyjama hat! You should have taken the other turn to the lunatic asylum.'

'If I have made mistake the apologize is terrific. But if this is not the lunatic asylum what are you doing here, my esteemed friend?'

This stung Bulstrode to cry 'Nigger!' whereupon the Nawob speedily showed that he had the necessary basic training to hold his own at Greyfriars.

If he had one ambition, it was

'to induce my esteemed and ludicrous chums ceasefully to stop talking slangfully and to use speakfully only the pureful and honoured English language as taught by my learned and preposterous native tutors in Bhanipur.'

Charles Hamilton did not mind saddling himself with a character who spoke Babu English, or for that matter with characters who spoke pidgin English ('Me tellee whoppee. Me solly. Only jokee'); German ('Vell, Bulstrode, I tink you vas vun pully and a prute,'); French ('Nom d'un nom d'un nom—I am smozzer viz somezing!'); or American ('I'm allowing those guys are sure loco'). Once the idiom was established it was only a matter of practice. At some early stage Hamilton (or his editors) had decided to standardize all exclamations. 'Oh haddocks!' 'Oh scissors!' 'Oh my hat!' and 'What the thump—' were suitable comments on almost any irregular happening. For special occasions there was 'Oh my only Aunt Sempronia!' Bunter's yells were rendered as 'Yarooh!' or 'Yaroop!' the number of 'o's' depending on the intensity of the anguish. Spluttering, as on a mouthful of soot, was denoted by variations on 'Gurrrrgh.' A typical exclamatory passage is this description of the punishment of Cardew, of St. Jim's:

Reilly picked a cricket stump out of the cupboard.
'Lay it on!' said Tom.
Whack, whack, whack, whack!
Cardew struggled furiously.
Levison and Clive looked on grimly.
Cardew had asked for it, and he was getting it now.
There was no mistake about that.
Reilly seemed to think he was beating carpets.
Whack, Whack, Whack!
'Oh! Oh! Yah! Oh! Leave off!' yelled Cardew.

'Word of honour wanted,' said Tom Merry.
'Go and eat coke!'
Whack, whack, whack!
'Yow-ow-ow! Leave off! I—I—I—I'll promise if you like.'
'Good enough! Honour bright?'
'Yes,' panted Cardew.
He slid from the table, flushed and furious.
The jury filed out of the study.
Justice was satisfied.

There can have been few readers of the *Magnet* and the *Gem*—
in the humblest or the highest schools of London or Glasgow,
Calcutta or Singapore—who could not find one character with
whom to identify themselves, or their playmates. Periodically
were published character studies of all the leading figures, with
pen and ink drawings. In these potted biographies it was to be
noted that no one was insufferably good or irredeemably bad. Even
Vernon-Smith, the Bounder of Greyfriars, son of a *nouveau riche*,
was by no means without virtue. Recklessness, not viciousness,
was his failing; and that was why he was never expelled, though
that fate constantly threatened.

Charles Hamilton declined to allow his style to be cramped by
preserving the unity of place. The boys of St. Jim's and Greyfriars, like those of St. Frank's, were for ever touring the globe
on their holidays, though Hamilton seems to have drawn the
line at El Dorados and Lost Valleys. A St. Jim's party went to
America, for instance, to visit the ranch of Tom Merry's uncle,
and had numerous excitements in the Wild West. On a treasure
hunt in wildest Africa Bunter became king of a fierce cannibal
tribe, and seems narrowly to have escaped the pot.

Refreshed by travel, back the lads would come for a new round
of priceless japes, dropping soot-bags from windows, squirting
ink through keyholes, filling each other's toppers with treacle,
upturning the desks of swots, ragging new masters, breaking up
love affairs, clashing with militant suffragettes, capturing spies,
tracking down ghosts, and rescuing each other's sisters from gypsies.
Once the Fourth Form at St. Jim's suffered the excruciating ordeal
of being taught by a woman, who called the boys by their Christian
names. Sooner or later every boy in the school would be accused

(and later acquitted) of theft. Every now and again a crook would be appointed a master, or an old boy who had been expelled in disgrace would return to plot a cunning revenge. One such committed a 'standing offence to Greyfriars' by erecting a sign near the school stating that he, late of Greyfriars, was prepared to repair boots and shoes with efficiency and dispatch. Periodically some too-enterprising youth would be dunned by bookmakers. Periodically some boy's father would lose all his money, through trying to pay off liabilities incurred by dishonest fellow-directors, and the boy would be threatened with a transfer to a more modest establishment. When this calamity threatened the editor would never fail to invite the sympathy of all his elementary school readers. Tom Merry had a bad spell. He spent his Christmas holidays down and out in London, too proud to tell his pals of his plight. The Head of St. Jim's heard about it and offered him a job as temporary form master—a job he was gratified to accept. But if Merry thought the boys' sympathy was such that they would refrain from japing him in his new role, he was disappointed.

New boys from the outposts of Empire were constantly arriving at Greyfriars and St. Jim's. If it wasn't an Australian bringing his own kangaroo it was a young cowboy riding a horse bareback. These Dominion recruits were always well received and soon conformed to pattern.

It would be ungallant as well as misleading to omit mention of Cousin Ethel, who at one time (c. 1911) cropped up in almost every story in the Gem. D'Arcy, whose relative she was, used to invite her to St. Jim's whenever he could. She was a great favourite with the Terrible Three, who were prepared to scratch from a football match in order to entertain her, even if it meant losing the match. And well might they be loyal to her, for did she not once personally intervene to save them from a flogging, herself receiving a sharp cut on the arm in the process?

According to the illustrations, Cousin Ethel had a pretty face, a smart feather in her hat, and a skirt only a few inches from the ground. Figgins, of the New School, had an especial weakness for her. In the story 'Figgy's Folly' he ran away from school in order to see her safely to Paris, where she was to attend finishing school.

o

Ethel was travelling with an elderly female relative who, Figgins felt, was an inadequate protection against the attentions of Frenchmen. In the train to Paris the lovesick youth became furiously jealous of an elderly Frenchman who entered the compartment and started to make conversation. Figgins' feelings towards Frenchmen were those of all right-thinking fellows at St. Jim's:

That a man old enough to be the father of a big family should take such minute care of his personal appearance offended Figgins' notion of the fitness of things . . . that a man of elderly years should cram his feet into boots too small for them filled Figgins with disgust . . . that an elderly gentleman should have no better business than to get himself up as a young fellow and go about making himself obnoxious to decent and sensible people seemed an outrage to Figgins. . . .

But that was not the full indictment against this unseemly foreigner:

The elderly Frenchman moved with grace and elegance but at the same time with a slight suspicion of stiffness, and once or twice Figgins thought he heard a slight creak—which confirmed him in his suspicion that the Frenchman wore stays. Figgins had heard that Frenchmen wore corsets to improve the elegance of the figure. Words could not adequately express Figgins' opinion on the subject.

Cousin Ethel had preserved a certain coolness towards Figgins so far. Their fingers had overlapped for a second or two on the boat, but she still called him 'Figgins.' When the train was wrecked (as it was bound to be on a French railway) and Figgins had distinguished himself in rescue operations, Ethel went so far as to catch both his hands and press them to her lips. Figgins came back with 'Ethel, dearest!' which made her blush and turn away. Later when he apologized for his jealousy in the train, Ethel 'pressed her hand to his lips,' though whether to silence him or to let him kiss her fingers is not clear. Finally Figgins expressed the wish that someone would punch his head, but all that happened was that Ethel pressed his hand. Figgins, of course, returned to St. Jim's a hero, instead of a disgraced runaway.

Girl cousins and sisters caused a number of embarrassing moments in these stories. 'Ashamed of His Sister' (*Gem*) told of the ordeal of the poser Valentine Bishop when he learned that his sister was going to visit him at St. Jim's:

Maud with her sweet and patient face, her plain dress of materials cheaper than those worn by the maids at St. Jim's, and her long fingers showing only too plainly signs of long, long sewing which she did partly that her brother might have pocket money in his pockets. . . .
Ashamed of his people!
To what lower depths of meanness could he have descended? Ashamed of the sister, the kind patient sister who worked for him and who regarded him as the finest and the grandest fellow the earth held!
Oh hang! Oh dash it!

There were other boys who were ashamed of their brothers, or ashamed of their fathers. One had the mortification of seeing his convict brother in handcuffs at the local railway station. The ending to this story does not read like vintage Hamilton:

Strangely enough the shout [that the convict was innocent] rings through the stone wall to the convict. But Convict 79 does not shout. The tears are thick upon his eyelashes and he sinks upon his knees on the stone floor, his hands clasped together, to render thanks for his freedom to the Giver of all good. And Lynn, after a moment's silence, joins him there. In that moment all is atoned for; it is light—light and happiness—after long darkness, for the man who has been pent in the convict cell shunned by his friends and disowned by his brother.

There was a third academy created and maintained by Charles Hamilton under the name of Owen Conquest: Rookwood, in the *Boys' Friend*. While St. Jim's boasted the Terrible Three and Greyfriars the Famous Five, Rookwood offered the Fistical Four (Jimmy Silver & Co.). It was a typical Hamilton school, in that only the unwary sat down without first brushing away the bent pin, or entered a room without first throwing open the door to bring down the can of paint balanced above it.

The code was the same: no sneaking—that remained the ultimate crime; no gambling, drinking or wenching; ragging of French and German masters tolerated, ragging of games masters discouraged.

The secret of the common identity of Frank Richards, Martin Clifford and Owen Conquest was carefully—and most successfully—preserved. Many a false trail was laid. At one stage Martin

Clifford had a series describing the school days of 'Frank Richards & Co.' at a backwoods school at Cedar Creek. One editor is said to have written a piece of whimsy about meeting Hamilton, Richards and Clifford together in the flesh.

Since the story of Charles Hamilton's aliases has been told in recent times in such diverse organs as *Hutchinsons' Pie*, *Picture-Post*, and *Saturday Book*, not to mention Forces' publications like *Gen* and *Soldier*, he probably no longer has to settle arguments about whether he is a man or a syndicate, or whether he is alive or dead. Collectors of old boys' magazines claim to be well-informed now on his pseudonymous activities; in amateur journals his works are discussed with affection verging on reverence.

A certain tendency to repetition is to be seen in the Hamilton style. At times a sub-editor surgically disposed could have cut out every other sentence without impairing continuity; it would have been a futile labour, however, because indignant readers would at once have exclaimed, 'This is not the genuine article.' They revelled in the repetitious style. Here is a characteristic passage:

Argument was waxing warm among the Famous Five of the Greyfriars Remove.

Four members of the famous Co. were trying to dissuade the other member—Bob Cherry! Bob was not to be dissuaded.

Bob's face, generally as bright and cheery as the spring sunshine, was clouded. It was grim with wrath. For once, the best temper in the Remove had failed its owner!

Bob seldom, or never, remembered offences for long. But it was not ten minutes since a heavy hand had boxed his ear! That ear was still scarlet, and had a pain in it!

Not that Bob was a fellow to make a fuss about a spot of pain. But ears were not boxed at Greyfriars School. It was an indignity. It was one of the things that were not done. . . .

As against that Hamilton brought in an occasional allusion or piece of out-of-the-way learning. So-and-so would choose, like Agag, to read delicately . . . 'The glory had departed from the House of Israel, so to speak . . .' 'Contempt, the Oriental proverb says, will pierce the hide of the tortoise.' But how many readers were able to relish the enormity of the howlers which d'Arcy and the others perpetrated when construing Latin?

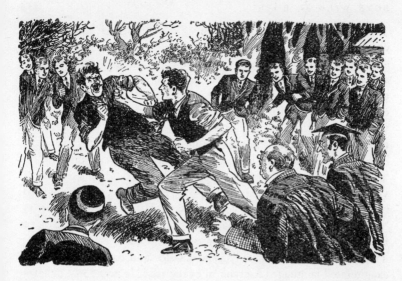

The Greyfriars games master deals with the cad who came back to disgrace his alma mater.—The Magnet

The astronomical output which Hamilton sustained for thirty years does not seem to have tied him down to a desk for an eighteen-hour day. (If a million and a half words—his yearly stint—is hard for the ordinary reader to imagine, it is about nineteen times the length of this book.) He has said that being naturally idle he worked only in the mornings. Throughout, his characters never lost their verve, their essential boyishness. That their adventures were sheer escapism it would be hard to deny. Hamilton's answer might be, 'And why not?' Only those who believe that schoolboys should be reared on stern and bitter realities will attempt to explain why not.

It is not correct to say that World War Two killed Billy Bunter. In 1947 he could be found inviting himself to tea at Sparshott School, in a shilling series published in London by William Merrett. Hamilton also launched Oakhurst and Ferndale Schools for a Manchester publisher, and his 'Chronicles of Carcroft' have run in *Hutchinsons' Pie*. Anyone in doubt about the present-day status of Bunter might like to know that his adventures are available in Braille.

St. Frank's School has already been touched upon in the chapter dealing with Nelson Lee, the detective who became a schoolmaster there. In many ways it was modelled on Greyfriars and St. Jim's, though there was never quite the same light and carefree atmosphere about the place. The characters included such derived types as Hussi Rangit Lal Khan, 'a dusky son of India with typical, characteristic features' (lacking more specific information than this, the artist was hardly to be blamed for representing him as an English boy with a dark complexion); Yung Ching, 'a typical Chinese boy of the upper class, thoroughly westernized, very tricky, although pretending to be innocent. Good-natured, but difficult to understand; very deep'; the Hon. Douglas Singleton, 'languid by nature, generous and easy-going and a slacker in form'; Sir Montie Tregellis-West, out of the same stable; Timothy Tucker—'speaks in a peculiar shrill voice and uses grotesque and exaggerated language. A crank in every way. Is popularly believed to be "touched," but is really well aware of all he is doing. Is a bold agitator . . .'; and a remarkably unattractive character called Enoch Snipe—'slightly hunchbacked, long neck, protruding head, habitual foxy expression, protruding red-rimmed watery eyes, scanty hair, a crawly cringing nature, will take a blow from a fag and creep away, but is cunning, vindictive and venomous . . . an out-and-out worm.' Perhaps it was part of the secret of Charles Hamilton that he did not admit quite such out-and-out worms to Greyfriars and St. Jim's. But Edwy Searles Brooks, who turned out most of the St. Frank's yarns, wrote a brisk and always readable story.

One of the more memorable episodes at St. Frank's was the Communist revolt of 1921, when the school was divided into Rebels and Loyalists. The revolt was the work of agitators, of course, and behind the agitators was Mr. Trenton, one of the masters. Smooth-tongued but a 'black-hearted scoundrel,' he was trying to cause the downfall of Dr. Stafford, 'the dear old Head.' He had succeeded in secretly doping the Head with a drug each dose of which resulted in an exhibition of terrible violence and savagery. These outbursts had an unfortunate effect on the less disciplined members of St. Frank's. There were meetings of protest. Then at the close of the Christmas holidays some of the dissidents, arriving a day or two earlier, stormed the Ancient House and refused to leave it until their demands for reform were granted. Timothy Tucker was the ringleader. When Nelson Lee expostulated with him he retorted:

'You do not seem to realize that the regime of tyranny and bloated autocracy is over. In fact the time has now arrived when the humble slaves come into their own. Hitherto the modern schoolboy has been downtrodden and enslaved. We have decided to end this state of affairs. This great blow has been struck with the intention of setting an example for every other school in the kingdom to follow.'

At this Nelson Lee 'laughed outright,' and the Loyalists, lacking his sense of humour, 'yelled with anger and shook their fists.'

Tucker and three of his confederates put their heads together and called themselves the Supreme Council of the Revolution. Their word was law. They issued a manifesto entitled 'For the Cause of Liberty,' which read:

'The Rebels in our command are all members of the new schoolboy union, a body which has been organized and invented for the good of every British schoolboy. . . . Masters must unconditionally surrender all control to the boys. Form councils will be inaugurated and we, the Supreme Council, will undertake to supervise the whole work of propaganda and organization. . . .'

Stating that the Council was willing to send a deputation on condition the members were not seized, the manifesto ended:

'Freedom is demanded! Liberty is the right of every one of you!'

Surprised—very surprised—were the Rebels when a notice was posted up in the Head's name stating that he had seriously considered the proposals advanced, and had agreed to the formation of Form Councils as an experiment. This notice, like most notices at St. Frank's, was a hoax. Nelson Lee, who knew that the Head had not issued it, nevertheless advised the Head not to disown it. Far better, he argued in his new role of political adviser, to let the Communists come a cropper of their own accord, rather than to try to suppress them by force, and thus breed the sense of injustice in which Communism would thrive.

The cover of the next number—'The Communist School'—showed a class of boys behaving as Communists. One was out in front arguing with the master, two others were half-sitting on their desks chatting, and a fat boy was scoffing a tray of jam tarts on a small table beside him. The desks were in irregular rows. Only the Loyalists sat to attention.

But the blackest hour was yet to come. One of the Head's more unfortunate outbreaks coincided with a visit of the heavily-titled Board of Directors, on whom he committed grave assault and battery. Shortly afterwards he and Nelson Lee were removed from office for their incompetent handling of the situation, and the rascally Trenton was appointed headmaster.

St. Frank's was not the only school in the grip of Communism. Explained one of the conspirators to his associates:

'It is in the great public schools of England the young mind receives its education. And if we can only commence our propaganda at school and thoroughly get our doctrines fixed in the minds of the coming generation the results of our efforts will be far-reaching and abundant. It will be a long process, but that is only to be expected.'

'Too long,' said one of the plotters, who wanted to see bloodshed.

It turned out that Nelson Lee was right. The schoolboy Communists and the crooks exploiting them overplayed their hand. At the end Lee was able to explain to the juniors:

'The whole thing is an insidious propaganda among the youth of this country. Quite a number of people may laugh at the whole thing and say that it is an absurd scare. They will declare that the boys of Britain are too sensible to listen to such rubbish. But people who talk in that way are all wrong. When the mind is young it is liable to get wrong ideas fixed. And such ideas stick. . . . The boys grow up with these notions firmly instilled, and although they may not actually know it they have a certain secret sympathy with this revolutionary movement. Such an affair is liable to be extremely dangerous. There is nothing so deep-rooted as a secret propaganda of this kind. I am very thankful to say that I have been successful in bringing the whole scheme to an untimely end.'

Luckily next week there was a great flood at St. Frank's (which

'Ow! Ooooogh! Aytishoo! Grooooogh!' gurgled Bunter.—The Magnet

had already been ravaged by a great fire) and the whole unfortunate episode was rapidly forgotten. Except, perhaps, by Mr. Orwell.

When their school was not in the throes of revolution or being machine-gunned under searchlights the boys of St. Frank's had friendly contacts with Irene & Co. of a neighbouring girls' school. Edward Oswald Handforth, who was affluent enough (and old enough) to run an Austin Seven, was at an advantage here. Such fraternization, however, was too much for Master T. E. Pattinson, of Walthamstow, who wrote in to protest. He was in a minority. Shortly afterwards the author of the offending story wrote:

In the November 22nd issue I had occasion to point out to Master Pattinson that his dislike of Irene & Co. in the stories was a little selfish and unfair. . . . But it now gives me the greatest pleasure to report that Master Pattinson has acted like the real sportsman I always hoped him to be. . . . He agrees that Irene & Co. have a perfect right in the St. Frank's district and that any girls have an equal right to be readers of the Old Paper.

It was in 1933, when the boys of St. Frank's were cruising on the yacht of Lord Dorrimore (the biggest schoolboy of them all) in China Seas, that the announcement was made:

Last issue of *Nelson Lee*.

But our chums of St. Frank's and our editor invite you to meet them again in the *Gem*. From now on *Nelson Lee* and the *Gem* are one paper.

That kind of merger (this was for 'policy reasons') usually bodes ill for one or other party. St. Frank's stories went to the back of the book, but they fought strongly. In the winter of 1933 Lee found himself in charge of the flying section of St. Frank's touring the unknown Amazon in an airship. (Parents had in all cases been consulted and an examination had been held to select the lucky lads.) From these operations, as from all their far-flung operations, all our schoolboys returned. They were still around in 1939, drilling in uniform and getting ready for a smack at Hitler.

A feature of the Greyfriars, St. Jim's and St. Frank's weeklies was the incorporation of a 'school magazine' purporting to give latest news and gossip, and to be edited by a different boy each week. Here solemn arguments went on over 'Should tuck shops be abolished?' Here tables of fictitious sports fixtures were meticulously kept. And here, in response to repeated demands, were printed the names of all the fellows in the Remove, the Fourth or the Shell, sometimes study by study.

In World War One there was a separate publication called the *Greyfriars Herald*, which tempted its readers with offers of 'monster tuck hampers,' the kind which in normal times were broached nightly in the dormitories of Greyfriars and St. Jim's. To William Bunter this open-handedness with foodstuffs must have seemed the final injustice, for already he had been paraded by his more patriotic chums with a notice on his chest reading: 'The Prize Hog. This animal has been caught helping the Germans by wasting the food supplies.'

The *Greyfriars Herald* was 'edited by Harry Wharton,' and listed as 'fighting editor' Bob Cherry. One early issue advised schoolboys not to read it under the desk but to 'show it to your schoolmaster.' It added:

Schoolmasters are sometimes regarded as preoccupied, narrow-minded individuals who take no personal interest in the fellows committed to their charge; but I know that such is not the case. As a general rule a master is also a friend and a jolly good friend.

Some of the answers to correspondents in the St. Frank's Magazine read oddly:

Lord Thomas (Wisbech): Haven't had time to read your letter . . . the pencil was too faint. Write it again in ink, and I'll answer it. You are the first Peer of the Realm I've known to write in this slovenly fashion.

But in face of a statement in an official history of the Amal-gamated Press that Royal princesses had written letters to the Rainbow it would be ungracious to suspect the bona fides of Lord Thomas of Wisbech.

Other replies to correspondents were slanging matches, or studied facetiousness:

Larry Brown (Sussex): It's a good job for you there was no proper address on your letter or I'd run you to earth and spiflicate you. Of course I've got as much sense as a busted-up hosepipe. I've got more . . . .

Archibald D'Arcy (E.C.): What's the idea of sealing your letter with a blot of blood?

Joan of Arc (Bradford): Here, I say! Do I write love-letters ? ? ?xxx!!! What next? I should jolly well think I don't. It takes me all my time to answer all those other letters. Besides I don't believe in it.

Then there were the 'Pen Pals' pages, which gave an illuminating picture of where the Magnet and the Gem circulated. Readers were invited to state with whom they wished to correspond and on what subjects. Here are typical entries:

Abu Baker bin Ali Bashah, Kampong Kuchai, Ipoh, Perak, F.M.S., Malaya: age 14–17; photography, fretwork, cycling.

Miss B. Srini, 20, Pulau Tikus Lane, Penang; girl correspondents, age 15–18; views, autographs, books, film stars and films. America, England, Australia, Egypt, Persia and Honolulu.

Miss R. Cheater, 171, Upper Newtonards Road, Belfast, Northern Ireland; girl correspondents, age 16–18; any topic; anywhere except British Empire.

G. Hershkovitz, 18, Beit Hasheva Street, Tel-Aviv, Palestine; age 14–16; stamps, sports, postcards; Eire, Australia, Canada, South Africa, British West Indies and Pacific Islands.

It was noteworthy that girls usually wished to correspond only with girls. Other readers, by design or accident, gave no hint of their sex.

Finally, let no one go away under the delusion that the kind of things which happened in school stories never happen in real life. The newspaper files of early 1947 contain a report of a court case in which one headmaster was alleged to have banded his boys together to storm and seize another headmaster's school.

CHAPTER XIV

DUNDEE SCHOOL

THE AMALGAMATED PRESS were still seated firmly in the saddle after World War One. Paper shortage had had surprisingly little effect on their boys' publications. True the *Boys' Realm* had been forced into suspended animation in 1916, and the *Dreadnought* had been merged with the *Boys' Friend*. On the other hand new publications had been launched during the war—among them the *Sexton Blake Library*, the *Nelson Lee Library*, and the *Greyfriars Herald*. Towards the end of the war the *Magnet* and *Gem* had carried urgent appeals to 'Eat Less Bread' and even Bunter had been forced in the national interest to curb his consumption of tarts and doughnuts. But no one in Greyfriars or St. Jim's emerged noticeably emaciated. It had been a jolly war.

There was little time for self-congratulation, however. Another kind of war was brewing. Soon the first shots of a broadside fired from nearly 500 miles away began ranging on Fleetway House. This was the half-expected assault from Scotland. For once the Scots were attacking Fleet Street from their native heath instead of from Fleet Street itself. In the van of the assault was the *Adventure* (1921), the first of a string of new weeklies which the publishers were to describe—on occasion—as the 'Big Five.' All had vigour unhampered by tradition and unfettered in imagination.

It may, and it may not, have been coincidence that in the following year the Amalgamated Press published the first number of the *Champion*,[1] which was to have more in common with the *Adventure* than with the pre-1914 weeklies like *Boys' Realm* and *Boys' Friend*. In the same year the Scots, undaunted, produced the *Rover* and the *Wizard*. Two years later Amalgamated Press put out the *Champion's* companion paper, the *Triumph*. Not till 1930 did the newcomers launch the *Skipper*, and three years later they 'went nap'—in their own language—with the *Hotspur*.

The headquarters of the 'Big Five' was in Dundee, traditional centre of jute, jam and journalism. Over many years the firm of D. C. Thomson & Company had acquired a reputation for shrewdness, hard-headedness and giving the public what it wanted. Its newspapers and weekly journals had a down-to-earth, forthright quality; they made no pretence at aiming at a highbrow public.

Similarly, the boys' papers now launched by this firm had no false airs about them. They were produced by young men of fertile mind who had undergone a course of indoctrination and knew all the house taboos. From the irruption of these weeklies dates the modern period of boys' thrillers; already there is a generation which remembers them with affection, in some cases to the exclusion of all others. (To-day the Thomson boys' papers are still flourishing—or as well as paper restrictions will allow them.)

Perhaps the editors of the *Adventure*, the *Rover*, the *Wizard*, the *Skipper* and the *Hotspur* might have been able to point to differences between their journals, but the boys who bought them almost certainly could not. All five dealt with sport, adventure, school, historical and futuristic stories. All five had a similar format, the same type of coloured cover and line illustrations which always seemed to have been drawn by the same hand, with everything—particularly shoulders, chests and biceps—a little larger than life.

Whereas the journals of the Amalgamated Press were frequently produced with an eye not merely on boys, but on old boys, the

---

[1] The *Champion* survived World War Two.

Thomson 'Big Five' appeared to be aimed exclusively at boys—
and rather younger ones at that, if such lures as 'A hundred biff
balls free' are any guide. To judge by the illustrations, the schoolboy heroes of the Dundee magazines were a year or so younger
than the boys of Greyfriars and St. Jim's, and the general get-up
and presentation of the stories was just that shade nearer to the
'comics' which the readers had begun to outgrow. Incidentally,
the drawing of 'The Editor' at the head of the Editor's Chat usually
showed a smooth, handsome young man who could not have
been using a razor for more than five years, even though—as in
the case of the editor of the *Rover*—he might claim a knowledge
of the odd corners of the world which put him right up in the
Commander Campbell class.

The Thomson papers were—and are—a curious mixture of
inhibitions and lack of inhibitions. The problem of sex was very
simply solved: girls did not exist. Occasionally, but very occasionally, there might be a reference to some fellow's sister being rescued
from a fire, but it could just as easily have been a tame goat or a
sack of flour. This ban on females was probably the most absolute
in the history of boys' magazines. The existence of an opposite
sex was admitted only in the advertisements of magazines which
catered for a fellow's sister: 'Famous Perfumes Free—This week
Phul Nana—with every copy of the great new story paper the
Mascot Magazine.'

Though they refused to admit that girls had any part in the
daydreams of adolescence, the Dundee School recognized such
innocuous aspirations in a boy's subconscious as the desire to fly
with bird-like wings, or to make himself invisible. It was a bad
week when not one of the Big Five could produce a story about a
boy who could walk about unseen. These were not the first invisible
boy stories by a long way, but hitherto the exploitation of this
idea had been left to the 'comics.' In Dundee they recognized the
evergreen appeal of the invisible boy and promoted him from the
comic strip to the adventure columns. One week it was a boy
who sniffed at a mysterious phial from the East and dissolved into
thin air. The next it was a lad who rubbed himself with a literal
brand of vanishing cream. Happily this cloak of invisibility was

employed as a rule only for the discomfiture of the pompous and oppressive; bad boys and Peeping Toms never got access to it (though sometimes master crooks did). Closely allied was the kind of story in which a likely lad got possession of a 'magic box' or a 'magic mixture' which would allow him to shrink objects to a fraction of their real size, thus giving him a tremendous pull over objectionable relatives and interfering policemen. There was another kind of magic box which contained the antidote to the law of gravity. Not only could the hero ascend vertically to escape from embarrassing situations, but he could suspend an unpopular form master in mid air, with his feet trying desperately to reach the ground. There were also X-ray spectacles (already encountered in Sexton Blake stories and elsewhere) enabling a person to look through opaque objects; an embarrassing device which once again happily never got into the hands of Peeping Toms.

Thus did the *Adventure, Rover, Hotspur, Skipper* and *Wizard* dream their readers' dreams for them. The Amalgamated Press had tended on the whole to respect the laws of Nature and Science; but plausibility and probability never worried the writers from beyond the Tweed. Their chief concern seems to have been to avoid any charge of conventionality, or of getting into a rut. Possibly that explains why they have not succeeded in establishing any one fictional character who can claim to be a household word; with the possible exception of Dixon Hawke. Most of their characters have lived brief and furious existences and then have sunk without trace.

None the less, certain very marked fashions are to be noted in the Thomson stories. For example, there is the vogue for the short series of stories based on the recovery of a specified number of objects, all of which are necessary to provide the solution to some puzzle. The first number of *Adventure* in 1922 carried a story of this kind. Next time it would be a story of twelve sea-ports scattered all over the world in which were twelve sailors each with different portions of a map tattooed on their backs; all would have to be traced before the sunken galleon with the gold aboard could be located. Another time it would be a casket which could be opened only by seven keys, all of which were distributed in Hidden Cities and Lost Temples. To the obvious objection: 'Why not break open the casket?' would be furnished the answer: 'Because any attempt to force the casket will release powerful acids which will at once destroy the contents.' A variation was the story in which Chief Sitting Bull would distribute seven feathers from his headdress to each of his seven sons, with the proviso that war might not be declared until all seven feathers were brought together again. It did not follow that a series involving seven feathers or twelve pieces of map would necessarily run for seven or twelve instalments. If the series was a flop the hero could recover two or more keys or pieces of map in one instalment; if it was a success he could be tricked out of the whole lot and have to start again. Quick success on the part of a hero is always a suspicious sign; the most popular performers receive the most set-backs. There would appear to be no justice in this.

Another favourite seam was that of a boy, or a pair of boys, travelling the world (and making a comfortable living) with some ingenious and improbable machine. Perhaps a super-bulldozer, which would help explorers to excavate for hidden treasure, or dig a river bed to prevent a town being engulfed by flood; perhaps an out-of-date and battered · double-decker bus pressed into commission in a gold rush; perhaps a desert yacht, towed in calm weather by camels; perhaps a new type of amphibian or a soundless helicopter (useful for rescuing chums from eagles' nests); perhaps an undersea tractor, just the thing for recovering five silver ikons from five sunken ships. None of these youthful adventurers seemed to have any difficulty in raising capital to launch their highly speculative enterprises. Any promising pair of 14-year-olds could acquire a streamlined motor cycle combination (and a licence to drive it), a movie camera (and the ability to operate it) and then tour the world taking photographs of assassinations and revolutions which the film companies fell over each other to buy.

They were a godsend, the film companies. Thus a 'strange car crawling up the steep slopes of the mountains of Hawaii' turned out to be the property of a daredevil who toured the world collecting noises for film and broadcasting companies—anything from the song of a nightingale to the roar of a Hawaiian volcano.

P

Another adventurer who seemed to have no difficulty in finding clients, even in the heart of the jungle, was Crispin Gaunt, who ran a portable light railway for the benefit of members of eclipse-viewing expeditions who might find themselves stranded with their heavy equipment, or zoo-stocking parties anxious for assistance in transporting their heavier and more obstreperous mammals. The portions of his locomotive and track were carried by indefatigable natives of the highest morale. Gaunt, who personally carried no portion of the railway, strode in front, a powerful figure wearing speckless silk jacket and shorts, a monocle and (in rotation) the ties of the twelve schools which he had been asked to leave, but for which he still cherished a loyal affection.

Perhaps it is unnecessary to add that, as they sweated through the jungle bearing the white man's burden (which never turned out to be the white man's white elephant), Gaunt's retinue argued incessantly about First Division football.

Gaunt, it will have been observed, wore the usual jungle monocle. The natives were invariably distrustful of any white lord who did not carry a window in his eye. Even jungle animals accepted this convention. There is an illustration in one of the 'Big Five' showing an ape proudly wearing a monocle.

Which leads to another favourite seam—the animal story Caligula may have made his horse a consul; in Thomson's Wild West they made horses into sheriffs and dogs into deputy sheriffs. Husky stories seemed especially popular; there were dogs which did everything but talk, and there may well have been dogs which talked too. Certainly there were dogs which wrote their own first-person stories of their adventures. There were dogs which became king of all the other dogs, and organized dog revolutions against savage masters, and raids upon their masters' towns. Running dogs a close second in popularity were kangaroos. Not only were they required to fight human beings, but they had to put on the gloves to fight goats, ostriches, apes and anything on two feet or four which could be persuaded into a boxing ring. But standing head and shoulders above boxing kangaroos, sacred ostriches, wild bulls and super-sagacious horses was O'Neil, the Six-Gun Gorilla. O'Neil's master, a Colorado prospector, had taught him

Dirk Reid balances the Rocking Stone—and starts a war in Africa.—The Rover

to dig, fetch firewood, haul up buckets of water from the mine
shaft and generally make himself useful about the shack. Unfortunately he had also taught the gorilla how to load and fire a revolver.
All went well until O'Neil's master was murdered. Then the
gorilla strapped on pistol and bandolier and set off on the trail
of vengeance. For a hundred miles he followed the murderers,
picking them off one by one. He discovered a quite remarkable
talent for holding up stage-coaches, and his hairy presence filled
the occupants with more alarm than the descent of any Spring-
Heeled Jack. On one occasion he held up a coach, mounted the
driver's box and drove the terrified horses on the heels of a flying
gunman. It was the highwayman story brought up-to-date.

In school stories the *Adventure* and its companion papers strove
hard to be different. The schools were boarding establishments,
without the aristocratic pretensions of Greyfriars and St. Jim's.
They were 'tough' schools and on the whole they produced
tougher pupils; but the boisterous extroverts they bred had no
vice in them. The usual crooked ex-pupils came back to ruin the
name of their *alma mater*: outbreaks of ventriloquism and invisibility were chronic; and no school was without its terrible twins
or tricky triplets. One journal even produced a headmaster who was
twins: the clever one conducted the classwork and the athletic
one organized sport, and whichever one was not on duty hid in
a cottage in the woods.

Burwood College, where this neat piece of integration went
on, must have been a much more smooth-running place than
St. Jude's, where the Head turned out to be a savage who suffered
from attacks of atavism, during which he dressed up in a leopard
skin and swung about the roofs.

Beachcomber's Narkover and Dickens's Dotheboys Hall were
saintly seminaries compared with some of these schools; but
discipline caught up with them all. There were schools in which not
merely one master, but every master, was a wanted man. There
were schools in which both masters and boys were starved. There
was one school—especially got together, regardless of expense, by
a tyrannous father anxious to discourage his son from being a
schoolmaster—in which cretinous boys tried out Spanish In-

quisition practices on such masters as were rash enough to go
about unarmed by clubs and red-hot pokers. The masters appeared
to be less interested in achieving a state of discipline than in wreak-
ing their personal revenge. To such schools would be sent new
masters, clean-limbed young men with a straight left, who would
try to fight everybody single-handed. They would be lucky if,
additionally, they did not have to fight sixteen Tibetan priests
looking for a jewel stolen from a monastery. Small wonder that
the new teacher at one inordinately tough school resorted to the
ever-popular device of making himself invisible.

The trick of introducing eccentric pupils was not overlooked.
There was the remarkable academy in which the boy king of
Manavia was installed with a £5-a-week whipping boy to take
his punishment for him. Pug, the whipping boy, had got the job
by walloping all the other applicants. When the boy king mis-
behaved the Headmaster flogged Pug, and Pug in due course
took it out of the 'dratted monarch.'

Nor was the vogue for schools in strange places forgotten;
rather was it extended. There was, for instance, an international
school in France, with English boys, Eskimos and Red Indians,
and there was a treetops school run primarily for the study of wild
animals, with precarious catwalks running all over the roof of the
forest.

In the next chapter is told how the *Rover* introduced the Sweeney
Todd disappearing chair motif into a story of the Wild West,
and brought Red Indians from their happy hunting-grounds to
act as fighter pilots or sleuths in New York's underworld. You
had to hand it to the Thomson five—they tried their hand at
every kind of story, and had no hesitation in combining two or
three kinds of story in one. If readers could swallow a serial about
a huge stone statue which came to life and strode about the mountain passes of India, why should they jib at the statue being called
upon to fight a prehistoric animal in a lake? The Dundee School
saw no objection to winning the Great War with sensational
inventions which had never been invented, or if they had, had
been kept remarkably quiet. One of these was the Snatcher, a
super tank with an enormous grab which could as easily pick up a

German staff car, complete with occupants, as lift a hundred tanks from an enemy laager and drop them one by one into a lake, or bring down a viaduct by nibbling away at the centre arch. To get through a forest it pulled up trees by means of its grab or felled them with its rotary saw.

Nor did the 'Big Five' turn up their noses at tales of Roman legions, of Red Macgregors or of Robin Hood. The latter stories were calculated to shock the traditionalists; they were possibly the first Robin Hood stories which did not make a feature of atrocious ballads. Quite often, by breaking with tradition and mixing one type of story with another, the 'Big Five' hit on an adventure series which could stand comparison with the best of boy's stories.

Dixon Hawke, the Thomson detective, proved to be fairly conventional in his methods. His exploits have been chronicled in the *Adventure* since 1921 and also in occasional 'casebooks.' They are still being chronicled to-day, like those of Sexton Blake, but those who follow Hawke rarely follow Blake, and vice versa.

Hawke conforms to the orthodox pattern in that he is tall, aquiline, wears a dressing-gown and smokes a 'blackened briar.' His rooms in Dover Street are run by Mrs. Benvie. His assistant is Tommy Burke and his bloodhound is called Solomon. In general his cases call for a minimum of deduction and a maximum of action. Sometimes he is required to solve a picture puzzle hardly more difficult than those in the mammoth competition on the next page. As with Falcon Swift, sporting mysteries occupy a great deal of his time. Why did the winning team fall asleep after half time? Why did so many horses mysteriously fall at the fourteenth jump in the Grand National? And so on.

The firm of Hawke and Burke are never happier than when chasing round the world picking up a ruby in each country. On one of these jewel hunts by way of New York, San Francisco, Yokohama, Tibet and the usual Hidden City the detective and his assistant got off to a good start, recovering four jewels in as many instalments. Then Hawke was confronted with a cruel choice: the master crook who was chasing round the world as fast as he was, and often faster, offered him the alternative of handing over the four jewels or letting Hawke's Japanese assistant freeze to death. There was the boy pathetically curled up unconscious inside a block of ice the size of a tea chest. Hawke handed over the rubies, then angrily smashed the block of ice open. The Japanese, a hardy youth, survived this ordeal by frost and sledge hammer.

Hawke was unlucky in his assistants during this world tour. He had discovered almost all the jewels when Tommy obligingly told the arch-crook, who was made up to look like Hawke, where they were. But Hawke recovered them all in one swoop on the last instalment.

Dixon Hawke rarely expressed surprise at the kind of adversary he was called upon to face—whether it was a white-washed orang-utan or a levitational crook like Marko the Miracle Man. Modestly described as 'a rather amazing type of criminal,' Marko had equipped himself not only with a device which enabled him to defy gravity but with X-ray spectacles as well.

With a man like that around, it was not surprising that Hawke should try an old Baker Street dodge and leave his dummy in the window seat; though why Marko should have wasted ammunition on the dummy when he ought to have been able to see Hawke lurking in a corner is not clear. That Marko was a determined fellow is shown by the fact that even when handcuffed by Hawke to an area railing, and tugged upside down by his anti-gravitational device, with all the money falling out of his pockets, his attempt to harpoon the detective with a concealed knife missed by only an inch.

The style of writing in the Dundee stories was starkly simple, with odd scraps of idiom occasionally betraying its Scottish origin—'other four men' instead of 'four other men.' There was no attempt to explain improbable situations; the facts were stated and the reader could take it or leave it. Usually he took it. A certain amount of slang went into the presentation of the stories—'a beezer yarn next week, boys'—but the stories themselves largely avoided slang and avoided also the stylized exclamations of the *Magnet* and *Gem*. No one cried 'Oh haddocks!' The characters in the 'Big Five' managed to get along with hardly any expletives. It is difficult for a student of style to say that a story in the *Adventure* was written by such-and-such a person, and a story in the *Rover* by another. All seem to have been written by the one person. That was a tribute to the Thomson coaching. Very rarely were authors' names mentioned.

The Thomson stories published during World War Two came in for criticism in the *Library Assistant* (1941) by a writer who felt it was undesirable that the up-and-coming generation should be encouraged to believe that one resolute youth aided by a comic Indian with a cricket bat could rout an Axis division in Libya week after week, throwing tanks off the road by the simple expedient of laying ice-cream in front of them. Was this the kind of fancy to be implanted in the minds of lads whose brothers had gone through the bloody ordeal of Dunkirk and Crete?

Every thriller penned is open to the same charge. It is just as absurd to portray a detective's boy assistant routing criminal gangs single-handed, or a boy explorer beating off swarms of Martians from a threatened space ship. But adolescence will not, and should not, be baulked of its heroic fancies. Reality comes all too soon.

To-day collectors of old-style 'penny dreadfuls' shake their heads sadly at the *Hotspur* and the *Wizard*, but there is no doubt that the tattered copies which they despise will be as eagerly sought after fifty years hence as are the works of Edward Lloyd to-day.

CHAPTER XV

WILD WEST

SOONER OR LATER, a fictional hero had to pit his wits against Red Indians. The only exception to this rule seems to have been Jack Sheppard. Dick Turpin was shipped to America by the Blue Dwarf and found himself caught up in some stirring adventures with the Mohicans. Jack Harkaway had numerous bloodthirsty encounters with redskins, and was fortunate perhaps to be able to fight them with the aid of a balloon. Sexton Blake undertook at least one enquiry on behalf of a Red Indian chief. Jack, Sam and Pete were as happy and self-possessed in an Indian reservation as in a Hidden City or at Margate. And the boys of Greyfriars were as certain to be embroiled with Apaches on their trips to North America as they were on their trips to Paris.

The 'penny dreadfuls' did not go in for redskin stories to any outstanding degree; Blueskin was nearer their mark. But the Brett, Emmett and Fox journals began to feature Indian tales. Some were just plain bloodthirsty; others played up the chivalrous master of woodcraft, like Deerfoot. And for the last quarter of the nineteenth century the Indian tales of Edward Sylvester Ellis—originally published in American dime novels—were being re-published in Britain.

Relish for Indian stories usually came at an early stage in a boy's reading. At first gulp it was intoxicating stuff—the flaming arrow over the wall of the compound; the white men tied to the stake while the braves roused their passions on firewater; the knife-throwing test of courage in which the hero, as target, was safe only so long as he did not flinch; the smoke signals on the horizon, the circling of the caravan by howling Sioux, Comanches, Pawnees, Cheyennes, Navajos and a score more tribes with magnificent if not always pronounceable names; and, of course, the scalping parties. (Just what *did* happen to a man when he was scalped? There was always a great deal of controversy about this.)

But in good time the youthful reader would find that older boys tended to sneer at simple tales of Red Indians. They were to be seen reading stories about Buffalo Bill, Wild Bill Hickok and Deadwood Dick, and these stories were said to be at once more exciting and more adult.

So the young reader would lay aside his Deerfoot and take pains to acquire his first Buffalo Bill. If he got hold of an unedited American version he probably made pretty heavy weather of the dialogue at first, for it would be full of words like pizen, ginuwine, purty, p'ticklerly, animile and so on. With a little practice he would be able to take passages like this in his stride:

Buffler. Come ter wonst. Injuns thet is said ter be Aztecs has hooked onter Little Cayüse and kerried him away. I follers em immejutly, on ther trail leading south from Eagle Pass. This I sens ter you by the hand of a red what belonged to ther band which his name is Ilhuat, er something like et; he's ther clear quill, I b'lieve, an he'll get this ter ye at Calumet Wells quick's he kin, tho he's hoofin' et.—Yer ole pard in trouble, Nomad.

It was of considerable assistance that correspondents like Nomad usually spelled place names correctly.

When he grew really proficient the reader might even be able to translate the following, from *The Tribunal of Ten, a Tale of Mystery and Love on the Rolling Prairie, Washington Territory*:

'I want ye to understand that I'm Lion Lije, the vigilant chief of this burg, and I'm bizness. Thet, corpus-going ter whoop out who war the Capting's Tribunal of Ten only he were shet off, an bein's he couldn't let us know no other way his sperit helped ter pint ye out.'

There was a foolish sort of competition between publishers to claim the only genuine, or ginuwine, Buffalo Bill stories. Foolish, because nobody really cared whether the tales bore even a fleeting resemblance to the exploits of 'Colonel' W. F. Cody. It would have been more sensible if there had been a common agreement to regard Buffalo Bill as a free-for-all legend like Dick Turpin or Robin Hood.

Before they buried him in the solid rock of Lookout Mountain Cody had had the unsettling but by no means distasteful experience of seeing himself become a schoolboy's legend. At first he had read the outpourings of the Wild West writers with tolerant amazement; latterly he must have found it impossible even to keep abreast of the fictional flood. He himself took no strenuous steps to dispel the more extravagant fancies spun about his name, and a good many to increase them. Dying a septuagenarian, he must have been in almost as much doubt at the end over what constituted fact and fiction in his life as are his biographers.[1]

The Aldine Company ran some of the liveliest Buffalo Bill stories in the late 'nineties—including stories 'by' Buffalo Bill and such unexpectedly literary pards of his as 'Colonel Sutliffe, United States Army.' One which appeared in the *O'er Land and Sea Library* under the title 'Oath-Bound to Custer' showed the 'Hon.' W. F. Cody, knife in hand, waving aloft the scalp of an Indian brave who lay on the ground beside him. Cover pictures were often deliberately misleading, but the text in this case supported the artist:

Buffalo Bill, dragging off the Chief's war bonnet, scalped him in the twinkling of an eye, and waving the red trophy and its attachment of feathers and head-dress in the air, shouted in ringing tones, 'The first scalp for Custer!'

An apologetic footnote explained:

It was not the custom of Buffalo Bill to scalp redskins, but knowing how highly Indians prize their scalp lock, and embittered by the Custer massacre, he determined to do so on his trail of revenge.—Author.

---

[1] The *Encyclopedia Britannica* says that W. F. Cody (1846–1917) was a Pony Express rider and a scout and guide for the U.S. Army; that he got his name Buffalo Bill when, in 1867, he secured the contract for supplying buffalo meat to workmen on the Kansas–Pacific Railway; that he killed the Indian chief Yellow Hand in single combat in the battle of Indian Creek in the Sioux–Cheyenne War of 1876; and that in 1883 he organized his Wild West Show. Another 'Colonel' Cody, often confused with Buffalo Bill, was a pioneer aviator.

In the last chapter Buffalo Bill rode in triumph into the camp of a United States general, who looked inquiringly at the 'string of ghastly souvenirs of death' hanging from the Scout's belt.

'Oh, these are the dead roofs of the braves who felt my grip, general. I intended to have a rope made of them to hang Bill Bevins with, but he persuaded me with a knife to give him a soldier's death.'

'You killed him?'

'Yes, general, I had to do it, so I'll have the scalp locks made into a bridle for you.'

The reader who expected the general to wave aside the offer with deprecating gesture did not know his United States generals. The answer came:

'Thank you, Bill. It will be a unique present and one most highly prized.'

Another story in this series portrayed Buffalo Bill and his comrades in a more mellow mood, yarning around the camp-fire. Their yarns were less remarkable than the language they employed. Buffalo Bill had said that he once knew of a snake being used as an instrument of murder, and Wild Bill Hickok had begged for further information:

'In Hayti and Martinique,' said Cody, 'the venom of the terrible serpent indigenous to those islands, the formidable *fer-de-lance*, which is far more deadly than the rattlesnake, has been often employed by the negroes in disposing of their enemies.'

Wild Bill showed no surprise, so Buffalo Bill continued in the same vein:

'A horrible but well authenticated instance of negro ingenuity and malevolence is told in Martinique. . . .'

He went on like this for column after column. His whole speech could have been lifted out of the story and used with hardly a word of editing as an article in a magazine. Wild Bill had to cap his comrade's tales of snakes with some personal reminiscences of scorpions, and he too chose to speak in the same language.

After alleging that scorpions, failing to achieve their objective, often sting themselves to death in disgust, he said:

'Brandy taken till stupefaction follows is a favourite remedy for scorpion bites in Mexico, and ammonia has also given very good results.'

Buffalo Bill came back with a story about a tarantula-versus-rattlesnake encounter described in the language of an old-fashioned provincial football report, and eventually the two men fell asleep. Perhaps the strain of talking old-fashioned journalese had been too much for them; or perhaps they had bored each other stiff.

Just how that kind of padded story crept into the Aldine series will never be known. It would be charitable to assume that the mails were held up, with the result that an inexperienced pen had to vamp up a story at short notice. Most of the Aldine Wild West stories were good value for money. The scarcity of copies to-day tells its own story.

Occasionally there was a dying flicker of Gothic in the early Buffalo Bill tales. There were hags in haunted canyons, and spectral riders ranged like the riders of Apocalypse, with phosphorescent hounds at heel. It was surprising how eerie an effect could be worked up against a background of wide open spaces, with no aid from clammy ruins or ancient burial grounds. One point worth noting was that the Things which appeared on the prairie usually had a satisfactory physical explanation in the end—they were, in fact, the work of the villain.

Guaranteed not to shock 'the most fastidious,' the Aldine *New Buffalo Bill Library* which began in 1899 started off with a story in which the heroine in the opening chapter received a parcel containing her lover's scalp and eyeballs. On the coloured cover of each number appeared the King of Scouts, looking like an arrogant Stuart courtier in Wild West dress—pointed beard, pointed moustache and a long mane of hair which must have been a standing temptation to every brave with a scalping knife. Wild Bill Hickok wore his hair even longer—it hung below his shoulders uncombed and uncouth.

These, too, were full-blooded stories. It was a dull day on which the Scout did not come across one of his old pards being crushed to death by a b'ar, or strapped Mazeppa-fashion to a wild mustang and burning like a torch; or catch a glimpse of a train of covered wagons, likewise flaming, racing into a petroleum-covered lake. (An editorial footnote pointed out that petroleum was so plentiful in North America that hundreds of lakes were oil-logged with the fuel which ran to waste.)

He was no sentimentalist, this Buffalo Bill. *Pour encourager les autres*, he had Cunning Fox tied to a sapling and flogged with buffalo hide whips, Surgeon Frank Powell being in attendance. His aides were no amateurs:

> They laid their stripes in a beautiful regular way, crossing each other's strokes until the redskin's back was a mass of bruised and quivering flesh.
>
> From time to time Frank Powell felt the redskin's pulse but always found it steady and strong. The man had a huge capacity for taking punishment.

Excess bravery in a brave had its drawbacks, however. Indian admiration was apt to take an embarrassing form:

> 'Take him alive! Take him alive! He must die by the torture; we must eat his heart hot, for he is a brave chief!'

So often was Buffalo Bill called upon to undergo the knife-throwing torture that he developed an almost sure technique to deal with it. He looked at the eyes of the brave who was at the head of the queue, and if he saw the death lust in the man's eyes he jerked his head to one side at the last second. If not, he stayed still and put his faith in the warrior's fear of the ridicule which was reserved for those who threw clumsily enough to maim. Occasionally he would be rescued at the eleventh hour by an Indian maid with a delightful name like Picture Eyes or Feather Feet. They had a weak spot for a white man, these Indian maidens; and the braves never seemed to bear any grudge.

Every now and again the editor came gallantly to the rescue when the author seemed to stretch the probabilities. At one point, after a man fell into a vitriol pit and died instantly and unpleasantly, it was found that a previous victim's body, already in the vitriol, was excellently preserved. Said the editor:

> The properties of vitriol are such as to render it a terribly corrosive agent when brought suddenly into contact with a living body; while at

the same time it will arrest decay in a corpse. Captain Wolverton's body
was slowly permeated and so preserved; whereas his enemy, falling alive
into the vitriol, met with a terrible end.

A rather more restrained Buffalo Bill appeared in *Buffalo Bill
Stories, a Weekly Devoted to Border Life*, which reached this
country about 1909 under the auspices of Street and Smith. In
these tales the Scout rode the Border like a knight errant, concluding
peace treaties with Indian chiefs and confounding the knavish
tricks of renegade whites. He shot to wing, not to kill. He would
break up a lynching party by firing two guns simultaneously,
hitting each of about seven gunmen in the wrist or arm, causing
them to drop their weapons, and inflicting wounds which, the
reader was assured, 'would heal in a few weeks time.'

Buffalo Bill's pard was perhaps the more colourful character of
the two, even though his conversation was largely limited to 'Er,
waugh!' Probably it was a habit he had picked up from the Indians,
who were always saying 'Wah!' The phrase served for all occasions.
If they found a dead man hanging from a tree he would say 'Er,
waugh!' If they lost their way he would say 'Er, waugh!' As he
sank his teeth into a juicy steak he would say 'Er, waugh!' When
greatly moved he would exclaim 'Hallelujer! Glee-ory! Er,
waugh!' His terms of opprobrium, when he could be bothered
voicing them, were drawn straight from Nature: coyotes, skunks,
tarant'lers, warty toads.

Another hard-working but hardly more articulate aide of Buffalo
Bill was Little Cayuse, who had been a bugler in Uncle Sam's
Army. His speech was complicated by an admixture of pidgin.
Thus, his comment on seeing an intermittent flash away in the
plain was, 'Mebbyso um horse soldier have um light box.'

Another 'pard' who assisted Buffalo Bill besides Nick Nomad,
Wild Bill Hickok and Little Cayuse, was a Baron von Schitzen-
hauser. This meant grafting a German-Dutch accent on to the
Western original. The result was 'Py yiminy!'

'Aber I ain't afraidt uff Inchuns. I tondt vandt any such exberiences
ag'in as vot I haf had. Nodt in dot vay, eenhow.'

For bloodthirstiness and lurid adventure the Deadwood Dick
stories tended to outshine those of Buffalo Bill. The Aldine

Company imported these by the hundred from the 'nineties onwards. Once they were moved to assure their readers in a foreword:

Trappers and Scouts are prone to the use of emphatic expletives, most of them racy with humour, all of them harmless; but there will not be found here or in any of the Aldine world-renowned libraries a single unchaste episode—and this latter is of great importance.

There is said to have been an original Deadwood Dick in the person of a Pony Express rider called Richard Clarke. Like Cody he enjoyed the privilege of being able to read a great deal of sensational literature spun about his name. He seems to have enjoyed his notoriety; at all events he rode in a pageant attended by President Coolidge at Deadwood in 1927. He was 83 when he died.

There was an insatiable thirst for alliteration on the part of the Deadwood Dick editors which extended far beyond the hero's name: 'Deadwood Dick's Dozen,' 'Deadwood Dick's Ducats,' 'Deadwood Dick's Diamonds,' 'Deadwood Dick's Danger Ducks,' 'Deadwood Dick at Danger Divide,' and so on for scores of titles.

The fictional Deadwood Dick had many phases: he was outlawed, he was reinstated, he married at least twice, he sought vainly to settle down, and finally he was killed, in an adventure rather callously entitled 'Deadwood Dick's Dust.'

In the Aldine illustrations Deadwood Dick did not greatly differ in appearance from Buffalo Bill or any of the other Western heroes. But much more handsome and dashing was Calamity Jane. She wore men's breeches, a saucy jacket buttoned with ten-dollar gold pieces, a boiled shirt and collar, and a belt containing 'self-cocking five-shooters.' The pair of them were described as 'two wild spirits who have learned each other's faults and each other's worth, in lives branded with commingled shame and honour.'

It was a long time before Jane was able to bring her true love to the altar. She would be referred to as 'poor, sore-hearted, but brave and true Calamity Jane.' Sometimes she was not very quick in the uptake. For instance, she suffered herself to be rescued by the masked Unknown and rode beside him for two days before he removed his mask and announced that he was Deadwood Dick, and reminded her that he held a 'mortgage of betrothal' against her.

Decapitation, or the threat of it, or the false report of it was a favourite theme in the Deadwood Dick series. One cover showed Calamity Jane intervening to protect a gambler who had rashly wagered his head and lost. The winner was approaching with his knife at the ready. It was characteristic of Calamity Jane that she kept her head when others were about to lose theirs. Then there was the time a showman put up a placard:

Startling Curiosity
The Wonder of the World
The Genuine Head of Deadwood Dick
Preserved in spirits.   On exhibition within this pavilion
The head of the greatest road ranger that ever lived!
Come one!   Come all!
Admission only 30 cents

Dick knew of this fraudulent display but took no action; he was masquerading at the time under the not inappropriate name of Hard Cheek.

In the Aldine *Boys' First-Rate Pocket Library* Calamity Jane was killed at least twice. Number 64 had Deadwood Dick kneeling beside her grave—she had been slain trying to cut down the enemy flag. Number 68 had Calamity Jane being hanged at the end of a rope by a group of desperadoes, in company with Mormon Bill; surely the first time in this type of fiction that a good-looking, God-fearing heroine ever came to such an ignominious end. Deadwood Dick, after cutting her down, swore a great oath to destroy the camp in which dwelt her murderers. This he did at the cost of his life. No undue sentiment was expended on his passing, which was described in no more than 150 words. He was buried in a quiet valley beside Calamity Jane, whose tombstone said, 'Frank with friends, fearless of foes.' His own said, 'Brave, honourable and kind in peace, cool, daring and fearless in war.' There were no editorial crocodile tears; somebody had decided that both characters were to be despatched, and

Q

despatched they were. The next issue started off with a tale of
Deadwood Dick, junior.

The Aldine *Boys' Own Library*, which started in 1909, had
Deadwood Dick, senior, married to a girl-wife called Leone:

Deadwood Dick, the Prince of Outlaws once, was now a reformed
man, leading the life of a cattle herder with his loved and loving wife
and boy, and servants enough to do the work in the house and upon
the stock lands; for Dick was annually receiving handsome profits from
a gold mine in the Black Hills and could afford to live luxuriously.

Leone, who frequently called him Prince, could not believe that
this placid, well-regulated life would last; nor could the reader.
Though she adored him, Leone was worried about the other
women in her husband's life (though not about Calamity Jane):

'Ah, Eddie, you know not what moment that Edith Stone may come,
for she is your lifelong enemy. Do you really believe that she is crazy,
dear?'

Edith came back, and she was crazy all right. Deadwood Dick,
from a hidden position, watched her hang a dead man from a tree.
She had always wanted this man's blood, but someone had beaten
her to it, so she was getting what satisfaction she could by stringing
up a corpse.

The call came to Deadwood Dick to clean up his old stamping-
grounds. He returned with his Eagles, whose names only he
himself knew. The war was bitter. Came the day when Edith laid
hands on Dick. She had him tied to a stake, and then made this
memorable proposal of marriage:

'Deadwood Dick, I have come to give you one more chance for life.
Wed me and take me East to live and we will omit this burning at the
stake and ever live happily together. What shall it be—will you accept
me, or what you will find ten times more unendurable, a horrible death?'

Edith must have entertained some doubts about her charms,
since she assessed death by burning as only ten times worse than
marriage. Deadwood Dick's answer not only dispelled all hopes
of marriage but put a more realistic rating on the proposition:

'Death, a thousand times death, in preference to linking myself with
you! Go ahead, you will find I am not afraid.'

As Edith, who knew when she was beaten, turned away to help the Indians gather some more tinder, Leone arrived. She had been reported dead, so by rejecting Edith's offer Dick had also saved himself from bigamy. Leone's relief at finding her husband, who had also been reported dead, was equalled by her fury at the other woman.

'Stand, you fiend!' cried the wife of Deadwood Dick, hurling a long narrow sword at the feet of Edith, and retaining a similar one in her own hand. 'Pick up your sword and stand on your guard, for it shall be your life or mine.'

Leone knew her own strength, or she would hardly have put this encounter on a duelling basis. In no time her sword was 'deep in Edith's black heart.'

Deadwood Dick, junior, was not the son of the outlaw, but a young and rather whey-faced namesake who arrived with his dying mother thrown over the saddle at the still-fresh graves of Deadwood Dick

Blue Blaze and Eagle Eye leap to attack the crooks' convoy.—The Rover

and Calamity Jane. There, taking brief respite from his pursuers, he swore to be worthy of the man whose name he thereupon assumed; a more exciting name than his own, which was R. M. Bristol. The adventures in which he was involved were not at first very different from those of his distinguished namesake; but in the Aldine *Life and Adventure Library*, many years later, he had become just another detective. No demon lovers lay in wait for him. The West was taming down. And just as Sexton Blake was required to undertake assignments from time to time in provincial cities of Britain, so Deadwood Dick, junior, tackled cases in Detroit, Cincinnati, Boston, and even Coney Island. One of his adventures ended on a particularly unromantic note:

> Dear reader, this is not a love story; consequently there are no heroes or heroines to be married off in the stereotyped manner, and therefore there is little left to add.
> Ben Brice was buried at Dick's expense, while the expenses of Mrs. Redfern's funeral were borne by the Coroner. . . .

In their heyday the Deadwood Dick stories were good value. The arts of suspense were well studied, even if the arts of grammar were neglected. Each short chapter worked up to a tingling climax, then the writer switched to the other characters. The reader had to fight down a temptation to read alternate chapters.

Meanwhile those who had lost their appetite for 'straight' Westerns could revel in the bizarre exploits on the prairie of Frank Reade and his steam men (Chapter X), once again in an Aldine coloured cover. The author was undeniably more interested in the performance of his mechanical wonders than in the ways of the West; but now and again the youthful inventor would fall into the hands of red or white desperadoes. He narrowly escaped being flayed alive, with the promise that boiling water would be poured on his stripped flesh; he was tethered in front of a rattlesnake which lunged nearer and nearer as the thong retaining it expanded; and he was made a pin-cushion for porcupine spines, alkali being rubbed into the wounds afterwards. But every ordeal only fired him with the desire to go back to Readestown and invent something better.

Early numbers of the Harmsworth magazines carried a variety

of Indian tales, sometimes Buffalo Bill, sometimes Deadwood
Dick, occasionally both in the one story, but there were no early
Amalgamated Press publications which were specifically Western
in appeal. Detection had become the obsession. In 'Trapper Dan'
(*Boys' Herald*, 1903) George Manville Fenn shed some light on the
great puzzle: is scalping always fatal? Old Dan, the grizzled
trapper, was seeking to impress his young assistant with the ruthless ways of redskins. Suddenly he decided to give a practical
demonstration:

'. . . he snatched off his square skin cap, making the boy spring to his
feet aghast with horror, while the dog started back glaring at the visitor
and bursting forth into a deep angry bay.
    Horrible! came from Wat Waring's lips—one word only but meaning
so much, for the sight he gazed upon was terrible indeed, his visitor
standing transformed into a hideous object as with one quick motion
he laid bare the trace of a frightful act of triumph of the savage redskin
over his defeated enemy, the trapper's head, with its long-healed scars
looking strangely white above his sun-bronzed face, telling the tale in its
frightful bareness of the rapid placing round of the savage's knife and
the tearing away of the scalp.

Not until 1938 did Amalgamated Press put out a short-lived
Wild West Weekly. The cover was as colourful as the contents.
Promised the editor:

'. . . We will put a hot rifle in your hands and make the sweat run
down your face. You shall look down the long smooth barrel of a gun
and, with nerves strung tight as a bow-string, you shall feel a bullet
spatter the dry earth into your face.'

After that it seemed a bit of an anti-climax that the free gift
selected for permanent subscribers should have consisted of a
shove-ha'penny board.
    It was left to the Dundee School to break all traditions and
work out some really original angles on the Wild West. Deerfoot
padding through the undergrowth was no use to them. The *Rover*
produced Hawkeye, the redskin detective, padding up Fifth
Avenue in all the glory of his native costume, seeking to do battle
with the Black Bat, King of the New York underworld. The *Rover*
also took pleasure in presenting Blue Blaze, Demon of the Air,

who in company with Hawkeye had done much to win World
War One in a phantom aeroplane. An illustration showed him
half out of the cockpit, pointing downwards. The artist had been
to some trouble to indicate, by means of the usual striations, that
the plane was swooping rapidly, but the eagle feather in Blue
Blaze's hair remained miraculously vertical, and his pig tail drooped
in a dead calm. After the Great War Blue Blaze and Hawkeye
brought their phantom plane home to their native hunting-grounds
in the Great Barrier Mountains, complete with machine-guns and
apparently limitless ammunition, and there found plenty of gainful
and spectacular employment.

But the *Rover*'s masterpiece was probably the Demon Barber
of Six Trails, in which the sinister apparatus of the disappearing
chair was used, probably for the first time, as an instrument of
high purpose. Crooks were lured into the barber's shop and then
dropped on to a pile of straw in the cellar for subsequent removal
to the town jail. And who was the Demon Barber? The evidence
was strong that it was Wild Bill Hickok himself.

CHAPTER XVI

VIVE LE SPORT!

Any historian of the remote future relying exclusively on old volumes of boys' magazines for his knowledge of the British way of life in the early twentieth century—notably the nineteen-twenties and the nineteen-thirties—will record that the country was the battleground of an unending civil war between a small vigorous race known as Sportsmen and a large, sluggish and corrupt race known as Slackers. The Slackers had a great deal in their favour—Wealth, Cunning, Ruthlessness and an unlimited supply of Secret Drugs. The Sportsmen had nothing but a clean pair of fists. Yet the Sportsmen always won. They would have won in half the time and at less injury to themselves if they had used knuckle-dusters, but then they would have forfeited their status as Sportsmen.

Collectors of old boys' books tend to fall into two camps: those whose loyalties lie in the late Brett and early Harmsworth era, and who look on Sport as a creeping blight which overtook and paralysed many a long-established magazine, driving well-loved authors into retirement; and those who, launched at an early age on a sea of sport, took sporting stories, no matter how preposterous, in their stride.

It is hard to trace just when the preoccupation with sport began. Desmond Coke in his chapter on 'Penny Dreadfuls' in *Confessions of an Incurable Collector*, quotes exultingly from *The*

Oxford and Cambridge Eights (published by Brett) in which a punters' plot to poison the entire Cambridge crew miscarries and Oxford is poisoned instead. This admirable story appears to have been ahead of its time.

Edwin Brett's *Boys of England* described itself as 'A Magazine of Sport, Travel, Fun and Adventure,' but the reader would require to do a good deal of researching to find a story which, by any standards, could be called a sporting story. It was in 1866 that the *Boys of England* was launched. That was the same year that the Queensberry Rules were drawn up in an attempt to purge professional pugilism of some of its more scandalous abuses. Three years previously the Football Association had been formed with the object of cleaning up contemporary football, in which hitherto hands and feet had been used impartially, and hacking and tripping were normal tactics. Bracebridge Hemyng, who contributed the first Jack Harkaway stories to *Boys of England*, would seem to have overlooked the Queensberry Rules; the reader has already read a description of a fight under the Harkaway rules (Chapter V).

In one of his later publications—*Jack Harkaway's Journal for Boys*—Brett set out to encourage what he called 'The Manly Sports of Britain,' which included football, cricket, sculling, fencing, cycling and even golf. He sponsored Jack Harkaway Cycling Clubs. In italics he emphasized that his encouragement was extended only to participants in amateur sports. Presented free with his *Journal* were large coloured plates showing boys playing football—a bigger bargain, it might seem, than those small 'real glossy' photos of players which the next generation were to be stampeded into collecting. The most interesting development, perhaps, was the offer of £20 to the next-of-kin of any boy killed playing football or cricket, or riding a bicycle. If this could not make the youth of the country sport-minded, what could?

But the stories in *Jack Harkaway's Journal for Boys* were in the old pattern. There is little doubt that most of the authors who wrote for Brett and his rivals knew nothing about sport and cared less. When it came to describing a schoolboy fight there was no talk of hooks and uppercuts, only of blacked eyes and bleeding noses. One popular author of school stories would content himself, though perhaps not his readers, by saying, 'With the details of the fight we need not concern ourselves.' Again, the Old Guard could no more describe a football match than they could describe the Otto Cycle. They had been reared on, and in many cases had helped to write, 'penny dreadfuls,' and the gulf between the Gothic Obsession and the Sporting Obsession was an almost impossible one to bridge. It may be that somewhere in the archives is a story in which the rightful heir to a haunted castle turns out to be the crack centre-forward of Mountjoye Wanderers; if so, the present writer would be happy to hear of it. Certainly such a plot would be not nearly as extravagant as some of those which were later encountered in sporting fiction.

The *Boy's Own Paper*, launched in 1879, was determined to strike a sporting note from the outset. The first story in the opening number was entitled 'My First Football Match.' It was a rather breathless—and entirely plotless—description of the sensations of a youngster chosen to play for the first time in an important match; of his apprehensions lest he should commit some unfortunate act which would cost his side the match; and of the glow he felt at the end in having contributed to 'the glorious victory of the Old School.' A few months later the *Boy's Own Paper* repeated this story in terms of cricket. Once again there was no plot; the climax was merely eleven boys riding home in ecstasy because they had won a good clean game.

This naïve kind of sporting story was not enough to hold the attention of boy readers avid for thrills, and Dr. James Macaulay must speedily have realized as much. He was up against the hard fact, unquestioningly accepted by editors of a later day, that a sporting story pure and simple is unreadable. A sporting encounter became interesting only when an element of crookedness or comedy was injected into it.

The *Boy's Own Paper* and its sport-minded contemporaries therefore decided to administer sport in neat doses, that is, un-mixed with fiction. Thus began the practice of praising famous men in the sporting world. The *Boy's Own Paper* and *The Captain* were among the first in the field, though their emphasis was rather on public school sport. Other journals struck a more democratic note.

James Henderson's *Nuggets*, in the eighteen-nineties, featured a players' gallery, with pen and ink sketches of footballers. The feature was part of the editor's weekly chat, but it is clear that he did not stir himself unduly to ferret out biographical facts. A paragraph about 'Williams,' for instance, did not even give the man's initials and could have referred to almost any player in the country, being full of phrases like 'He is easily recognizable as a player of more than ordinary talent.' The pen-and-ink likeness could have been attributed with perfect safety to any young footballer between the ages of twenty and forty. In *Nuggets* also appeared a football competition—not as yet a question of forecasting results of matches but of translating cryptic pictures into the names of teams.

The twentieth-century editors were quick to see that a sporting story needed a great deal more than sport. The paradoxical result was that while real life sport was only moderately dirty, fictional sport—in which boys were encouraged to revel for their health's sake—was vastly dirtier than in real life. No one is likely to forget the long and unflagging sequence of stories about football matches in which the lemons were poisoned at half-time, in which rascally backs hacked the home forwards with boots containing poisoned nails, and in which bogus referees blew poison darts at the star players. There was the goalkeeper who had to lose the match or lose £1,000, and the centre-forward who had to score a hundred goals in the season or lose his life. There was the forward who turned out to be a convict, and the honest forward arrested at half-time on a trumped-up charge. There were the spectators who loosed mad dogs, snakes and even menagerie lions on to the pitch.

If a club was winning it was because a crook had got control and was bribing down all opposition. If a club was losing it was because a crook had got control and did not want it to win. The only honest men among the directors were those who were being blackmailed or threatened with foreclosure of mortgage. The one honest player in the team spent the week shaking off kidnappers and trying to clear his own or his father's name. It was all he could do every Saturday afternoon to break through the crooks' blockade and reach the football ground in time to score the winning goal.

The theme of the 'wonder player' or the 'mystery player' was ever-popular too. The masked forward took the field with unfailing regularity, and the Football Association never seemed to mind, nor did they take any exception to the fielding of blind forwards, forwards who had lost their memory, Red Indians, Hottentots or Boy Tarzans. The Empire was always contributing brilliant players who had learned to play in peculiar circumstances—such as boys who had been shipwrecked for years on a desert island with a party of footballers, and had had nothing else to do except to perfect their technique among the palm trees.

When World War One arrived the sports writers continued unabashed. Any players with Teutonic antecedents were drummed out of the team and were later convicted of espionage. Teams joined up wholesale in Footballers' Battalions, and were promptly moved to key positions in the line, where they earned the personal thanks of Kitchener and Foch. As soon as they had hurled back the Big Push they would celebrate with a rousing game of football on the fringe of no-man's-land, watched by the men of half a dozen Allied divisions. 'Ach, those English sportsmen,' Hindenburg would say as he licked his wounds, 'they do not take war seriously.'

It was left to the Dundee School to take the sporting story and throw into it everything on the shelf. A story entitled 'The One-Man Forward Line' in the *Wizard* started with the team of Prestfield United going out to West Africa to prevent a massacre, the Africans believing the team to be a powerful ju-ju worshipped by the people of Britain. In Africa the team recruited the exiled son of the Earl of Kilblane, who turned out to be a talented footballer. The Earl declined to have his son back in England, and his rascally lawyer Kripp blew up the United ground as a mark of aristocratic displeasure. That was only a minor upset; the real fun started when the throb of war drums began to be heard at Prestfield, and it was remembered that the earl's son had in a weak moment in Africa carved his initials on the Golden Chair of Seremba, the penalty for which was death. Whatever this story may have lacked, it did not lack plot.

In Dundee they had a weakness for sporting ju-jus. Outstanding among these was the cricket bat, which natives venerated even to the point of seeking to do human sacrifice in front of it. In any clash with cannibals a cricket bat in the hero's strong right hand rated half a dozen Excaliburs or a hundred maxim guns.

Boxing stories tended to follow the same fictional pattern as football stories. Crooked managers were the rule, and dope, drugs and poison were their weapons. The towel wafted in front of the flagging hero had been steeped in a debilitating drug, the sponge was alive with germs. A man was lucky to leave the ring suffering from simple concussion, and not from anthrax, infantile paralysis and the Black Death. It was a tough school.

A common trick in boxing stories was to make one's fighter a member of an improbable profession. Arthur S. Hardy ran a long series of 'vocational' boxing stories in the closing days of the *Marvel*. One week he had the boxing parson hanging up his surplice in the vestry and rolling his sleeves ready to do battle with a Sykes-like intruder; the next he had a boxing editor forsaking pen, paste-pot and proofs to do likewise. Boxing dockers, boxing Chinamen, boxing farmers, boxing millionaires, boxing plumbers, boxing taximen and boxing barmen—the author was nearly as hard put to it to find new occupations for his boxers as the Sexton Blake authors were to find new disguises for their hero. As an editorial device for tapping new fields of readers it was perhaps just as successful as moving the hero to a new provincial city each week.

By the nineteen-twenties the *Marvel*—in the pages of which such notable characters had been born—had become a sporting magazine. Its title was *Marvel and Sports Stories*. Many of its older readers were not happy about this change of policy, and were disappointed without being surprised when, in 1922, they were informed that the *Marvel* was ending and that henceforth they must ask for *Sport and Adventure*.

The editor of the new magazine indulged in no lamentation for

'Jimmy the Dodger's training was amazing to watch. With one hand strapped to his side he took on two sparring partners at once.'—The Wizard

the old *Marvel.* In his first issue (addressing readers, as he hoped, of from ten to seventy) he said:

To those who do not greatly care for footer this may seem the wrong time of the year for giving away counterfeit presentments of Buchan, Clay, Meredith and the rest of the League heroes. But we believe that those who do not care much for footer are in a small minority among our readers; and we know that to the true enthusiast there is no close season of interest.

Those former *Marvel* readers who continued to take *Sport and Adventure* through the summer of 1922 may have smiled cynically when in October they were again promised a 'big surprise' and then found themselves being invited to ask, not for *Sport and Adventure*, but for 'Number One of a Great New Paper' with a name almost as old as that of the *Marvel—Pluck.* There were no fewer than ten separate announcements of the new *Pluck* in the final issue. It was to be a companion paper to the 'tremendously successful' *Champion*, and was to carry a detachable 'long complete' story. The short life of *Sport and Adventure* did not mean that the policy of running sport had proved unsuccessful, or was to be abandoned.

Meanwhile the pink *Boys' Realm*, revived from suspended animation, was carrying as many as six sporting stories in each issue—boxing, football, horse racing, motor racing and sometimes cricket. It was a leading protagonist in the competition to see who could give away the largest and glossiest photographs. Portraying of players had come a long way from the very free pen-and-ink sketches in *Nuggets*. First it had been a case of a single matt-finished black-and-white photograph of a player given away; then had followed a 'real glossy photo' given away with each number; then two glossy photos; then two coloured photos; then two glossy photos in an envelope, and so on. Collecting of these photographs eventually came to rival the collecting of cigarette cards. Stimulation came from the firm of Thomsons who took hero-worship a stage farther and published stories bearing the signatures of famous footballers. In those days the giants of sport did not hesitate to perform in even the humblest of literary arenas.

All this time the Aldine firm was putting out one sporting library after another; notably a racing library (most of the tales being written by Bat Masters), a football library and a boxing library (to which Sidney Horler contributed).

Motor racing does not appear to have been honoured with any notable library of its own (though in America a 'Motor Matt' Library had enjoyed a considerable vogue in the early years of this century). Here again was a sport in which the deeps of criminality were plumbed. Revolutionary new carburettors had to be invented almost weekly to make up for those which were stolen. A new alloy was hardly cold before the formula was being scrutinized in Berlin and Barcelona. The hero's home-made racer was a target for saboteurs: the stub axles would be filed three-quarters through, or an infernal machine fitted to the accelerator pedal. At the very least his petrol would be sugared. Even if these hazards were circumvented and the car started to circle the track there would be a concerted effort to side-swipe it over the banking; the standard of track discipline was akin to that displayed in a New York taxi cab 'war.' The same practices were liable to crop up in tales of dirt-track racing.

In the *Champion*, just before World War Two, sport grew from a fetish to a frenzy. Through the 'eighties and 'nineties the editor of the *Boy's Own Paper* had tried his hardest to sell his readers the idea of a daily cold bath. The *Champion* played up almost impossibly hearty types who were always sluicing themselves under icy showers. Take the frightening case of Smudger Smith, the Cruiser Bruiser:

Big, brawny and powerful, and the heftiest middleweight aboard the *Turbulent*, Smudger bore down like a battleship upon the fellows who were racing to beat him.

He tackled them like a rugger half-back, slinging them aside as he waded into their ranks, and chuckling with glee as he was the first to sluice himself down in icy water.

Smudger Smith was always the first dressed, the first tidied up and the first to fall in; in spite of which he was the most popular man on board his man-o'-war.

He was no isolated case. On board the S.S. *Carolia* was 'Sporty' Dawson, whose day started just as explosively:

'Scrape my barnacles. This is great!'

'Sporty' Dawson, late of the Royal Navy, bounded from his bunk and inhaled the fresh morning air from his open porthole. Then he started punching away at a punchball fixed between the ceiling and the floor of his cabin.

The walls of the cabin were covered with sporting pictures and a stack of sports gear stood in one corner.

As he thumped violently at the punchball Sporty Dawson grinned.

Tall, splendidly muscled, square-chinned and determined looking; he was a perfect specimen of physical fitness.

Sporty had been a schoolmaster before going to sea and, on leaving the Navy, he had found a good job. He was to be Fourth Form master aboard the s.s. *Carolia*, the mighty cruising liner which had been commissioned to take two hundred schoolboys on a tour round the world.

Warmed up by his morning exercise, Sporty quickly changed into shorts and sweater, tucked an old Rugby football under one arm, and picked up a battered muffin bell.

'Bet none of the scalliwags are up yet,' he chuckled. 'I'll soon rouse 'em.'

Bounding out of his cabin, Sporty raced along the Fourth Form cabin passage, ringing his muffin bell.

'Show a leg! Show a leg, you young landlubbers! You're at sea, and it's a fine morning for a game of rugger on the main deck!'

'Gosh, it's Sporty Dawson, our new Form master!' cried Chirpy Morgan, one of the Fourth Form. 'I didn't think we were going to have much sport on board ship. But rugger on the main deck's a good idea. Come on, chaps, let's join in.'

And Sporty Dawson kept up this tempo right through the day, increasing it if anything towards nightfall. Even the fat boy was co-opted in the cult of heartiness. There were Slackers, of course, but their opposition was mown down like corn before a whirlwind.

In the other *Champion* stories someone was always trying to suppress Sport, and coming off second best. Assistant Commissioner Macnab, wearing his monocle in the jungle, spent much of his time trying to teach the natives to play Rugby, to the unaccountable annoyance of the Commissioner. In the Royal Flying Corps Rockfist Rogan's major was always putting obstacles in the way of holding boxing matches, especially the kind which involved two men slogging it out in an open cockpit in mid-air while the Richthofen Circus banked for the kill. Other sportsmen in unexpected places were Q9, the Boxing Spy, who introduced a touch of clean fighting into a notoriously dirty profession; Bulldog Blade, the 'biggest sport in the Foreign Legion'; the Boxing Boss of the Convict Castaways, who ruled an island of convicts with his fists; Serjeant Dunn and his Fighting Sportsmen in the Flanders trenches; and Square-Deal Samson, the Strong-Man Sheriff, who upturned caravans with one hand and brought in desperadoes two at a time lashed to a pole across his shoulders.

Always the heroes punched hard and clean. Only a cad would wish to conjecture how many would-be heroes in real life have been needlessly maimed through trying to dispatch ruffianly assailants with a clean right to the jaw rather than a straight right in the stomach.

CHAPTER XVII

DICK BARTON

Hitler's war killed off, perhaps for good, a score of legendary heroes who had survived the Kaiser's war, and one at least who had survived the Boer War. When the publishers, faced with crippling paper cuts, issued their first casualty lists the names of the boys' thrillers were high up on the page. It was the old problem of throwing the least essential passengers from the raft first; sentiment did not determine the order of sacrifice. To-day the unbiased student of the bookstalls may feel that some of the survivors could more easily have been jettisoned.

It was a meagre ration of romance which awaited the schoolboy when Hitler's war was over. Yet out of the disenchantment which followed this war was to be born a new mythical hero with a following of scarcely credible dimensions, a hero whose popularity was unaffected by paper rationing (though not entirely unaffected by fuel rationing): Dick Barton, Special Agent.

Let no defender of the printed word under-estimate the pull of Dick Barton. In the welter of world problems there was one constant but ever-changing problem which nightly drove an audience variously estimated at between one in five and one in three of the population to tune in to the B.B.C. Light Programme. The problem was: What will Dick Barton do next?

In a matter of weeks Barton became a national phenomenon. He has been called everything—an entertainment, a stimulant, a relaxation, a drug, a safety valve, a social menace, a fascist plot and a pattern for parasites. The important thing is that he has never been called a bore.

Nor can he be called a corrupter of morals. The clergy and the teachers who were horrified at the rake's progress of Charley Wag would have found it uncommonly hard to frame an indictment against Barton. For the B.B.C. have been as much concerned to ensure a hero *sans reproche* as a hero *sans peur*. His personal life was soon seen to be ascetic to a degree—even the odd glass of beer was cut out at a fairly early stage. His vocabulary did not contain even the words they use at Girton. His sex life was wholly sublimated in the ceaseless war on evil. He did not lie. In no circumstances did he break the law of the land. He did not even call on nervous citizens for aid in his headlong pursuit of crooks, even though failure might mean the destruction of half the population. His methods, though forceful and forthright when required, were less forceful than those which they taught him in No. 20 Commando. Garrotting and the knife in the dark were out; the clean sock on the jaw was his only weapon. Unlike Jack Harkaway, he did not deliberately slice off his adversary's ear to teach him manners. The only lesson Dick was allowed to remember from his Commando days was that one resolute man need never fear being outnumbered. Indeed, Barton statisticians will tell you that he has never entered a rough-and-tumble without being outnumbered, or at least physically matched.

On what grounds, then, could the cult of Barton be attacked? This was the question which worried those who knew that anyone so popular with the rising generation must be an unhealthy influence. Within eight weeks of his radio début, which was in October 1946, they had found what they wanted. Barton was distracting the youth of the nation from that stern assessment of the postwar world and a realization of their function in it which alone constituted the country's hope of salvation.

Hostilities were opened in *The Times* by Mr. W. Wright-Newsome, who complained that the B.B.C. were turning children into 'some form of drug addict.' Boys were more concerned about how Dick Barton would escape from his next predicament than

about their own futures or the future of Britain, and they regarded
adults who expected them to continue with their homework at
6.45 p.m. as 'insensate and tyrannical giants.' To which Sheelagh
Hardie retorted: 'Heaven postpone the day when our priggish
offspring forsake such unsophisticated thrills for a sober contemplation of their own importance in the future of a planned economy.'
After all, who grudged the bishop his detective novel and the
business man his *Times* crossword?

Others plunged into the correspondence, including Noel Johnson, the actor who was playing Dick Barton five nights a week.
Mr. Johnson recalled the tedium of his own prep. days, and said
he had always felt the better for a break in the middle. 'Let the
children of to-day enjoy themselves as much as possible,' he wrote,
'for I fear they will not have much entertainment in the planners'
Brave New World of the immediate future.' A placatory move
by the B.B.C., announced by Mr. Norman Collins, to run a Barton
'omnibus' on Saturday mornings did not placate Mr. Wright-
Newsome, who again trespassed in *The Times* to point out that
while this was welcome news to day schoolboys it showed dis-
crimination against boarders. As for the evening broadcasts, the
baneful influence of Barton was not confined to the fifteen minutes
of the broadcast; one had to allow for time lost in anticipation
and in backward contemplation. Dr. M. L. Jacks, a former headmaster of Mill Hill, thought that the craze for Barton was no
worse than the craze for the *Pickwick Papers* when these came out
in monthly parts.

The correspondence spread to other newspapers. It was like a
leaky fire hose, spurting up somewhere else whenever a closure
was applied. A disillusioned reader of *Picture-Post* in October
1947 described Dick as 'a lower middle-class spiv.' In the same
month Miss Marion Seddon informed the readers of *Illustrated*
that children had no business to be listening, at the homework
hour, to the exploits of Dick Barton 'and other characters leading
abnormal lives.' Seemingly, it did not worry Miss Seddon that
in the history books in which she was seeking to bury the heads
of British schoolboys there was hardly a character who could be
said to have lived a normal life.

In the *Daily Telegraph* of January 1948 Gwen M. Owen rejoiced that Dick Barton set an example of 'initiative, quick decision and private enterprise'—'Can anyone see Barton referring any matter to a committee?' Sourly, Mr. R. J. Austin complained of the number of simpletons of mature age who listened to Barton—'a disturbing phenomenon.' He was smacked down the same day by a Cabinet Minister in a public speech. 'I like Dick Barton and listen to him when I get the chance,' said Mr. Herbert Morrison. 'I listen because I like it, which seems a good reason for doing a thing provided you don't get yourself into trouble. There are too many people going round publicly trying to psycho-analyse other people.'

It is time to take a closer look at Dick Barton, instead of at his critics. He was sired in no light-hearted fashion; if ever there was a carefully planned birth, this was it. Edward J. Mason, the first script-writer (who can thus make fair claim to be the creator of Barton), based his hero strictly on the official Barton dossier; so did subsequent script-writers like Geoffrey Webb and Basil Dawson. It was important to have uniformity. Editors of thrillers with modest five-figure circulations know what a sharp reaction can be provoked from readers by errors and inconsistencies in the tale of a popular hero. How sharp, then, might be the response from an audience running into millions?

All the facts of Barton's life were meticulously set out. Some of them were printed for the benefit of admirers in the *Radio Times* of February 14, 1947. Even the place and date of his father's birth are on record—Sheffield, November 23, 1887. Barton *père* was an errand boy for a flour-milling firm. On June 22, 1911, he had sufficiently advanced himself to be able to marry Mary Ann Smith, of Ealing. The union was blessed at 5 p.m. on December 10, 1912, when Dick, a brown-haired, hazel-eyed baby, was born in a rented home at High Wycombe. The day was mild and cloudy, and rain had just begun to fall.

Young Dick, who proved to be an only child, was described by neighbours as 'a clever, dogged little chap,' who excelled at toys of the kind that fit together. 'They ought to make him an engineer,' was the general view. On his first day at King Edward

Grammar School Dick intervened in an unfair fight. His resource-
fulness and habit of quick thinking led to his appointment as
school football captain. From 1930 to 1933 Dick was a pains-
taking student at Glasgow University, then he worked for a year
at a drawing board in Liverpool. After that he felt the urge to
travel and found himself jobs in Peru and Persia. In 1937 he became
the maintenance inspector of the International Construction
Corporation Ltd., a job which lasted him until the war came.
On October 10, 1939, he volunteered for the Royal Engineers,
and next year was commissioned at Colchester. He joined the
350 Field Company in France, earned the M.C. for plucky demo-
litions and came out via Dunkirk. At once he joined Combined
Operations and served with No. 20 Commando in almost all
theatres of war. He was released with the rank of captain in
November 1945. His old job was waiting for him but a better
offer came along—the job of Special Agent.

Dick's background would seem reasonably democratic; if
bourgeois, not offensively so. Nevertheless he has not escaped
criticism from the *Daily Worker*, which has charged him with
selling ideology. All his villains, it was complained, were foreigners
or fuzzy-wuzzies. On another occasion (January 1947) the *Daily
Worker's* radio critic, Jack Oliver, wrote:

I personally am enthralled by the politics of the current episode. Dick
has descended on a primitive people with the object of stealing their
most treasured possession. He and his companions have been having
twinges of conscience about their mission. Will they rob the Princess
Maroa? Will Dick turn out to be a crypto-Fascist? Or is he just a fine
boneheaded young Englishman who does not know the meaning of the
word Fear?

Dick has never been interested in politics. That was not stated
in the article in the *Radio Times*, but it is none the less irrefutable.
He fights in no controversial or dubious cause, his only cause
being that of white right against black wrong.

What sort of cases has Dick Barton tackled? Aided by
his two faithful henchmen, he has hounded smugglers, black
marketeers and bullion robbers. He has defeated a crook who sought
to establish a reign of terror over London—one of those super-

confident, exhibitionist crooks who publicly announce the time
and place of their next outrage. He has confounded the plans of
those who seek the green eyes of little yellow gods. He has
tackled a super-smuggler who, profiting by the tactless disclosure
of World War Two secrets, had built himself a synthetic, gun-
defended iceberg on the Habakkuk plan out in the Atlantic. Dick's
first adversary was possibly the most melodramatic—a mad scientist
who sought to wield a radio-active secret weapon against the
population of Britain. It is worth noting that no Gothic horrors
·beset the path of Barton. Radio-active rays, yes; vampires, no.
Barton is firmly in the twentieth century.

   Naturally the pursuit of his resourceful adversaries has taken
Dick many times round the world. In Tibet he got to the spot
by helicopter, a feat which produced a letter from a reader saying
that helicopters could not be used in the conditions and at the
altitudes described. The script-writer laughed that off by making
Dick exclaim to his comrades, as they were flying over a particularly vertiginous range, 'Look, here's an article by a professor
who says you can't fly a helicopter over these mountains. Well,
we're doing it.' There was a notorious occasion, too, when Barton
was trapped by a rising tide in the Mediterranean. The script
writer, confronted with the facts of Nature, said that what he had
meant was surface drift.

   The naming of Dick's adversaries became something of a problem. The first was Kramer, a name which at that time enjoyed
considerable disrepute. Others have borne names like Weimar
and Schwarfschmidt. The 'Vulture' turned out to be a Signor
Patelli. But Dick has also taken on a de Flaubert. Doubtless the
best names from the B.B.C.'s point of view are those like Ra-Mo
and Zorio—names unlikely to evoke protests from excitable
gentlemen at the Court of St. James.

   There was a brief period when it looked as if Dick was going
to be seriously involved with Jean Hunter, an auburn-haired
lassie from Dundee, six years younger than himself. The threat
of matrimony was unpopular with both old and young. Nobody
wanted to see Dick dragged down into domesticity. The script
writers, on the whole, were relieved; in this kind of story girls

only hold up the action. To-day Dick and Jean admire each other from their respective pedestals. With other girls Dick is on tennis club terms, nothing more. A psychologist has predicted that some day he will break out spectacularly, in a manner which will horrify Kraft-Ebbing.

To say that the Barton programme was bound to succeed, since it had a monopoly of an all-pervading medium, is not fair to the team responsible for its slick presentation. True it is that Dick has gained some adherents from those who listen because they cannot bear to have the radio switched off, or who were forced to listen, whether they liked it or not, because their sons or young brothers insisted on having the Barton programme turned on during the evening meal. There were others who came to scoff but stayed to listen, and others who habitually listened for a joke, in the same way that they studied the cartoon strips of Jane. But when allowance is made for all these, there is no denying that it is the élan and clever teamwork of the Barton team under Neil Tuson, the producer, which has compelled such an unprecedented proportion of the population to listen.

The word 'teamwork' is used advisedly. Success in the case of a printed story is the result of a mere three-man collaboration—between author, editor and artist; sometimes a felicitous combination, sometimes an uneasy one. Often the editor never sees the author, and the artist sees neither. But the success of the Barton programme has depended almost as much on the alertness of the 'effects' girls as upon the fecundity of the script writers. A motor chase with a 'near squeak' at a level crossing involves not only a lot of excited dialogue round a microphone but split-second slamming of car doors by a girl in the studio and the simultaneous operation by another girl of as many as half a dozen turntables which, at the touch of a knob, will provide the required sounds of screeching tyres, screeching brakes, an engine tick-over, an engine at speed, a locomotive whistle and the roar of an express. The technique of blood-and-thunder has come a long way from the days when (allegedly) a hard-up publisher commissioned a still more hard-up author to write a gory romance around a set of second-hand blocks.

As these lines are written the Barton programme is being 'rested' (it lost none of its popularity during an earlier rest). Will Dick be remembered sixty years hence as Harkaway is still remembered to-day? It is an impressive thought that in the year 2000 there may be a Dick Barton Club at which old recordings—secured by heaven knows what backstairs influence from the B.B.C.—will be played over in reverent silence. And sentimental greybeards will shake their heads and wonder why Dick never married Jean Hunter in the end.

It is idle to speculate whether the radio thriller will oust the printed thriller. The latter has at least these powerful advantages: it can be followed under cover of a school book or on a bus top; it can be treasured and re-read at will; or it can be sold at half-price or even at a profit to the boy next door. As against this, Dick Barton costs the youthful listener nothing—it is the parent who pays for the radio licence.

If boys' thrillers come back in pre-1940 strength—and given the paper there is little doubt that they will—the editors will have learned one lesson from Dick Barton: namely, that even a non-smoking, non-swearing, non-controversial paragon is still the target of drivelling criticism. Galahad and Turpin alike are condemned as anti-social, if their adventures are exciting. If they are wise, editors of boys' papers will give their heroes full rein, and drop all protests in the waste-paper basket. Their justification is in the words of Chesterton (and the writer makes no apology for quoting him again):

The vast mass of humanity, with their vast mass of idle books and idle words, have never doubted and never will doubt that courage is splendid, that fidelity is noble, that distressed ladies should be rescued and vanquished enemies spared. . . . [Their literature] will always be a blood and thunder literature, as simple as the thunder of heaven and the blood of man.

INDEX